THE ROOTS OF
BLACK NATIONALISM

Kennikat Press
National University Publications
Series in American Studies

General Editor
James P. Shenton
Professor of History, Columbia University

RODNEY CARLISLE

THE ROOTS OF
BLACK NATIONALISM

National University Publications
KENNIKAT PRESS • 1975
Port Washington, N.Y. • London

Manufactured in the United States of America

Published by
Kennikat Press Corp.
Port Washington, N.Y./London

Library of Congress Cataloging in Publication Data

Carlisle, Rodney P
    The roots of Black nationalism.

    (Series in American studies) (National university
publications)
    Bibliography: p. 174
    Includes index.
    1. Black nationalism—United States—History
I. Title.
E185.C19   320.9'73   75—25609
ISBN 0—8046—9098—7

FOR NATHAN AND BONNIE

CONTENTS

PREFACE

This book is intended to provide an introductory synthesis of the state of historical knowledge of black nationalism in the United States, and to provide both the student of the subject and the general reader a comprehensive view of the place that the doctrines of black nationalism have had in American life.

Black nationalists for the most part have been studied in a compartmentalized way. But history is not lived as a series of separate biographies. Rather, lines of influence and personal contacts between men active in the development of ideas overlap in never-ending intricacy. Thus, the tendency of historical scholarship to cut subjects into ever smaller frames for close examination may have contributed to the myth that each black nationalist stood alone, unique, and unrelated to any discernable political tradition. Yet it is the very existence of a vast body of excellent and diligent original research by scores of scholars which makes possible such a work as this. I have attempted to acknowledge sources for particular pieces of information through the annotation, of course taking responsibility for errors of omission or commission.

This book searches for a pattern of development of black nationalism based on these premises: 1. Black nationalists fall within an integral tradition which has had the same kind of vitality and continuity as the liberal or radical tradition in American life; 2. Black nationalism was motivated and structured in ways which may have paralleled nationalisms among European groups; 3. Black nationalists developed ideas, doctrines, and specific plans which have been unique to black nationalism; 4. Political black nationalism aiming at the development of sovereignty was not a fantasy, but in fact was a body of ideas with considerable practical impact.

PREFACE

Black nationalism shares with other nationalisms the effort to evoke loyalty and pride, to shape a sense of national identity and to develop sovereign government of a territory. Yet the black nationalist tradition in the United States grew in a unique environment of uneven political suppression coupled with racial proscription, and out of those conditions took on qualities of its own, such as a special relationship with black Africa, and a leadership frequently drawn from the ranks of clergy. The cluster of black nationalist ideas, at once a means of protest within the American political framework, and potentially a force for breaking out of that framework, engendered special dilemmas for its major spokesmen. Although radical in its premises, black nationalism often attracted men of conservative views, as did some other 19th and 20th century nationalisms. During several periods in American history, black nationalism declined in popular following and its spokesmen seemed lonely voices in the wilderness. But at other periods, the doctrine flowered in a profusion of conflicting organizations and mass followings.

The author's interest in looking for patterns and attempting a developmental treatment of the subject was particularly aroused by a reading of Harold Cruse's *The Crisis of the Negro Intellectual.* The author is more personally indebted to Professors Elbert Harris and Bernard Dehmelt for their encouragement and suggestions. The Library staffs of the Schomburg Collection of Negro Literature and History in New York, the Library of Congress, and the Library of Rutgers University were most helpful and their assistance is deeply appreciated.

Portions of the work have appeared in different form and acknowledgment is gratefully made to the *Negro History Bulletin* and to *Black World* for allowing the use of material published in these journals.

I am grateful too for the support and encouragement of my wife Anna in seeing me through the drawn-out process of research and writing of the book.

1

BLACK NATIONALISM
AS A TRADITION

developing /evolving tradition (handwritten annotation)

When the evidence from different periods is viewed consecutively, American black nationalism is revealed as a group of ideas which had a continuous development, a tradition. The tradition had its precursors, its pioneers, its demagogues and charlatans, its statesmen and intellectuals. Rather than being a random collection of ideas, when seen as a whole black nationalism developed and was passed on from generation to generation. Nationalism has been seen by most scholars as a minor theme in American black history, running at cross purposes to the major theme of the struggle for integration and recognition of rights as American citizens. However, a few scholars in recent years have contended that black nationalism was much more widespread, if less "respectable," and expressed the aspirations of the black masses better than the pursuit of justice within the American system. The vitality of black nationalism over two centuries of American life suggests that its advocates should not be studied in isolation, but as men possibly linked by some common ideals, a unique situation, and a developing tradition.[1] Biographers' interest in single individuals and scholars' work in the form of monographs may account for the slow development of a comprehensive outlook on the history of black nationalism.

To think of nationalists as interesting but isolated cases has been less challenging to the American dream than an approach which shows the nationalist doctrine as a two-hundred-year-old body of thought based on rejection of the superficial optimism of American life. Black nationalism opposes the myths of American life because it presumes a black nation existing unassimilated alongside the American nation. When we set out to study the doctrines of black nationalism in the United States, we do not necessarily present a brief that a black nation exists here as such. Yet the concept that the black people of the United States form a nation has a degree of objective justification. Blacks in America have had not only a separate economic status and a more or less clearly separate ethnic identity, but also a degree of separate culture, separate religious structures, and separate social institutions which give support to the idea of a national existence.

Despite the fair claim to a national identity, black nationalism has faced a number of severe obstacles to implementation. Viewed either as a nation or as an oppressed minority, blacks have generally lacked power to effect fundamental change. Black leaders and potential leaders were often rewarded by whites for their talents by being bought off into supporting the notion of justice through American nationality rather than through a separate nationality. Whites who did support the idea of separate black nationality did so usually out of hostility to blacks, simply regarding separatism as the logical extension of segregation. With supporters among the worst enemies of the black man, the nationalist found his position difficult. Perhaps most fundamental of the black nationalist's handicaps has been the fact that, like the Jews in nineteenth-century Europe, the American black nation controlled no territory. The nationalism of black people had first of all to come to grips with the question of geographic location.

While such handicaps have been severe, they are not unique. In one form or another, similar problems of undermined leadership and powerlessness were faced by Irish nationalists under British rule, various central Europeans under Austrian rule, and colonial peoples in Africa and Asia. The similarities of black nationalism to other nationalisms suggest that the definitions and concepts developed by scholars to deal with European nationalism might have some applicability. Boyd C. Shafer, in *Nationalism: Myth and Reality*, offered a concise summary definition based on the European experience which can provide us with a sense of how much black nationalism conforms to the patterns and problems of Europe's nationalisms.

To reduce Shafer's definition to a brief ten points, nationalists believed in and worked towards these goals: a territory, a language and culture, common institutions, sovereign government, a common history, love for fellows, devotion to the nation, common pride, hostility to opponents, and hope for the future. The goals of territory, common institutions, and sovereign government are political ones. Language, culture, and history are cultural goals. The rest of the goals might be described as emotional states.[2]

The most striking obstacle for American black nationalists has been the question of where the nation should locate—point number one on Shafer's list. The alternatives facing black nationalists seemed impossible at first: *emigrationism* entailed large-scale population removal either to Africa or to some relatively unsettled part of the Caribbean or Latin America; *territori-*

alism required the establishment of an autonomous enclave within the United States. While both plans have been labelled fantasies by some of the critics of nationalism, it should be remembered that several modern states were created in just such ways.

In the antebellum period the emigration idea attracted large numbers of followers. Despite the expense involved and all the difficulties in the way of those hoping to emigrate, tens of thousands of free blacks emigrated to Liberia, Haiti, Canada, and Mexico in the period 1820–60. The total emigration, by even conservative estimates, was 15 to 20 percent of the total free black population. Many more were interested in emigration, as evidenced by letters of inquiry received by organizers of the emigration efforts.[3]

Despite parallels with the experience of other nationalists, black nationalists developed doctrines which are unique and which grew out of their particular situation. Most notable is the close association of religion with American black nationalism. In the American context there were very few institutional settings where blacks could meet and develop ideas free of white control or influence. One such setting was the black church, including both the major denominations and the minor cults. The relationship between the black church and black nationalism was reciprocal—the church provided a fertile field for nationalism, and some nationalists even founded new religions and separate churches. If blacks were to justify the political choice of nationalism, the existence of a separate nationality had to be demonstrated through emphasis on separate religion, culture, history, destiny, literature, lore, manners, and style of life. If pride and identity in those elements could be evoked, a political following would cohere more readily. The church provided both the forum and the model for separate identity through separate culture.

After 1822 the existence of Liberia, first as a colony of the white-funded American Colonization Society and after 1847 as an independent republic, created another special situation for American black nationalist thinkers, especially those who sought political sovereignty. While not all nationalists had to believe in emigration, nor particularly in Liberian emigration, from an early date they were faced with the fact of a black-governed state. Black settlers there developed a *Liberian* nationalist doctrine out of their own experience. When the most intellectually notable of those settlers, Alexander Crummell and Edward Wilmot Blyden, imported that nationalism to the United States, their ideas, advice, and interests profoundly influenced a generation of American black nationalists. To a much lesser extent ideas developed by black settlers in Canada were also imported to the United States. Thus, from early in the nineteenth century American black nationalism had, paradoxically, an international character. The flow of ideas across the Atlantic, especially in the crucial early stages of the development of the black nationalist tradition, is one of the factors examined in this work.

Several specific traditions and ideas peculiar to this form of nationalism can be distinguished. Black acquisition of shipping facilities in order to establish trade, cultural exchange, and passenger routes to Africa is one such idea which grew directly out of the Liberian experience. In addition, the following points have recurred with regularity in the writings of black nationalists: emphasis on African past glories, rejection of white association, rejection of miscegenation, advocacy of high personal morality, interest in pan-African unity, elevation of black womanhood, pride in standards of beauty unique to the black race, and interest in and support for the education of blacks.

Black men with nationalist ideas and belonging to movements devoted to the implementation of those ideas have disagreed on tactics, politics, and attitudes. Unlike Marxism, nationalism offers no specific economic policy, and black nationalists have ranged from private-enterprise conservatives through proponents of cooperative ownership to socialists. While some have been intellectuals, others have been nonintellectual or even antiintellectual. A few have made pure black ancestry a sine qua non of black nationality. On the other hand, some leading black nationalist figures have been themselves of mixed ancestry and light-complected.

As a tradition, black nationalism has a history, but beyond a shared national identity there is little which can be said to unite black nationalists. In the sense that the doctrine challenges the status quo and American mythology, black nationalists have been "radical," even when conservative in their economics. Perhaps the most common feature of those advocating black nationalist ideas has been the ideal of overcoming black powerlessness in the American context by setting up mechanisms of self-determination. For some, revolution or emigration to a black state seemed the proper approach. Others preferred the slow and careful building of separately controlled black institutions. All sought control of their own destiny and liberation outside the white-dominated society.

2

PRECURSORS

When nineteenth- and twentieth-century black nationalists set out to write a national history which would inspire and be a source of pride, they could rightfully claim a heritage of black self-government in the powerful African states of the Sudan, and in the glories of Egypt and Ethiopia. Yet American blacks could not as a group trace their ancestry to any single African homeland; the diaspora had not only produced a wide dispersal, it had so obliterated and mixed ancestries that the American black race, if excluded from American nationality, was effectively a stateless race. As white political control of both the Americas and Africa extended and tightened through the nineteenth century, blacks in the diaspora could only obtain a homeland in the Americas at the expense of white control either through force or concession, or in Africa by means of a grant conceded by a European power at the expense of indigenous African peoples. Prior to the nineteenth-century development of nationalism, forerunners and models of such alternatives could be found in the attempts of escaped slaves to seize land for themselves, and in white-developed plans for resettlement in Africa.

Rebellious escaped slaves, or maroons, had established independent black states ranging in size from small outlaw camps in the United States through internationally recognized nations in the West Indies and Latin America. The idea of a newly created black state was advanced by several white Americans in the late eighteenth century. Another, more practical effort was that of a group of London philanthropists and abolitionists who planned and established Sierra Leone as a refuge for free blacks from Great Britain and for black Loyalists from North America.

Black States

The Palmares Republic retained its independence for nearly the whole of the seventeenth century in northern Brazil. Unlike the smaller fugitive slave settlements that Brazilians called *quilombos,* Palmares was regarded as a *mocambo,* or a permanent hideout. There were at least ten major *quilombos* in Brazil; most of them were destroyed by military expeditions after one or two years of existence, although one of the *quilombos* in the Mato Grosso region did last from 1770 to 1794. However, the *mocambo* of Palmares was of an entirely different order of magnitude.

In the 1640s, during a Dutch occupation of northern Brazil, unsuccessful expeditions against Palmares reported that about eleven thousand blacks lived there in several separate communities. The Dutch found organized settlements with farmlands, irrigation, churches, smithies, and a foe they described as "invincible."[1]

Palmares reflected essentially African political institutions. It was a kingdom with an elected ruler, delegated territorial government, and a system of courts and laws. As such, it was a de facto state. In 1678 the Portuguese signed a treaty with Palmares which recognized its local sovereignty, but within a year the treaty was ignored as Portuguese planters led raids on the area to obtain slaves.

By the time the Portuguese destroyed Palmares in 1697, after several unsuccessful expeditions and a two-year siege, the *mocambo's* large size could be partly attributed to two generations of births within the state as well as a steady influx of fugitives. Significantly, Palmares was not the creation of a single ethnic group of blacks, but cut across tribal lines, including blacks born in Brazil, mulattoes, and mestizos, as well as some recently arrived African slaves. The names of the rulers and bits of reported vocabulary indicate that many of the founders of the state were Bantu slaves originally from Angola. The fact that the state was made up of blacks of a variety of backgrounds brought its ethnic composition closer to that of the black race of the Americas as a whole than to any particular tribal group in Africa. More than any African kingdom, Palmares was the kind of state which black nationalists would later envision: it was created by force; it preserved elements of African culture; it was black rather than tribal in makeup; it was antislavery and antiwhite in its "politics."[2]

Although Palmares was destroyed and never served as a place of destination for nationalists, it demonstrated that blacks sought, and could establish, an alternative to white domination. In fact, Palmares was a transplanted set of African institutions in the prenationalist era; yet the sovereign quality of the state represented the logical end product of the drive for self-government. Haiti, although it appeared a century after the destruction of Palmares, was in its essentials much like the earlier Brazilian *mocambo*. The slave uprisings which merged into a revolution in the mid-1790s grew out of the disrupted conditions produced by the French Revolution. French planters in Haiti were reluctant to see the rights of man, proclaimed in France, extended to mulattoes or free blacks in Saint-Domingue. When French Girondists and Jacobins declared such an extension, blacks in Haiti overthrew slavery as incompatible with the new ideals. By 1798 abolition was an accomplished fact under the emerging black leaders including Toussaint L'Ouverture and Jean Jacques Dessalines. However, L'Ouverture made it clear that he fought as a Frenchman; he resisted the offers of the British to grant him aid, regarding such a course as a betrayal of France. He took the Spanish end of the island in the name of France, and promulgated a constitution which gave the blacks autonomous power, retaining only a nominal link with France. Napoleon rejected the constitution and sent armed forces to suppress the black army. L'Ouverture discovered that the French intended, once his own army was dispersed, to reestablish slavery; thus, the war for abolition and autonomy became in 1801–03 a war for national independence. The creation of a national state was an afterthought to abolition and escape from slavery, as in Palmares. Independence in both cases grew out of resistance to white attempts at reenslavement.[3]

Haiti maintained its statehood, despite interventions by other powers. It soon became a possible place of refuge and settlement, and thousands of black colonists from America emigrated there as soon as some stability was achieved in the 1820s. White deportationists and black nationalists alike considered Haiti a suitable location for a black homeland, and its continued independence served as a point of reference and an inspiration to black nationalists through most of the nineteenth century. Haiti was the creation of a black revolution, and as such its history could be read with pride; it could attract black immigrants without apology regarding its origin.[4]

Smaller maroon communities in Latin America, the Caribbean, and the United States became part of the later nationalist history of the black race in America; their existence illustrated that black statehood and black independence were sought from the earliest period of slavery in the New World. There is evidence for at least fifty maroon settlements within the present limits of the United States, but only rarely did the maroons achieve a settled life rather than a fugitive or migratory one. The largest settled community consisted of about two thousand fugitives in the Great Dismal Swamp on the Virginia-North Carolina border. The number of settled communities that carried on a peaceful life of crop and stock raising and trading with other communities may have been greater than the documentary sources reveal, since such communities did not attract the notice that more hostile outlaw bands did.[5]

Of sixty-five slave rebellions and conspiracies in the United States from the colonial period through 1860, at least four conspiracies were directed at the creation of an independent black state: in Virginia in 1722, in Maryland in 1739, Gabriel Prosser's Plot of 1800 in Virginia, and Denmark Vesey's Plot of 1822 in South Carolina. These plots and rebellions, like the maroon settlements, showed that the urge to national self-determination had deep roots, and that even where chances of success were slim, the idea could emerge.[6]

Slave revolts and communities of maroons received treaty recognition from the British in 1739 in Jamaica, and from the Dutch in several revolts on the Cotticas and Moroni rivers in Surinam in the late eighteenth century. The maroon republics of Jamaica and Surinam, although far smaller than Palmares or Haiti, were militarily successful. The colonial powers found it easier to accept their local sovereignty than to waste troops in vain attempts to defeat black armies in remote fortresses.[7]

Like their European counterparts, nineteenth- and twentieth-century black nationalists assumed that heroically written history would evoke the emotive responses essential to the sustenance of political nationalism. Rich sources for such a history could be found in a whole range of action from small-scale rebellion through the variety of maroon enclaves to the *mocambo* and the internationally recognized state of Haiti. Understandably, it was Haiti which received most of the attention; but it was only the most successful of a whole range of efforts.

American deportationists

White planners of black deportation and colonization worked out, on paper, precedents for the idea of black sovereignty; yet their motives were at odds with those of blacks. In the period following the American Revolution, many whites viewed emancipation as a logical outcome of the ideals of the Revolution; but for those who believed blacks and whites could not live compatibly as free men with equal status, deportation seemed a necessary consequence of emancipation.

Deportation of blacks upon emancipation had been suggested as early as 1714, when a British visitor to New Jersey reported that a native of America proposed such a plan. There developed a scattering of deportation proposals, including one in 1768 in a Philadelphia newspaper proposing a colony on the southern frontier of the American colonies. Another, in 1773, by Anthony Benezet, a Quaker who worked for the rights of black men, proposed a colony in the territory between the Allegheny range and the Mississippi River. Benezet considered African emigration, but rejected it on the grounds that it would expose blacks "to greater difficulties than many of them labor under at present."[8]

In 1787 Thomas Jefferson, in his widely read *Notes on Virginia,* suggested expatriation of blacks upon their emancipation, and their replacement by white immigrants. Following the publication of the *Notes,* discussions of deportation, emigration, and colonization of blacks in either a separate territory on the frontier or Africa appeared in a flood of pamphlets and newspaper treatments. In 1788 Othello, reputedly a free black man in Baltimore, proposed a western colony. In 1790 Ferdinando Fairfax a Virginia planter and protégé of George Washington, published an extensive plan for deportation of freed slaves to Africa and submitted his ideas to Congress. In 1793 Noah Webster, who had read Jefferson's work, published a treatise on slavery in which he discussed the problems of colonization; he favored the assignment of territory within the United States.

In the period 1786 through 1790 William Thornton, a medical doctor and a native of Antigua who was later appointed by Jefferson to head the Patent Office, corresponded with British and French planners of freedmen's colonies. He wrote to and met Samuel Hopkins, pastor of the First Congregational Church in Newport, Rhode Island, who was also interested in the British ideas. In 1793 Hopkins published a comprehensive deportation and colonization plan, incorporating various notions current in the suggestions of prior planners.[9]

In the writings of a variety of antislavery people at the turn of the century, the idea of colonization was closely linked to emancipation. Saint George Tucker, president of William and Mary College, proposed in 1795 that blacks when freed be denied any of the rights of freedmen, as a kind of negative incentive to their emigration. Deportation at state expense would be too costly, he believed; the freedmen should simply be induced to leave by severe treatment and conditions.[10]

The Virginia legislature in 1800, 1804, and 1805 passed resolutions supporting the idea of expatriation. In 1805 Thomas Branagan, an opponent of the slave trade and of slavery, suggested the establishment of a black homeland in the Louisiana Territory. In 1806 John Parrish, a Maryland Quaker and abolitionist, proposed voluntary colonization in the West, beginning with those blacks already free. The existence of such a colony, Parrish believed, would provide a stimulus to abolition.

During the twenty years preceding 1806 the atmosphere of social reform had been conducive to this kind of discussion of emancipation and its consequences. Deportation was a lively topic, cropping up not only in formal treatises, in pamphlets, and memorials to legislatures, but in both private and public debate. The kind of problems discussed at this stage by white proponents of deportation were later to have practical consequences. Where was the black colony to be located? How would freedmen be induced to accept removal? Who would bear the expense of transportation? Could a black colony be healthy and self-supporting? Would a settlement of ex-slaves represent a threat to the security of the United States? How would such a colony or settlement be governed?

Although deportationists concocted various theoretical answers to such questions, a pattern emerged in their discussions, containing these elements: a colony in Africa or on the southern or western frontier of the United States; manumission on condition of accepting emigration as a means of inducing removal; federal or state taxation to support the cost, with former masters accepting some of the expenses; careful selection of location and sufficient initial funds to assure a prosperous colony; sufficient distance from the United States to reduce the threat to security; a period of white control while the machinery of self-government was developed and while black settlers gained governing experience. When the American Colonization Society was formed later, these ideas in fact formed the basis for its activities.[11]

In the period between 1806 and 1816, interest in the idea of deportation and colonization of emancipated slaves fell off, perhaps because of the rising international crisis and the War of 1812. Winthrop Jordan has shown that the motives of the deportationists—both the planners of the prewar period, who were largely in favor of emancipation, and the activists of the American Colonization Society in the period after 1816, who were more frequently proslavery, were based on the pervading prejudices of white America. Yet many of the specifics of the utopian plans of colonizationists of both periods coincided with plans later made by black nationalists. The alternatives considered by the whites, despite their hostility to blacks as equals, were precisely the alternatives considered by active black nationalists seeking national liberation: Africa or an American enclave; colony or nation; oppression in America or freedom in a black state. Deportationists and later black nationalists agreed that the American ideal of equality could not or would not be extended to blacks.

British philanthropy and Sierra Leone

The British counterparts of American planners in the period 1787–1806 considered the alternatives and reached similar conclusions. The plan for Sierra Leone apparently originated with Henry Smeathman, who had accompanied Dr. John Fothergill, a naturalist, on a voyage to West Africa. On Smeathman's return he was captured by American revolutionaries and taken to the West Indies. Fothergill had planned a settlement on the west coast of Africa which would engage in commerce in goods as competition against the slave trade. Smeathman took up the idea and expanded it by proposing in 1783 that such a colony be "intended more particularly for the service and happy establishment of blacks and people of color, to be shipped as freemen, under the direction of the committee for relieving the black poor, under the protection of the British Government."[12]

The "black poor" to whom Smeathman referred included two groups. Some blacks in England had been freed by a court decision of 1772 which formally ended slavery in the British Isles. In 1783 their numbers were increased by blacks evacuated from the United States by the retreating British army. This group of black men was made up of veterans of the War for Independence who had served with the British and secured freedom as a reward. Other black Loyalists had been sent to the West Indies and Canada.

British philanthropists, including Granville Sharp, heard of Smeathman's plan. Sharp, working with William Wilberforce and Thomas Clarkson, reorganized an existing company to form the Sierra Leone Company, which implemented the colonization idea. The new company began embarcation of blacks from England in late 1786, and by April 1787 about four hundred black men set sail. The ship also carried sixty white women, wives of some of the men. This first group of colonists did not fare too well, and the directors of the Company were eager to supplement their number. The chance soon arose.[13]

Among the Loyalist blacks shipped to Canada was Thomas Peters, an African-born veteran. He had escaped slavery in 1776 and joined the British to serve as sergeant in a pioneer unit. He settled in Nova Scotia, where he expected to receive a farm promised by the British to blacks evacuating with the army. Peters was then sent by a group of his fellow black émigrés to London to present grievances regarding treatment: only a few refugees had received land, often uncleared pine forest; some white Loyalists from the United States had tried to reenslave the blacks; the black settlers were denied trial by jury; all the available farmsites were too far from market centers.

Peters arrived in London in early 1791, where he received the assistance of Granville Sharp and other reformers. He spoke before several groups on the black Loyalists' difficulties. Abolitionists drew up a proposal in Peters's name, which he signed, asking either for land as promised, or for assistance in emigrating to any country which would provide homesites. Peters met the board of directors of the Sierra Leone Company, accepted their suggestion of emigration to Africa, and returned to Nova Scotia to promote the idea. He was followed by two agents assigned by the directors, Lawrence Hartshorn and John Clarkson, younger brother of Thomas Clarkson. Young Clarkson vigorously sought settlers, despite the opposition of Canadian administrators who feared the removal idea would strip the colony of labor. But Clarkson never made clear that the settlers would be expected to pay a quitrent for the new lands in Sierra Leone, a gap in his propaganda which later produced an uprising among the emigrants.[14]

Thomas Peters personally recruited eighty-four emigrants, and Clarkson interviewed hundreds of applicants. David George, a black Baptist minister who had evacuated from Charleston, South Carolina, with the British in 1782, had emerged as a leader in the Nova Scotia group. He brought his family and fifty-nine members of his church to join the African emigration. Other ministers also urged their followers to emigrate, including David Wilkinson, Boston King, and Cato Perkins. By the end of 1791 the group was ready, and in mid-January, 1792, 1190 emigrants sailed for Sierra Leone in a fleet of four ships, nine brigs, and two schooners. It was the first organized return of free blacks directly from North America to Africa.[15]

In 1800, 550 Jamaican maroons were shipped first to Nova Scotia and then on to Sierra Leone. On their arrival in Africa they were immediately put to work suppressing the rebellion among Cato Perkins's followers over the issue of the quitrent. The maroons received a thousand-acre grant and settled down. After the British outlawed the Atlantic slave trade in 1807, their government assumed direct control of the colony. The first two thousand settlers of Sierra Leone were soon augmented by slaves taken by the British from traders along the coast.

Peters, George, and Perkins might be regarded as the prototypes of black nationalists, even though their motives were immediate and economic, rather than ideological. These men were leaders, they did help in the founding of a new society, and the new society was pan-African in that it eventually took in blacks from England, North America, and the West Indies, and later recaptives from several areas of West Africa. The community which they established was thus a living example of a newly created pan-African homeland.[16]

In 1801 Jefferson, as president, suggested to Governor Monroe of Virginia that Sierra Leone might serve as a possible location for slaves who had participated in Prosser's Plot of 1800. Jefferson made inquiries through Rufus King, United States minister to Great Britain, as to whether American blacks might be sent there. Both the Sierra Leone Company and the British government preferred stable settlers, if such could be found, to rebels, and the suggestion was put off.

Sierra Leone was more than an abstract precedent or precursor to the development of black nationalism. Like Haiti, Sierra Leone served as a living society which could inspire pride and act as a potential homeland for American blacks. Further, it stimulated American proponents of a freedmen's colony by proving that such plans could be implemented. In later decades the exchange of experience, ideas, and individuals between Sierra Leone and Liberia would lead to a continuing influence of the British colony on the thinking of both white colonizers and early black nationalists.

3

PAUL CUFFE

Personal background

The British precedent in Sierra Leone might have had far less influence in the United States had it not been for the activities of Paul Cuffe, who publicized the Sierra Leone experiment and by his energies aroused both blacks and whites in America to convert abstract discussions of emigration into action. His work initiated both American black nationalism and at times the uncomfortable bedfellow, Liberian colonization.

Cuffe was born on the island of Cuttyhunk, in Massachusetts, in 1759. His parents were Cuffe, or Cuffee, Slocum, a freed slave, and Ruth Moses, an Indian, both of Dartmouth. After his father's death Paul, the youngest of four boys and six girls, led the others to drop "Slocum," which had been the name of their father's one-time owner, and adopt their father's first name as a surname.

Paul Cuffe became a seaman at the age of sixteen with a whaling voyage. During the Revolutionary War he was captured by the British and held in New York for several months. After his release Cuffe built two boats; each was seized by pirates on its maiden voyage in the New England coastal trade. After the war, with the decline in privateers Cuffe engaged again in the coastal trade and whaling. With the profits from these voyages Cuffe ordered a sixty-nine-ton vessel to be built at Westport, Massachusetts.

From the period 1795 through 1806 Cuffe continued his commercial ventures, trading as far afield as the Chesapeake and later Gotenburg, Sweden. By 1806 "he was posessed of one ship, two brigs, and several smaller vessels, besides considerable property in houses and lands."[1]

Cuffe, like his father and at least one of his sisters, married an Indian. Settling near Westport, Cuffe raised a family and joined the local Society of Friends. He was dedicated to black education, for he financed the construction of a school, paid teachers' salaries, purchased school materials, and corresponded with relatives regarding the education of nephews and grandchildren. His own brief education included tutoring in navigation, mathematics, and geography.

Although Cuffe's ancestry included both Indians and Africans, and although he pursued a Yankee-style commercial career, he was clearly aware that he had to fight the disabilities placed on him by his status as a black man. Cuffe, a brother, and five other black men petitioned the 1780 legislature of Massachusetts for tax relief, using the principle of no taxation without representation:[2]

While we are not allowed the privileges of freemen of the state, having no vote or influence in the election of those that tax us, yet many of our color (as is well known) have cheerfully entered the field of battle in the defence of the common cause and that (as we conceive) against a similar exertion of power (in regard to taxation) too well known to need a recital . . . .

The Cuffe brothers later petitioned the county government for relief from taxation, claiming they were "Indian men and by law not the subjects of taxation for any estate, real or personal . . . ." Having both African and Indian ancestry, they had no clear status in Massachusetts; as they saw it, if they were to be regarded as black they suffered taxation without representation; if they were Indian, they were legally tax-exempt. Despite their logic, they were arrested. The case came before a judge in 1781, and the Cuffes paid their taxes and court costs. While the suit was pending, the Cuffes also petitioned the town meeting of Dartmouth for voting rights and government participation or exemption from taxation. While the various Cuffe petitions and court cases did not produce either tax relief or a grant of rights, their fight raised the same issues that, all over revolutionary New England, brought recognition of the rights of black men. A 1783 judicial decision, rather than the Cuffe actions, won recognition of black men's rights under the Declaration of Rights in the 1780 Massachusetts Constitution, which stated that "all men are born free and equal."[3]

Visits to Africa and England

Cuffe's concern with the rights of black men went beyond personal tax questions. An active Friend, he grew concerned that little had been done to convert Africans to Christianity. In the year of the legal closing of the slave trade between Africa and the United States, Cuffe wrote to James Pemberton, a Philadelphia acquaintance and fellow Quaker, that he felt "uncapable of doing much for brethren of the African Race," but "if God pleases to lay upon me to make an instrument for that service" he would submit.[4]

Pemberton replied by informing Cuffe of the activities of the Sierra Leone Company and the British African Institution. Zachariah Macaulay, director of the Institution, was interested in inducing stable, religious black freemen from the New World to emigrate to the colony. In contrast to Jefferson's inquiries regarding captured rebels, Pemberton's query about emigrants was appreciated. Macaulay assured Pemberton that Cuffe would be welcome to visit Sierra Leone and to encourage others to emigrate. Over the next two years Cuffe developed his plans, receiving encouragement from the Westport Meeting of Friends. He sailed his ship, the *Traveller*, to Philadelphia, where he spent the month of December, 1810, discussing his ideas further with Pemberton and other parties. On January 1, 1811, he set sail with a crew of nine blacks for Africa, arriving at Sierra Leone March 1.

Cuffe stayed at Sierra Leone over two months. While there he dined with the governor and toured the colony. He recorded discussions about the state of the colony, agricultural prospects, the degree of African civilization, and progress of the suppression of the slave trade.

Invited by William Allen and William Wilberforce, Cuffe went to England. There he met the leading supporters of Sierra Leone, including Clarkson, Macaulay, and the duke of Gloucester. Cuffe visited Friends Meetings, factories, Parliament, the mint, and the sights of London. He impressed the board of the African Institution, for their report indicated that they had high hopes he would settle in Sierra Leone and bring from America "free blacks of good character and some property who might settle in the colony and practice among the natives the mechanical arts and the cultivation of tropical produce."[5]

After two months in Britain Cuffe sailed again for Sierra Leone, with papers allowing him to trade there. On this second stay he diligently explored the country. He helped establish a Friendly Society, which was devoted to commerce, not religion, and he discussed with the governor the details of settling immigrants. He wrote up his findings in a letter, later published in the United States as a pamphlet.[6]

The first emigration

On Cuffe's return in early 1812 American revenue agents seized his ship for carrying an illegal British cargo. Cuffe gathered influential support and travelled to Philadelphia and Washington to clear the ship and cargo. Finding that his voyages to Britain and Sierra Leone were well known, he easily convinced President Madison and the secretary of war that his trip was innocent and arranged the release of the impounded cargo. In Baltimore Cuffe met with Daniel Coker, who taught in a school established by and for free blacks. Cuffe and Coker established a society to enter into correspondence with the London African Institution and the Friendly Society of Sierra Leone. In New York, Philadelphia, and Boston, he also laid plans for African Institutions which would correspond and plan commercial relations.

Cuffe's actions had some political overtones. Many urban blacks with small property or regular employment enjoyed the franchise and voted with the Federalist party at the time. Federalists for the most part opposed the War of 1812, and were decidedly pro-British. The thought of settling in a British colony, even in the midst of a war with Britain, coincided with the political leaning of free blacks who voted at that time.[7]

To further his plans, Cuffe petitioned Congress in June, 1813, for permission to trade with Sierra Leone, despite the war. He stated that he was a descendant of Africa who had been blessed by Providence with wealth. Upon learning of the efforts of many "pious individuals" in England and the United States to end the slave trade, he found it his duty to attempt to assist Africans however he could. One of his plans, he said, "was to keep up an intercourse with the free people of color in the United States, in the expectation that some . . . would visit Africa, and endeavor to promote habits of industry, sobriety, and frugality among the natives of that country." He had reported to "the free people of color in Baltimore, Philadelphia, New York and Boston," who gave him zealous support; several families, he said, were ready to emigrate. Accordingly, he petitioned Congress for permission "to transport such persons and families as may be inclined to go, as also, some articles of provision, together with implements of husbandry and machinery for some mechanic arts . . . ." He explained that profit was not a major concern, but that any proceeds from trade would offset expenses otherwise to be covered by philanthropy.[8]

Cuffe's petition was presented to Congress, but a bill which would permit the trade was defeated in the House of Representatives by a vote of 72 to 65. The British also denied Cuffe the necessary license, despite support for his petition by the British African Institution.

However, as soon as the war ended and trade with the British started to become normal, Cuffe sailed for Sierra Leone with thirty-eight emigrants, including twenty children. Eight of the passengers paid for their own passage, but Cuffe carried most of the expense himself. In addition to passengers, the ship took a sawmill, a wagon, grindstones, a plow, a collection of hardware and a cargo of grain. Arriving in Sierra Leone in February, 1816, Cuffe arranged for the sale of his cargo, saw that his passengers were settled, and stayed two months attending meetings and churches, and examining the country.

Cuffe's influence on colonization

Cuffe was pleased to find American interest in Sierra Leone high when he returned, and announced that he had received over two thousand requests for assistance in emigrating. He continued to work with the African Institutions he had established in Philadelphia, Boston, New York, and Baltimore. The leadership in the organizations included Prince Saunders in Boston, Peter Williams in New York, James Forten, Richard Allen, and Absalom Jones in Philadelphia, as well as Daniel Coker in Baltimore. Williams, Allen, Jones, and Coker were leaders in newly formed black churches, and through them Cuffe hoped to maintain interest among free blacks in the idea of emigration to Sierra Leone.

Cuffe's own interest in emigration was originally based on the idea of the Christian redemption of Africa. After his visits to Sierra Leone, it became obvious to him that blacks seeking to emigrate could escape the disabilities they faced in America and in his later writings he used that appeal. Cuffe regarded himself as obliged to his fellow blacks by his personal good fortune; on another level, he believed that free blacks in the United States shared African identity and that they were obliged to assist Africa. His personal sense of identity as an African clearly increased in his last years.

Cuffe's connection with the foundation of the American Colonization Society was tangential, but in some respects crucial. Although the ideas of deportationists were widely discussed in the decade before 1806, until Cuffe's party of thirty-eight emigrants arrived in Sierra Leone in 1816 the idea of black emigration had been purely an abstract issue. Cuffe's trips and practical success were newsworthy, and details of the emigration trip were published from Boston to Louisville.[9]

Probably stimulated by the publicity about Cuffe's efforts, white supporters of deportation gathered in a New Jersey meeting later in 1816. Robert Finley, a Presbyterian minister, grew excited by the proposal. He went to Washington, where he organized "The American Society for Colonizing the Free People of Color of the United States," which later shortened its name to the more familiar American Colonization Society. Judge Bushrod Washington, George Washington's son, agreed to serve as president. The list of officers included Henry Clary, Andrew Jackson, Francis Scott Key, and John Taylor. While in Washington, Finley wrote to Cuffe, asking information about prospects for settlement in Africa. Cuffe's reply gave details of possible locations: "Shaborow [Sherbro] layeth about 50 leagues S.E. of

Sierraleone, I have had the River of Shaborow much recommended by John Consell [Kizell] a citizen of Sierra Leone. . . ."[10] Cuffe recommended exploration of the area to find a precise location. He was already considering the larger question of "a general removal of the People of colour." He suggested that a larger area such as the Congo or South Africa might be more appropriate than small West African colonies in such a case. He also considered the possibility of two colonies—one in Africa and another in the United States—to "draw off the colored citizens." He pleaded with Finley to work against the slave trade.[11]

Another founding member of the ACS, Samuel J. Mills, wrote to Cuffe early in 1817, crediting him with "preparing the public mind" for colonization and asking his future assistance. Cuffe declined out of ill health to aid the new society directly but sent Finley and Mills to his associates in the African Institutions, Forten of Philadelphia and Williams of New York. Finley followed Cuffe's advice, met with James Forten and Richard Allen, and reported them enthusiastically in favor of emigration. However, a mass meeting held in Philadelphia to discuss Finley's proposals definitely voted against emigration and colonization in 1817.[12]

The ardent support already developing for colonization among plantation owners and the language used by such supporters was the factor which evoked the strongest opposition from the Philadelphia black community. Cuffe died September 9, 1817, before he had a chance to hear and respond to the arguments of the Philadelphia group.[13]

However, Cuffe's initial support for colonization proved useful to the ACS organizers in several ways. When Mills visited Sierra Leone, he worked with Cuffe's Friendly Society. Cuffe's brief correspondence with Finley and Mills was printed and disseminated by the ACS in hopes of winning black support for the Society. While some of the leaders of the African Institutions rejected the ACS, a few worked with the new group. Daniel Coker turned down his election as bishop of the African Methodist Episcopal church and later left with the first party of ACS émigrés for Sierra Leone and Sherbro in 1820. The Boston African Institution had taken care that only proemigration individuals be allowed to join, but Prince Saunders soon became an advocate of Haitian, not African, emigration.[14]

Cuffe as a nationalist

Neither Cuffe nor his associates in the American African Institutions were interested in ideological speculation, and their writings, whether in the form of letters or pamphlets, usually dealt with practical and immediate concerns. Yet, from those writings we can derive an implied and underlying set of ideas which have a definite nationalist character.[15]

Paul Cuffe's brother wrote to their sister Freelove when Paul first visited Sierra Leone, that Paul had gone for a "religious visit amongst the inhabitants of that land, our own nation." In the journal of his visit to England, Cuffe noted that his purpose was to assist Africa in its civilization. He later wrote to William Allen that he felt "in duty bound to escort [sic] myself to the uttermost of my ability for the good cause of Africa." Such statements confirmed not only Cuffe's Christian and philanthropic motives but his identification with Africa. As time went on, his sense of identification became more pronounced and explicit. He advised the Friendly Society in Sierra Leone to "not give up her [Africa's] commercial pursuits, for that is the greatest outlet to her national advancement. I foresee this to be the means of improving both your country and nation."[16]

When an impostor used Cuffe's name to solicit funds, Cuffe published an open letter directed at the fraud. His line of argument had an explicit nationalist tone.

The great evil that thou has embarked upon is not only against me as an individual. It is a national concern. It is a stain to the whole community of the African race. . . . Let me tell thee that the manumission of 1,500,000 slaves depends on the faithfulness of the few who have obtained their freedom, yea it is not only those who are in bondage but the whole community of the African race, which are according to best accounts, 30,000,000.

Taking Shafer's points common to nationalists, we find that Cuffe displayed many of them. He sought to establish a defined territory; he desired a specific Christian and commercial system to prevail there; he believed in self-government; he believed in a common history of all black men, in which the suffering of slavery was a central theme; he asserted a love for his fellow nationals and attempted to evoke national devotion to Africa; he spoke of and acted on a sense of common sorrow and common hope for Africans and blacks.

Cuffe's single-handed exploits lent credence to later historical treatments which showed him as unique and isolated. But because of his influence on the African Institutions and on the founders of the ACS, Cuffe was hardly an isolated figure. His visits to Africa in 1811 and 1815, his tours and studies of Sierra Leone, and his discussions in England made him the best-informed man in the United States about the conditions which would face emigrants to Africa. In his time he was not at all obscure, as evidenced by the queries sent him by Finley and Mills and by the press coverage of his activities. To suggest that Cuffe should be regarded as a spectacular and unique achiever is to ignore his significance as a black man who expressed black nationalist aspirations and communicated them to the total community. He served as a link between the speculations of earlier deportationists and the more practical colonizers of the ACS, and between the religious leadership of blacks and the philanthropists interested in black removal. Despite the War of 1812, Cuffe brought together the Sierra Leone experience and the Americans, black and white, interested in a similar and parallel enterprise.

In even the small details of his life, Cuffe foreshadowed some aspects of the later personality and psychological pattern of black nationalists. He changed his name, dropping his father's slaveowner's name, and he encouraged others to do the same. He spent part of his early political energies in a fruitless pursuit of political rights within the American system. He lived by the highest kind of personal morality and was an ardent supporter of education. He and some of his associates were devoutly religious; he abstained from alcohol.

In a broader sense, Cuffe's ideas and his style of life set the pattern followed by later black nationalists in America. He sought to redeem Africa through a mixture of business acumen and religious proselytizing. He acted on the premise that a good link between Africa and the blacks in the diaspora would be a black-owned and black-manned shipping operation. He briefly supported the concept of a separate black state within the United States. Like some later nationalists, he worked with and trusted some white allies, despite repeated incidents of insult and discrimination. But as the descendant of an Afro-Indian marriage and as the husband of an Indian woman, he never advocated racial endogamy.

Not long before his death Cuffe cautioned his friends in Philadelphia to examine the ACS plans carefully. His death removed a major obstacle to the takeover of emigration by whites who propagandized for the idea in clearly antiblack language. The ACS, while it attracted black emigrants, failed to utilize or express the separatist and black nationalist sentiments which motivated Cuffe and to which he had given expression. Without the contribution of men like Cuffe, the ACS soon lost black intellectual support, and for more than twenty years colonization operated largely without it.

4

THE IDEOLOGICAL FAILURE OF COLONIZATION

Black opposition to colonization

Black spokesmen quickly noted that the American Colonization Society's basic appeal was not to their interest, that it did not reflect even a rudimentary understanding of black attitudes towards emigration, and that it was based on prejudice. Meetings and statements of blacks throughout the North revealed that the reasons for distrust of the Society were neither local nor transient. In the period 1817–31 most of the agitation against the Society came from blacks and not from whites.

Defenders of the Society cautiously attributed the antagonism of black spokesmen to "some unguarded expressions of Southern men, at the first public meeting to form a Colonization society at Washington." At that meeting, called by Finley and organized by his brother-in-law Elias B. Caldwell, clerk of the Supreme Court, much of the distinguished leadership of Washington attended. The meeting adopted the principle that the new society would not interfere with or touch on the issue of slavery itself.[1]

Henry Clay observed that the condition that slavery and its abolition not be discussed had assured the attendance of representatives from the South and West. But it was the remarks of John Randolph of Roanoke that probably struck listeners as the most "unguarded." He stated that the proposal to remove free blacks[2]

must materially tend to secure the property of every master in the United States over his slaves .... It was a notorious fact that the existence of this mixed and intermediate population of free negroes was viewed by every slave-holder as one of the greatest sources of the insecurity and unprofitableness of slavery property ....

Such language among the founders would hardly endear the Society to northern free blacks. But more fundamental than the particular rhetoric used by ACS advocates was the fact that slaveholders clearly supported the Society out of the intention of removing what they saw as a troublesome element, not out of charity or philanthropy. Colonization was simply deportation, which amounted to exile.

The sentiments of some ACS supporters were often stated in more philanthropic terms. Caldwell said that blacks would necessarily be unhappy while denied rights, and their presence as an unhappy class tended to "injure the morals and destroy the habits of industry" among the rest of the population. Black men's happiness, he said, would be promoted by removal; the more they were exposed to culture and education in the United States, the more unhappy they became at their condition. Caldwell believed it was better to keep slaves and freedmen ignorant than to spend funds in education. Yet, in advocating a colony in Africa he included among his reasons the idea that the black settlers would introduce civilization and Christianity to Africa.[3]

To an observer, the hypocrisy might have been obvious. The hardheaded slaveholder would be glad to be relieved of the dangerous free black element; philanthropists would give the whole proceeding a cloak of idealism. Even within the arguments of Caldwell several contradictions were obvious: if blacks were unhappy, ignorant, and productive of low morals, how would their introduction to Africa tend to civilize and Christianize that continent? Clearly, Caldwell assumed that Africans were so low in culture that even the dregs of American society would benefit them; in this and in his whole position he reflected the set of prejudices, and the blindness to his own prejudices, common to whites of the era.

To men who shared Caldwell's values the Society held out appeal. The idea may have been compelling for several less-than-conscious reasons. White Americans dreamed of making America a white man's country. Removal of the "Negro problem" may have psychologically amounted to the removal of a whole set of problems in whites' outlook on sex, society, and race. The advocates of colonization tried hard to overcome the aura of fantasy and unreality surrounding the idea by repeatedly calculating practical issues such as the rate and expense necessary to transport all blacks from America.[4]

The arguments which the Society included in its early literature dealt with the issues of practicability, with the fact that the plan did not challenge slavery nor violate the Constitution, with the project's claim to philanthropic support, but never with the charge that its premises were prejudiced. While some philanthropic defenders of colonization regarded Randolph's comments as "unguarded" or irresponsible, they did not appear to recognize that their own views would also be seen as springing from hostility to blacks. In the period of the organization of the colonization effort, there was practically nothing in colonization literature to recommend the idea to black readers.

Blacks immediately raised the issue of the prejudices at the root of the Society's plans, and from the first blacks denied that they had any less right to live as citizens in the land of their birth than did Clay, Randolph, or Caldwell.

James Forten described the Philadelphia mass meeting of blacks which rejected the ACS, and revealed the dilemma he personally faced as a nationalistically disposed leader.[5]

Three thousand at least attended, and there was not one sole [sic] that was in favour of going to Africa. They think that the slave holders want to get rid of them so as to make their property more secure. . . . My opinion is that they will never become a people until they come out from amongst the white people, but as the majority is decidedly against me I am determined to remain silent, except as to my opinion which I freely give when asked.

The meeting passed a resolution declaring that the plan of the American Colonization Society represented "banishment" and a "direct violation of those principles which have been the boast of this republic." The assembly rejected the stigma of the Society's declaration that free blacks were "dangerous and useless," and asserted the sense of black identification when it further resolved "that we will never separate ourselves voluntarily from the slave population in this country; they are our brethren by the ties of consanguinity, of suffering and of wrong."[6]

Southern free blacks were more circumspect in their criticisms of the Society than the Philadelphians, yet it was clear, in 1817, that they too, regarded colonization under the auspices of the ACS as a form of exile.[7]

We perfectly agree with the society, that it is not only proper, but would ultimately tend to the benefit and advantage of a great portion of our suffering fellow creatures to be colonized; but while we thus express our approbation of a measure laudable in its purposes, and beneficial in its designs, it may not be improper in us to say, that we prefer being colonized in the most remote corner of the land of our nativity, to being exiled to a foreign country. . . . Be it therefore resolved that we [ask territory] either on the Missouri River, or any place that may seem to [Congress] most conducive to the public good and our future welfare, subject however, to such rules and regulations as the government of the United States may think proper to adopt.

Black clergy participated in and dominated many meetings devoted to condemnation of the Society. Nathaniel Paul, pastor of the African Baptist Church in Albany, New York, toured northern states arguing against colonization, and later lectured in England, raising funds for a Canadian colony and attacking Colonization Society Liberian plans. In both local protest meetings, and in the Annual Conventions of Free People of Color, held 1831–35, the names of black clergymen were prominent in the ranks of ACS critics. The Reverends Hosea Easton, Peter Williams, and many lesser-known ministers helped organize the meetings, usually held in AME or African Baptist churches.[8]

In increasingly severe language the Annual Conventions condemned the Colonization Society, while endorsing Canadian emigration. The third convention called the ACS plan ludicrous, unprincipled, and insidious, while the fourth called it "the great Dragon of the land" and discussed its prejudiced assumptions in some detail. The fifth convention urged blacks to petition state legislatures to stop supporting the Society; this convention renounced the term "African" and urged blacks to drop its use since it lent arguments to the advocates of African repatriation.[9]

White abolitionist opposition to colonization

Through the 1820s some whites who later attacked the hypocrisy of slaveholders and who came to be known as fire-eating abolitionists, remained moderately in favor of colonization. As late as 1828 William Lloyd Garrison spoke to a Boston audience, attacking slaveholders but supporting the Colonization Society. James G. Birney, Gerrit Smith, and other prominent abolitionists of a later period temporarily supported colonization before 1830. But Lewis Tappan opposed the ACS from its early days, and his brother Arthur, after making several contributions to the Society, turned against it because it continued to engage in selling rum in Liberia and regularly stocked liquor as a trade item. Whites involved in other reform movements of the period shared similar hesitations about the Society and criticized it for a variety of reasons in its first years. However, unlike black critics, whites were not at first concerned with the implied prejudices or the explicit attacks on free blacks in the Society's literature. It was the fact that the ACS armed its early settlers and that those settlers engaged in bloody wars with neighboring African peoples that turned a number of pacifists away from support of the Society. Quakers interested in colonization through the 1820s directed their support to plans which did not require forceful displacement of other groups, such as Haitian, Mexican, or communal settlement.[10]

In 1831 Garrison attended the first Annual Convention, hoping to raise funds for his newspaper the *Liberator*. He was accompanied to the convention by the white reformers Simeon Jocelyn, Arthur Tappan, and Benjamin Lundy. The convention passed a sardonically worded censure of the ACS, noting that if blacks were to be sacrificed to the cause of philanthropy, they would prefer to find their graves in the land of their birth. But the black opposition was directed at the ACS, and not at the principle of emigration, for another resolution approved the Canadian colony established the year before by blacks from Ohio.[11]

Garrison was converted to opposition to the Society by several black participants in the convention, including James Forten. When Garrison later travelled to Great Britain, he found abolitionists there concerned with immediate rather than gradual abolition, and already in opposition to the ACS. He had been preceded in Britain not only by the black preacher Nathaniel Paul but by Charles Stuart, a white evangelist from the United States who wrote several pamphlets to support and assist Paul. When Garrison returned to the United States, he developed the various arguments against colonization by Forten, Paul, and Stuart, and published them, together with a series of anticolonization resolutions previously passed by free blacks at twenty-two different local meetings, under the title *Thoughts on African Colonization*.[12]

While his was not the first anticolonization publication, Garrison's book did attract the most attention. Already notorious as an outspoken abolitionist through his newspaper, Garrison intended and achieved wide distribution for *Thoughts*. In the work he familiarized white abolitionists, clergy, and philanthropists with the criticisms, advanced from a black point of view, of the fundamental prejudices at the root of the ACS. He marshalled all the standing arguments: the Society sponsored persecution, since ACS supporters had argued that free blacks would be more likely to emigrate if their situation in the United States worsened; the ACS spread false propaganda by asserting free blacks were Africans; the Society was based on cowardice since it played upon fears of slave uprisings; it immorally held that prejudice was stronger than the power of the gospel; it perpetuated slavery, itself equivalent to robbery; it was congenial to slaveholders and to those "who avow undying hostility to the people of colour"; it was patently hypocritical in suggesting that the very people it described as dangerous to American society were to be sent to Christianize Africa; it indulged in war, commerce (itself the result of greed, asserted Garrison), and rum selling. Garrison omitted one popular criticism of Liberia, in that he stated that the location was fairly healthy for colonists. His purpose was to argue that regular missionaries, both black and white, could do the job of Christianizing and civilizing better than settlers.[13]

By extensive quotations from ACS literature he developed his arguments, showing that the Society was pledged not to oppose slavery; that it apologized for slavery and attempted to put slaveholders in a good light; that it accepted the premise that slaves were property and the claimed right of ownership by masters. He argued that the Society tended to increase the value of slaves and therefore made their eventual emancipation more difficult. He pointed out that the Society held free blacks in contempt, opposed their education, contributed to their abuse, and aimed at their expulsion from the United States. All in all, he concluded, the Society's plan was a deception.

In addition to such arguments, based on the Society's own literature, Garrison presented a selection of resolutions mostly passed in 1831 and 1832 in meetings of free blacks in cities from Boston to Washington. While all the resolutions condemned the Society, their major line of argument was the right to live in and die in the land of one's birth. Even so, several of the resolutions approved emigration to destinations other than Liberia. Seven of the twenty-two supported Canada, particularly the Wilberforce settlement. A few included support for locations in the western United States, Mexico, and Haiti. Garrison himself and later observers overlooked the point that the thrust of the resolutions was not antiemigration, but rather antiracist.

One reason for the vehemence of Garrison's attack and that of black clergy upon the ACS may be found in the fact that slavery itself was "not debatable" at the time. Arguments against slavery or against racism could be best directed at the ACS and its policies, and in the guise of a debate over the advisability of removal to Liberia both blacks and white egalitarians could express antislavery arguments.

Despite the clarity of Garrison's book and the criticisms levelled by blacks, the defenders of the Society claimed that such attacks worked against the interests of blacks. Since such arguments, they said, discouraged blacks from accepting offers of freedom linked to emigration, the arguments would themselves contribute to keeping blacks in slavery. Colonizers blamed Garrison for even greater evils—his work in the formation of the Anti-Slavery Society, although apparently well intentioned, had the effect of exciting slaveholders to a greater defense of the institution. The attack of abolitionists on colonization seemed unfair to some ACS supporters in that the two groups should be concerned with separate problems: abolitionists sought to free slaves, colonizers sought to remove free blacks. Why could not both reforms proceed side by side?[14]

The charges of black clergy, Garrison, and British critics of the ACS regarding the prejudices at the base of the Society's plans were patently true. The language and assumptions of the Society were those of deportation. Similar ideas lay behind the contemporary Indian removal and extermination.

What both supporters and opponents of colonization overlooked in the debates of the 1820s and 1830s was that the creation of Liberia could in fact coincide with black nationalist aspirations. The Society tried to find as many black defenders of its arguments as possible. The ACS reprinted materials from Paul Cuffe's journals and correspondence, from his funeral oration given by Peter Williams, from letters written by blacks interested in emigration, and from emigrants settled at Sierra Leone and Liberia. Even as the colonizers did so, however, the black nationalist implications of what they published eluded them. And on the other hand, Garrison and other white abolitionists also ignored the implications of the support of emigration and colonization even among the black opponents of the ACS.

The Society made no effort to enroll black spokesmen on its boards, nor even to develop black auxiliary societies. Contributions from whites were usually attributed by name; the rare notations of contributions from blacks were listed anonymously; no black churches or fraternal associations were listed among contributors. Even white abolitionists had difficulty bringing themselves to work with their black allies, but eventually integrated abolition meetings were held. Colonizers could never have achieved such liaison without offending both slaveholder supporters and the less explicitly bigoted philanthropic contributors.

Over the years colonization supporters appeared to remain blind to the appeal that the colony developed for blacks with nationalist and separatist ideas. Some black spokesmen, like the white colonizers themselves, regarded prejudice among whites as too permanent to be erased or altered in a few years. For such black men, the consequence was to turn to separatist or revolutionary alternatives. Abolitionists, particularly after 1830, held as an article of faith the premise that the force of moral conversion would overcome prejudice. But as slavery remained and increased its territory, the skepticism about human nature held by colonizers and black separatists seemed justified by the facts. The abolitionist view that prejudice would melt in the face of moral force became harder and harder to sustain as the moral force produced so few results. By the 1850s more black spokesmen would argue that blacks could reject the prejudiced view of themselves implicit in colonization, and yet accept emigration and support from the ACS to build an independent and self-governing black state. As the Liberian emigrants quietly set about doing that, they developed a set of ideas crucial to black nationalism in America, ideas which were eventually recognized and reimported to the United States.

5

LIBERIA

In the first decade of the Liberian colony, black separatist ideas rarely took
the form of explicit black nationalism and the construction of a sovereign
state; Liberian nationalism emerged gradually. In the United States explicit
nationalism and a definable group of black nationalists did not develop until
the early 1850s. As the black colonists in Liberia struggled through their
first trials of high mortality, disease, and negotiation and battles with the
native inhabitants, they began to demand power, shape institutions, and
develop ways of thinking about their experience which can only be called
nationalistic and which formed the basis for sovereignty. As they did so,
they drew on the experience of the Nova Scotia pioneers in Sierra Leone
and on that of Paul Cuffe. Particular Sierra Leone colonists and some contacts of Cuffe assisted in the founding of the new colony.

John Kizell

The American Colonization Society began its explorations of the African
coast in 1818, sending founding member Samuel Mills and Ebenezer Burgess
to Sierra Leone with instructions to explore southward. At Freetown they
met with the governor of Sierra Leone and with members of Paul Cuffe's
Friendly Society, among whom was John Kizell, a man largely overlooked
in the literature of black nationalism, who played a crucial role by bringing
the previous experience of Sierra Leone and Paul Cuffe to bear on the
foundation of Liberia. Burgess and Mills agreed that Kizell and another
member of the Friendly Society, William Martin, should accompany them

as interpreters and guides to assist in the negotiation for land.[1]

Kizell was a native of West Africa, born a few miles inland from the coast near Sherbro Island. His father and uncle had been chiefs of different towns, and as a child he was kidnapped during an attack on his uncle's village. Despite his father's offer of ransom, he was sold to a British slaver bound for South Carolina.[2]

After several years as a slave in Charleston, he found an opportunity to secure his freedom by joining the British forces under Sir Henry Clinton during the Revolution. At the end of the war he was sent to Nova Scotia, and in 1792 he returned to Africa with the founding group of Sierra Leone emigrants from Canada. Since he was from the area and knew the local languages, he was employed by the British governors in their dealings with chiefs, and he soon made a name for himself as an effective negotiator at the extended palavers held to settle questions of land use, trade rights, and justice. In 1810 the governor of Sierra Leone authorized Kizell to secure property in his own name at Sherbro Island, and to establish residence there. The governor expected Kizell to start a settlement which would have no European residents, and to develop the British influence in that region. Kizell carried out the task, making regular reports, and he tried to attract American black colonists both from Paul Cuffe and from the American Colonization Society to his own settlement.[3]

It was Kizell who suggested Sherbro Island to Cuffe so strongly that Cuffe in turn recommended it in a letter to Mills. Kizell had established in 1814 a community called Campelar. The town was on a site of five hundred acres which Kizell had purchased for about $150 in goods. At his settlement Kizell experimented with crops, introduced cattle, and in several respects acted as a modernizing influence. He saved six individuals from a trial-by-poison, by paying bribes of fifty to one hundred bars of iron—in trade the equivalent value of several slaves—for each. In addition, he rescued about twenty individuals from sale into foreign slavery, usually by purchase and emancipation.[4]

Kizell accompanied Mills and Burgess to Sherbro Island and helped them in their negotiations with local chiefs. Mills's report showed that Kizell already thought in terms of local and pan-African nationalism:[5]

Mr. K. is a second Paul Cuffe. . . . He has enlarged views, and he believes with the fullest confidence, that the time has arrived, when the descendants of Africans abroad shall begin to return to their own country. His mind relies on the promise of God, "Ethiopia shall soon stretch forth her hands unto God." He says, if we can fix on a proper place for a colony, our people may come out by hundreds and thousands, and we need not fear the consequences, only sending some men of education and piety to be their conductors and guides. Africa is the land of black men, and to Africa they must and will come . . . . As for land, he says, it belongs to Africans abroad, as well as those now in this country; and if they are disposed to return, land they must and shall have. They have not forfeited a right to the inheritance of their fathers, by being carried by force from their country. . . . Let any class of the people of colour come, only give us a few who will be good leaders of the rest. . . . Mr. K. thinks the greater part of the people of colour, who are now in America, will yet return to Africa.

A more clear-cut statement of the fatherland concept at the heart of nationalism would be hard to locate in that era. Kizell's experiences on the Middle Passage, in South Carolina, Canada, and Africa gave him a perspective on the black race shared by only a few men.

Burgess and Mills explored a number of attractive locations with Kizell's assistance, and negotiated for the site of a colony on the Bagroo River, about thirty miles inland from Campelar.[6]

In his conversations with Kizell Mills raised the question of who should govern; together they discussed a system of white custodial government for the period while black leadership developed. Mills said of Kizell's comments:[7]

Mr. K. . . . thinks it may be best for the first few years to have a white governor, a man of considerable age, and great moderation and prudence. If, however, a Paul Cuffe could be found among the people of colour, who was disposed to come out to this country, it might be well to appoint him governor. . . .

Mills indicated that he substantially agreed with this position, and supported the principle of eventually moving to self-government. But a definite note of skepticism about black abilities and of condescension showed in his remarks.[8]

If Paul Cuffe were alive, it might settle the question; but unless a judicious man of colour can be found, who will secure the confidence of all parties it will be best to have a white governor. Everything should be done to encourage the people of colour to make exertions and help themselves.

After the receipt of the Mills report, the Society appointed new agents and began to recruit emigrants. In February, 1820, thirty-nine families, eighty-nine individuals in all, sailed on the *Elizabeth* from New York. The groups stayed at Campelar while negotiations on the Bagroo site became bogged down over the colony's intention to interfere with the lucrative slave trade. The white agents died before the palavers were completed, and the governing of the colonists was left in the hands of Daniel Coker, Cuffe's associate from Baltimore.[9]

33

Daniel Coker

Coker was raised as a slave in Maryland; he escaped at an early age to New York, where he joined the Methodist church. He was ordained and returned to Baltimore to preach and operate a school run by the AME Bethel Church, and he arranged to buy his freedom. He was a coorganizer of the AME denomination with Richard Allen and Absalom Jones. He established the African Institution of Baltimore, with Cuffe. He declined the nomination as the first bishop of the AME to continue work in Baltimore, and emigrated to Liberia in 1820 on the *Elizabeth* as a missionary, with support from the Maryland Colonization Society.[10]

On the death of the agents and some settlers by disease in early 1821, Coker sought the advice of the governor of Sierra Leone, and shortly received aid from American naval vessels. Coker arranged to have the surviving colonists moved to a plantation at Fourah Bay, near Freetown. Almost a year after Coker took command, the brig *Strong* arrived with twenty-eight more colonists, who settled with the first group at Fourah Bay. New agents conferred with Coker and agreed that a new location should be established for the colony. The decision to move further south was partly based on a fear that an American colony at Sherbro would be too close to Sierra Leone and British control.[11]

After considering settlement at Bassa Cove, which had been explored by Burgess and Mills, agent Eli Ayres and Captain Robert Stockton of the U.S. Navy ship *Alligator* decided to negotiate for land at Cape Mesurado. Captain Stockton speeded up the protracted discussions at one point by placing a pistol at the head of the local chief. The transaction cost about $300, and the estimated value of the land by American standards was about $1 million.[12]

In January, 1822, the settlers were transshipped from Fourah Bay to Mesurado, although some of those at Fourah decided to remain in Sierra Leone, including Coker. Despite Coker's obvious ability and his promise of developing into "another Paul Cuffe," he was dropped by the ACS. Ayres noted that some of those staying on in Sierra Leone were "insubordinate" and he was glad to leave them. It was apparent that Coker's leadership ability did not coincide with white ACS conceptions of how a colony should be run.[13]

In the first months of the new settlement, a British naval cruiser with about thirty recaptured slaves aboard ran aground near the colony. According to local custom, such a ship and its contents, including slaves, became the property of the local people. In ceding the land for occupancy, local chiefs assumed they retained the right to salvage slaves for purposes of resale. The colonists viewed the matter differently and protected the ship and slaves until another vessel arrived to send them on to Sierra Leone. After this and other such disagreements the local chiefs launched an attack against the colony which was repulsed with British naval assistance; the matter was soon arbitrated by Boatswain, a powerful chief and himself a returned slave, who held some supremacy over local chiefs. He decided in favor of the colonists. The decision was reluctantly accepted, but elements of the indigenous Dey people believed that they had been betrayed, and the incident remained a casus belli for several years.[14]

Elijah Johnson and Lott Carey

The colonists took formal possession of Cape Mesurado in a ceremony on April 25, 1822. The rainy season set in immediately, and Ayres asked the colonists if they would prefer to return to Sierra Leone. Six accepted, but the rest, under the leadership of Lott Carey, decided to stay and secure the colony against further attacks. Ayres reported that Carey and Elijah Johnson, who had both come over in the 1821 ship, were devoted to the welfare of the colony and showed leadership capacity.

Ayres departed in June and left the colony in charge of Carey and Johnson. In August a new agent, Jehudi Ashmun, arrived to find the colony of about 135 settlers once again threatened by attack. He set up a form of military organization, assigning elements of defense to various colonists. Johnson was placed in charge of the colony's stores and Carey was appointed health officer. Others were put in charge of ordnance, picket stations, and artillery emplacements. They did their work well, for in November and December the local chiefs brought an army of between nine and fifteen hundred to attack the colony. The combination of fortifications, discipline, and rapid-fire artillery saved the colony. However, after the second severe attack the colonists ran low on ammunition, and a British naval vessel intervened to bring about an uneasy negotiated settlement. During the battles Ashmun was ill, and the conduct of the war remained largely in the hands of Carey and Johnson, both of whom had expected to serve as missionaries, not military officers.[15]

Johnson had been born in the North, probably New Jersey, and had a brief grammar-school education. He had served in the War of 1812 and had been a Baptist preacher before sailing in 1821. Later, in 1824, he again governed the colony in the absence of the white agent. He continued to distinguish himself, particularly in leading the militia. He served in the Constitutional Convention in Liberia in 1847.[16]

Carey had been born a slave, about 1780, near Richmond, Virginia. In 1804 he had hired out to work in a tobacco warehouse, where he soon took up heavy drinking. He underwent a conversion and pledged to reform himself, joining the Baptist church in 1807. He learned to read, in order to study the Bible. He began to conduct meetings himself, and local clergy encouraged him to preach. He did not confine his readings to religion, however, for a surprised white visitor once reported finding Carey reading Adam Smith's *Wealth of Nations.*

Carey began to make money by the sale of scrap tobacco, and by 1813 he was able to purchase his freedom. By 1815 he earned a salary of $800 per year and conducted his own business. In this period he grew interested in Africa, and led in the formation of an African missionary society in Richmond. As a Baptist preacher he won a devoted following, and he owned a farm on the outskirts of the city. When he resolved to give over his life to Africa, and to emigrate, his associates in the clergy and his tobacco employers attempted to keep him. His explanation of his decision had a nationalist tone:

I am an African; and in this country, however meritorious my conduct, and respectable my character, I cannot receive the credit due to either. I wish to go to a country where I shall be estimated by my merits—not by my complexion; and I feel bound to labour for my suffering race.

Together with Colin Teague, another Baptist preacher of the Richmond area, Carey volunteered to serve as a missionary to Africa under the direction of the Baptist General Convention, and applied to the ACS for passage. Before his departure Carey addressed a meeting of free blacks in Richmond, stressing his religious motives in emigrating: "I feel it my duty to go; and I very much fear that many of those who preach the gospel in this country, will blush when the Saviour calls them to give an account of their labours in this cause. . . ."

During the stay at Fourah Bay Carey engaged in barrel and tub making in order to buy provisions for his family. He later turned his talents to medical care, developing a reputation as a competent physician. Carey founded several mission stations and schools, and emerged as a leader, not only in the military defense of the Mesurado settlement in November-December, 1822, but as a spokesman of the settler position in relation to the Colonization Society.[17]

Settler rebellion

Carey soon participated in a small-scale rebellion against the authority of Ashmun and the Society, which had lasting influence. The source of the rebellion was that both Ayres and Ashmun attempted to enforce the Society's rule that lands should be distributed and cultivated, and that stores should only be issued during the pioneering of the land. Hoping to force the issue, Ayres and Ashmun set several deadlines on the distribution of stores. The colonists issued a "Remonstrance" in December, 1823, complaining of the decision and appealing to the board. Ayres commented that the settlers "went out expecting to govern themselves, and had no idea of having white agents. . . ."[18]

Carey led a group to take stores from the common storehouse, in direct contravention of Ashmun's orders. Ashmun read the Colonization Society's orders to the colonists, and achieved an apology from Carey and an uneasy peace. When the ship *Cyrus* arrived with over one hundred new settlers and inadequate supplies, Ashmun issued half rations for the whole settlement. Carey then armed his supporters with weapons from the stores. Ashmun found the protest against his rule taking on the proportions of an insurrection, and he left for a four-month stay in the Cape Verde Islands in April, 1824, putting Elijah Johnson officially in charge. The Board of Managers of the ACS, disturbed at rumors of trouble, dispatched its secretary, Ralph Gurley, to investigate. He proceeded by way of the Cape Verde Islands, where he picked up Ashmun. Once at Liberia, Gurley investigated the colonists' complaints, conferred with Carey, and then instituted a system of limited self-government and increased colonist participation. The storehouse rebellion of Carey, overlooked by historians of black nationalism, had forced the issue of self-determination and paved the way for the development of the first English-speaking black nation.[19]

The system put in effect was at first rejected by the Board of Managers. But within a few months, after receiving letters from the colony stating that the new policy was working well, the board reversed itself, accepted the new arrangement, and formalized developments of the previous two years. In the provisions of the original charter, the contrast between the stated long-range goal of black self-determination and the actual authoritarian structure established by the managers had been striking. The Society enacted the laws; the agents were the judiciary and appointed all local officers and decreed local law. After the rebellion the revised charter provided for limits on the power of the agents; set up an elective system with qualifications for voters; set a term of office of one year for civil officers appointed from among the colonists; and provided for the election of some officers, with the agent retaining a veto power. By 1824 experience suggested that the white agents would die or be absent with considerable frequency. Hence, one of the most crucial officers to be elected was the vice agent, who was to serve in the event of the death or absence of the appointed agent. Other elected officers included two councillors and a sheriff, while the agent retained control of the judiciary through the power of appointing judges and officers of the court. The colonists' pressure tactics had brought about an effective set of reforms and limited self-government.

The settlers accepted the new system and worked within it. Some, including Carey, found it very satisfactory.[20] A statement prepared two years after the new rules went into effect by the citizens of Monrovia praised the new plan. As structured, it gave voice to the inherent black nationalist appeal of Liberia.[21]

We are proprietors of the soil we live on and possess the rights of freeholders. Our suffrages and what is of more importance, our sentiments and our opinion have their due weight in the government we live under. Our laws are altogether our own; they grow out of our circumstances; are framed for our exclusive benefit; and administered either by officers of our own appointment, or such as possess our confidence. We have a judiciary chosen from among ourselves; we serve as jurors in the trial of others; and are liable to be tried only by juries of our fellow citizens, ourselves.

The emphasis on trial by jury was a particularly telling point. Even in those few states in the United States where blacks had the vote, they were excluded from juries.

But the statement did not recognize the powerful control of civil affairs retained by the Society through the agent, nor the control over essential parts of the system, such as schools, exercised by the missionary societies and churches in the United States. For continued immigration the colony remained strictly dependent on the Society; munitions and other stores were purchased out of Society funds. However, the force of the colonists' displeasure and harassment could remove an agent they did not approve, as it had Ashmun in 1824; in fact, the laws were administered, as the statement claimed, by men who possessed the confidence of the settlers. While independence was far off, the colony had achieved more significant self-government—at least for settlers, although not for indigenous people—than other areas of Africa were to achieve under European rule for more than a century. Americo-Liberians had far more rights of citizenship than did blacks in America.

The colonists demonstrated the triumph of their tactics and their control of the structure by electing Carey vice agent in 1826; two years later he took over administration of the colony when Ashmun, seriously ill, returned to the United States. After an eight-month administration Carey was killed while loading cartridges. Another colonist, Colston Waring, who had been elected to the vice agency when Carey became acting agent, took charge. Thus, for most of that year, the colony was entirely governed by black settlers.[22]

Francis Devany

As hostility to the Society mounted to a high pitch in the United States, the black colonists quietly continued to build their fortunes and to work towards fuller self-determination. Francis Devany, the high sheriff of the colony, visited the United States in 1830 to meet with both the Board of Managers of the ACS and a Congressional committee to discuss the state of the colony. Devany's warm advocacy of Liberia was rewarding to the colonizers; besides, he was the first black elected official from Liberia, or indeed from anywhere, to visit the United States; and he had amassed a fortune in Liberia worth between $15,000 and $20,000.[23]

Devany was ready to move to national independence, as a report of his statement to the board indicated:[24]

The colony experienced great inconvenience for the want of a national flag: several vessels are owned by the colonists—he himself owns one which cost one thousand dollars; and another person paid six thousand dollars for a vessel; but these and many other vessels are laid up and going to decay for want of a flag. . . . The people have great respect for the agents, but feel themselves to be at the head of their own society.

Such commercial reasons for seeking statehood eventually proved to be effective. The anomaly of a colony established and controlled by a private society became increasingly uncomfortable as Liberian officials sought to enforce trade rules against European merchants and attempted to suppress the slave trade.

The developing commercial interests in Liberia of men like Devany had other long-range consequences that contributed to nationalism. The colony expanded its territory through land purchase, through military expeditions, and through various treaties of protection in which weaker villages sought to protect themselves against stronger, slave-raiding neighbors. To protect outlying trade routes and stations as well as the expanding sphere of influence, the colony's militia was more formally organized, with ranks of captain, colonel and general assigned to officers. Often the officers were prominent men of commerce, and the military rank explicitly expressed the developing social stratification. While the elite that emerged only cautiously challenged the Society's control at first, such men were eager to run their own affairs and escape some of the more restricting policies of the ACS Board.

John Russwurm and the state Society colonies

During the 1830s a number of state colonization societies in the United States undertook to establish their own colonies near or contiguous to the Liberian colony. The most successful and important of these was the Maryland colony, whose territory centered around Cape Palmas, over two hundred miles southeast of Monrovia, and whose claims stretched from the Grand Cess River to the River Pedro. Maryland continued under separate government until ten years after the independence of Liberia, when it was merged into the republic as a county. Its eastern part was lost to the French in the Ivory Coast in 1895.

Partly because of financial aid from the Maryland Legislature and partly because of the experience gained in Liberia, the Maryland colony had fewer problems related to self-government than the original one at Mesurado. Voluntary emigrants were difficult to recruit, but eventually a total of about twelve hundred sailed. Within seven years of its founding ten emigrant ships had established a flourishing settlement of seven towns.

After brief administrations by two white agents, the Maryland colonizers appointed John Russwurm to be governor of the colony in 1836, and he retained the position until his death in 1851. Russwurm's governorship had more impact in the United States than did the administration of several other black chief executives in Liberia, for he was relatively well known in America prior to his emigration. He had been born in Jamaica of a white American and a black woman. When the father moved to the United States, he sent his son to Canada, but his white wife insisted that John be educated. Russwurm attended Bowdoin College in Maine and is presumed to be the first black man to receive a college degree in the United States. In 1827 he was the cofounder, with Samuel Cornish, of *Freedom's Journal,* the first black-owned newspaper in the country. From the beginning the paper opposed the Colonization Society, so that when Russwurm announced his decision to go to Liberia in 1830 he was publicly criticized by his partner and by other black leaders. However, he stated it was a "mere waste of words to talk of ever enjoying citizenship in this country."[25]

On his arrival in Liberia he took over a printing press sent there by public subscription in Boston four years before, and founded the *Liberia Herald,* which earned international repute as a well-edited and well-printed newspaper. Even the press's job printing received notice, as ship captains were obliged to fill out printed forms when clearing customs. Russwurm resigned the editorship of the paper before his appointment to the Maryland position, and served briefly as superintendent of education in Liberia. His term as governor in Maryland was a credit to the colony. Ship captains and other visitors found their prejudices challenged and expressed astonishment that a literate and distinguished black man governed the colony.[26]

From the beginning Russwurm's most serious problems were working out differences between indigenous people and the settlers, and straightening out the badly tangled financial accounts of the colony. He was instrumental in obtaining a patrol of the U.S. Navy to counteract slave-trading operations along the coast, and after 1841 naval ships regularly stopped at Cape Palmas. But conflicts with missionaries over military duty of missionary assistants flared into a major dispute, as several white missionaries, critical of a black governor, tried to have Russwurm removed. The problem took on a larger significance since the missionaries hired most of the talented settlers, leaving very few to serve in the civil administration. By 1844, after several clashes in the United States between missionary societies and the Maryland Society, the American Board of Foreign Missions removed its missions from the colony; independent missions under Baptist, Methodist, and Episcopal control stayed on, accepting colonial jurisdiction and Russwurm's administration. The Episcopal mission station there would later provide a post for Alexander Crummell.[27]

Russwurm experimented with the idea of a small fleet of coasting vessels to be owned by the colony. He purchased two ships but had to abandon the project after difficulties in obtaining sailors and repairs.[28]

Russwurm's interest in the colony's welfare and his careful administration soon served as a stimulus to developing autonomy. Other factors contributed as well. In order to insure that the colony not be seized in any dispute between the United States and Britain, in 1841 the Maryland Society declared that the colony was in no way under United States sovereignty. The sheer delay in communication between the capital town of Harper and Baltimore, usually at least six weeks in each direction, led to increased authority for the governor. The Board of Managers urged Russwurm to gain greater financial independence of the Society, and he sought revenues. He charged an anchorage duty on ships visiting Cape Palmas. In 1843 a system of revenues, including import duties and license fees, was temporarily suspended by the board, then reinstated after protest from the colony. On Russwurm's insistence, the function of presiding judge was separated from that of governor, and in 1843 a chief justice was appointed.[29]

When Russwurm died in 1851, he left behind a colony that had survived, expanded, and gained defined borders. While the colonists depended on the Society for support and resisted farming, the Russwurm administration had been a success. But about two years after his death the colony voted for independence. After making agreements with the Maryland Society, Maryland in Africa was proclaimed an independent republic on June 8, 1954, and William Prout became the governor of the new nation.

Prout was forced to resign in 1855 by angered citizens who wanted to adopt a more aggressive attitude towards the indigenous people. His successor, Boston Drayton, engaged the new nation in several battles, and when Liberians under J.J. Roberts came in response to calls for military aid, they found Marylanders on the verge of being wiped out. Roberts negotiated a peace settlement and an agreement which incorporated Maryland in Liberia as a county. By April, 1857, the unification was officially completed.[30]

Other colonies established by state societies did not fare so well. Pennsylvania and New York societies combined to establish a colony which expressed temperance and pacifism: no liquor or arms were to be allowed within its boundaries. This proposal raised funds from reform-minded philanthropists in those states. However, the absence of weapons at the settlement at Grand Bassa established by the joint societies invited attack from the the natives; Liberian militia forces came to the rescue. The Mississippi Society established a settlement at Greenville, on the Sinoe River, hoping to avoid the reformist, philanthropic tinge of the ACS and the northern wing of the colonization movement. Within a few years, however, the Mississippi legislature forbade all emancipation. Other state societies planned colonies which were never established, among them Virginia, Ohio, and Louisiana.[31]

In 1838 the ACS had invited the state societies with African colonies to form a union for mutual protection. In 1839 the Commonwealth of Liberia was formed, but Maryland refused to join. The other colonies were incorporated, retaining elements of their previous independent status. Prohibition of liquor remained in the Bassa Cove settlement, the Mississippi Society retained title to the lands in its settlement, and the right to appoint its own chief executive. "For the time being" the governorship was yielded to the governor of the whole commonwealth.

Anthony Williams and J. J. Roberts

The ACS abandoned the term "agent" in the early 1830s, and appointed governors were to serve as the colony's, and later the commonwealth's, chief executive officers, with elected lieutenant governors from among the colonists to serve in the case of death or absence of the governor. The practice, which had started with Coker and been regularized under Carey, continued to produce black self-government, and it became incorporated in the colony's constitution. Anthony D. Williams, first as vice agent, then as lieutenant governor, administered the colony in the mid-1830s. After the formation of the commonwealth Thomas Buchanan, the last white governor, served for two years until struck down with malaria. The commonwealth came under all-black administration again in 1841 with the succession to office of J.J. Roberts. Roberts was appointed governor in his own right by the ACS, and remained chief executive until independence. He was a light mulatto and a leader of the mulatto faction. Liberian political parties, like those in Haiti, soon developed along color lines. The antimulatto party emerged as the opposition to Roberts during his first presidency of the republic, as early as 1851.[32]

After 1827 the colony saw frequent and extended periods of black administration under Carey, Williams, Roberts, and several lesser figures; Maryland had a black governor almost from its inception. On at least two issues black governors developed policies which conflicted with the Society. Williams was more aggressive with the militia than the Society thought proper, and seized territory which the Society tried to renounce. Williams, Roberts, and the white governor, Buchanan, all enforced tariff regulations against the missionaries. By the mid-1830s the colonists preferred to run their own affairs, and the governor-in-council attempted to act as sovereign without consulting the ACS board.

The contrast between the experience in Liberia and that in Sierra Leone was striking. The British colony continued twenty-one years, from 1787 to 1808, as a private venture, before British government takeover. The early attempts at settler autonomy and rebellion were suppressed by the Jamaican maroons under British authority, and self-determination by the settlers was not tolerated, except in local situations such as Kizell's outpost. Despite continuing pressure for self-government and the advocacy of autonomy by occupants of the governor's house, the colony remained under the British flag until 1961. Liberia was technically under Society administration for only twenty-five years before independence. For at least twelve of those years, blacks administered the colony from the chief executive office through minor posts, and controlled interior commerce from the beginning. While from the settler point of view the Liberian pattern was preferable, the British arrangement in Sierra Leone may have offered the indigenous people more protection from exploitation by settlers and westernized recaptives.

Independence

The movement for Liberian independence was the result of factors created by the local situation and the demands of commerce, such as mutual defense, the death of white agents and governors, the rise of black settlers of wealth and influence in business, government, and the militia, and the rankling supervision of the ACS over local matters. The Society's preference that the colonists enter agriculture rather than commerce had been a sore issue from the beginning. The mounting problems of shipping, merchants, and the role of missionaries pushed the anomaly of Society control too far. In the United States sectional rivalry in the 1840s, the development of abolitionism and proslavery advocacy, and the dissolution of hopes for a united white approach to eliminating the black man's presence created a climate in which Liberian independence seemed practical. By the mid-1840s the ACS was willing to accept the idea of a Declaration of Independence for Liberia, although the board wished to retain ownership of lands.

A series of conventions met in Liberia, and a slim majority favored independence. The local convention at the Bassa settlement voted in favor of continued ACS control, declaring that if the sister colonies voted for independence, it would seek to dissolve the commonwealth and remain under Society patronage. When the Constitutional Convention met almost two years later, however, the Bassa colony had little choice but to accept the majority decision.

Hilary Teague, the son of Carey's associate Colin Teague, was a prominent advocate of independence in the public debates over the issue. Young Teague had taken over the editorship of the *Liberia Herald* on Russwurm's resignation in 1835 and served until 1849. As an orator and poet, as well as newspaper publisher, he emerged as a strong advocate of pan-Negro nationalism, giving emphasis to the themes of past black glories and the future mission of Liberia in regenerating Africa. He advocated that Liberia take "an honourable rank amongst the great family of nations" in 1846. Teague served as a delegate to the Constitutional Convention in 1847 and wrote the Declaration of Independence.

Several issues at the convention indicated that the transition to independence was not entirely amicable. The ACS sent a suggested draft of a constitution. While the delegates adopted the relatively mild Declaration of Independence drafted by Teague, which mentioned the ACS and American philanthropy as the origin of the colony, in the Constitution they adopted language which reflected their determination to run their own affairs: in the declaration of rights the Constitution referred to the right to "alter" the form of government when government failed to serve the needs of the people. This right had been repeatedly exercised by Liberian settlers in the past. The Constitution admitted only "persons of colour" to citizenship; it held as a goal the introduction of civilization to the "benighted continent" it postponed the question of Society title to lands.[33]

The development of Liberian sovereignty and nationalism proceeded in some isolation from the American public, despite the Colonization Society's efforts to publicize its successes. The Board of Managers tended to avoid giving emphasis to issues between the colonists and the Society, and continued to stress the prominence of white contributors more than black emigrants and their affairs. The agitation of Garrison, Paul, and dozens of other black and white abolitionists put every publication of the Society under a pall of suspicion. That suspicion remained justified, for the Society proceeded to raise funds and win support on grounds that appealed to white prejudices, and attempted to decide colonial policy without much understanding of black aspirations. The issues which were most embarrassing to the Society—colonist "insubordination," a disposition to speed progress towards self-control, aggressiveness towards white missionaries and merchants—were all elements which could have appealed to those blacks who condemned the whole effort as a white-dominated fraud.

Summary

Black executive power in Liberia was inevitable from the beginning, as Mills anticipated from his discussions with Kizell. Coker set the precedent of acting agent, which was repeated in 1824 with Elijah Johnson, forced by the storehouse rebellion, and formalized before Carey's administration of 1828. By the thirties mulatto leadership in the persons of Russwurm and Roberts emerged through the mechanisms of the separate state Society colony of Maryland and the lieutenant governorship of the commonwealth.

The colonists' control of their own military forces and their conception of the colony as a place of commerce rather than of agriculture contributed to the exercise of independent power. They recognized that more money could be made from trade than from growing crops in competition with native producers, and as black Yankees the emigrants were disposed to moneymaking. Commerce brought men like Devany to seek a flag as early as 1830. Military actions in defense of trade routes and outlying settlements, and against slavers, developed a cadre of officers, some of whom emerged as leaders in the early republic. From the ranks of the men of wealth and the officers of the militia, and from a handful of intellectuals like Teague, a nationalistic group of leaders was ready for a quiet move to independence by the 1840s.

In the United States opposition to the ACS among black spokesmen and whites working for abolition remained so strong that many black separatists and potential black nationalists turned their attention to other possible forms of political separatism. Some dallied with the idea of revolution, some with emigration, and a few with the possibility of local black sovereignty and self-control. Liberia would attract few such men until after 1847, and even then it remained in competition with other locations.

6

EXPERIMENTS WITH BLACK ENCLAVES

Emigration to Liberia was only one of several projects undertaken by white-sponsored and black-supported colonization in the period 1820–60. Suspicion of the motives of the ACS did not extend to efforts at settling freed slaves and free men of color in colonies within the United States and elsewhere in the Western Hemisphere. Migrations, both organized and individual, to Canada, to Haiti, and on a small scale to Mexico, swelled the volume of black emigrants. Together with the Liberian emigration, the total number of free blacks who had left the territory of the United States by the eve of the Civil War was between 80,000 and 90,000, a considerable number when compared to the total free black population of the United States in 1860, 488,000.

The extent to which these settlements, experiments, and emigrations derived from previous separatist ideas and precedents is limited; but their contribution to the body of nationalist doctrine, while tangential in comparison to the Liberian contribution, did involve some specific ideas and methods regarding economic self-sufficiency. Some of the settlements were specifically developed as refuges for fugitive slaves, especially after 1850. To an extent, their existence needed no further raison d'être than refuge, and hence little intellectual justification of separatism developed out of them.

Whether as refuges from discrimination or from slavery, the settlements were separate, not integrated. Founders explained temporary separatism as a mechanism through which training for life in an integrated society could take place; freed blacks were expected to learn manual and intellectual skills, to acquire habits of self-government, and to develop thrift and pride which would come from property ownership. The colonies and communities in the Unites States and Canada which were conceived of as training grounds for citizenship and which developed schools centered on manual and moral training clearly set the precedent for the kind of school which later reached full fruition under Booker Washington at Tuskegee. Even the relationship of the school to the surrounding community—a kind of economic interdependence in which the students learned skills in local industry and in which the industry contributed in one form or another to the school—was not original within Tuskegee, but developed in the earlier era.

Experiments in the United States

The planter who specified in his will that his slaves should be free assumed a large place in the legendary literature of the Old South, but relatively few records of large planters ordering such a course exist. Before legislation in the 1840s in several southern states made all emancipation by will illegal, some states required that slaves freed by will be removed from the state to prevent an increase in free blacks. While such laws in the end provided a source for the ACS in its recruitment, they presented a difficulty for planters who wished to free their slaves if they conscientiously sought a suitable locale for the freedmen. Southern hostility to freed blacks, even when not reflected in law, might give an intended philanthropist pause about resettlement in a slave state. Liberia's critics, mortality rate, and unsettled condition made that alternative unpleasant for some. Another alternative—freeing the slaves and sending them north or west individually or in family groups—might appear heartless.

For a few planters, a plan of manumission developed which seemed to meet most of the objections. The slaves would be freed, sent as a group to a site of land purchased on the western frontier of a free state, and there be established as a colony, either with individually owned or trustee-held land to provide them with homes and livelihood.

But some of these proposals, when implemented, fell far short of their planners' hopes. Like the Liberian plan, white philanthropy reflected little of black aspirations, and the convergence of white-sponsored separatism with black self-determination ideas was usually accidental, not thought through. Edward Coles, a Virginian who migrated to Illinois and later became its second governor, inherited seventeen slaves. He purchased land near Edwardsville, Illinois, and manumitted his slaves in 1819. His settlement, which provided no elaborate plans for the slaves or their well-being, apparently worked out quietly.

Another settlement in 1819 encountered difficulties. Samuel Gist, an

English owner of a plantation in Virginia, specified in his will that his slaves be freed and that they be provided for from the proceeds of his plantation. The executors of his estate took this to mean they should purchase new lands outside Virginia with the proceeds of the sale of his plantation land. The slaves walked overland to a pair of sites in Ohio selected by the executors of the will. Unfortunately, most of the land was untillable, proceeds from the sale of the original estate, after satisfying creditors, were quite small and although some of the slaves sought employment, others appeared to the local whites to be living as vagabonds. Despite hostility of white neighbors, the community and its school held together until at least 1835, and the group's dissolution came gradually.[1]

Several groups of freed slaves settled in this fashion were reported around the North, some thriving, others encountering severe problems. In 1827 sixty-five freedmen settled near York, Pennsylvania; there were at least five such settlements in Ohio between 1815 and 1858.[2]

As tensions between the North and South increased and antiblack sentiments became more explicit in many areas of the North, resettlement plans encountered more problems. John Randolph of Roanoke, despite his one-time endorsement of the ACS plan, specified in his will that his three hundred slaves should be freed and settled on a large tract of land with provision for housing and equipment. In 1846 his executors purchased a 3200-acre site in Mercer County, Ohio, but the arriving freedmen were kept from the land by armed whites and the group was dispersed. By 1847 the remnants of the group were again threatened with expulsion from the county if they did not leave peacefully, and the Randolph colony was never settled. Another effort in the 1840s was more successful. A Virginia planter by the name of Saunders took his slaves to Cass County, Michigan, in 1847 and settled them on a square mile of land he purchased there. Other free blacks moved to the settlement, and visitors reported after several years that the group was prosperous and that the farms did well.[3]

These planter-sponsored efforts predictably reflected paternalism and for the most part were not carefully planned. Those that succeeded did so because of a combination of good management, good land selection, and some dedication on the part of the freedmen. Some failed simply because of inattention to management and the hostility of local whites. Although there was no overall plan behind the colonies, there was a common intention. The planters saw separate settlement as necessary to protect and provide for the group, to keep the families and friends together, to provide for emancipation outside states either prohibiting or frowning on free blacks, and to serve as a school for freedom. The pattern that emerged was very much like the plantation in some respects, except that the settlements were managed in what the white trustees felt were the interests of the freedmen, rather than in the interest of the owner's profit. On some of the settlements blacks worked towards and achieved separate land tenure.

Frances Wright at Nashoba

One settlement which achieved wide notoriety in the late 1820s was that of the Scotswoman Frances Wright. Her settlement, unlike those of the planters, was conceived as a social experiment which, if successful, would be widely utilized as a means of providing for emancipation.

Frances Wright had grown internationally famous in 1821 with the publication of a series of travel letters she wrote during a two-year tour and residence in America in 1819-20. In Europe she was befriended by the Marquis de Lafayette, and she returned to the United States in 1824 in his company. Like other European tourists of the day, they visited a number of sectarian communities founded by Shakers and Rappites. In 1825 she published a plan for a community which incorporated some of Robert Owen's ideas, which were under wide discussion in that year. The community she planned was to provide a transition from slavery to freedom. The slaves would receive an education, work for their maintenance and for their purchase price, and then be freed for colonization abroad. Like the planners of the ACS, Wright did not care to challenge slavery with a method of emancipation which would threaten the institution, but rather sought to provide a transition which was gradual, compensated, and which removed the free black man from America.

The settlement she began with the cooperation of George Flower, an Englishman who had already expressed a similar idea and had lived in several experimental communities, was at Nashoba, on the Wolf River, near Memphis, Tennessee. She purchased two thousand acres and settled about a dozen slaves on the land, together with three white men.[4]

After seeing the settlement started, Wright toured several other communities and then left for Europe. In December, 1826, she reorganized Nashoba, setting up a board of trustees which included Lafayette and Robert Owen. The new plan placed more emphasis on cooperative communitarianism than on emancipation. Nonworking members could join the community on payment of a fee—an arrangement that soon produced a group of more or less idle whites and another group of hard-working slaves still aiming at their purchase price. Her doctrine was nonreligious, and she regarded extramarital sex as acceptable. When one of the white trustees publicly announced that he was living by mutual consent with a slave girl, he created a scandal that swept the press of both the United States and Britain.

Wright returned in February, 1828, to find Nashoba in serious internal as well as external trouble; the land had been poorly farmed, and the crops were meager. She once again reorganized the community, with emphasis on training schools. But in 1830 she took the slaves to Haiti and freed them there, ending the whole Nashoba experiment. The idea had been too loosely implemented to provide a true test of the economics of the plan. Like Robert Owen himself, whose New Harmony community collapsed in dissension and lawsuits, Wright failed to stay at the settlement and attend to management. But the attacks of a shocked public on the irreligion and immorality of the settlement did little to disrupt its inner workings. At Nashoba Frances Wright tried to act on two ideals: the utopian goal of a community free of religious and moral restrictions, founded on the basis of communally shared property, and the goal of providing a transition from slavery to freedom. The two goals were in conflict, and the revisions of Nashoba's organizational plan reflected that tension.

Haiti

At Nashoba, Wright responded to popular currents in the intellectual ferment of the 1820s. Owen's ideas regarding communal living, ideas of educational reform stressing the need for manual training and mass education, and the idea of colonization of freed slaves abroad were all under wide discussion. Her decision to take the slaves to Haiti can also be seen as a response to a vogue in reformist thinking.

One of the early advocates of Haitian emigration was Prince Saunders, who had been briefly involved with Paul Cuffe as secretary of the Boston African Institution in 1812. Saunders was born free in Vermont, attended Moor's Charity School at Dartmouth College in 1807–1808, and taught for a period at a school for free blacks in Colchester, Connecticut. He lived in Boston in 1812 and soon thereafter went to England with the funding of some white friends, in order to further his education. In London he met Thomas Clarkson and William Wilberforce. He emigrated to Haiti with the support of British abolitionists, to assist in establishing schools and to help forward the cause of Protestantism. Working with Christophe, Saunders took an office in the ministry of education. He compiled a collection of the laws and decrees of Christophe, translated them to English and returned to England in 1816 to see them published there.[5]

Returning to Haiti, he was shortly dismissed by Christophe after a dispute over financial matters. He then moved to the United States to give a series of lectures in Boston and Philadelphia. He returned to Haiti, and President Jean Boyer appointed him attorney general. Saunders remained in Haiti until his death in 1839.[6]

In an 1818 address he advocated migration to Haiti and set forth some nationalistic-sounding arguments.[7]

This magnificent and extensive island which has by travellers and historians been often denominated the "paradise of the New World," seems from its situation, extent, climate and fertility, peculiarly suited to become an object of interest. . . . If the two rival governments of Haiti were consolidated into one well-balanced pacific power there are many hundreds of free people in the New England and middle states, who would be glad to repair there immediately to settle.

Saunders noted the effort of friends of abolition and emancipation in the ACS to provide an asylum for free blacks, and saw that the "authorities of Haiti are themselves desirous of receiving emigrants from this country." He proposed to an 1818 Philadelphia convention that it should attempt to offer mediating services to help bring about a settlement of the war between Christophe's forces in the north and those of Boyer in the south. He suggested that the forces of British philanthropy headed by Clarkson, Wilberforce, and the duke of Gloucester, and the British African Institution, would be encouraged and would assist if blacks convened in Philadelphia attempted to bring about such a settlement. Clarkson and Saunders corresponded, and Clarkson supported the idea of black emigration, urging Saunders to work for it. Clarkson wrote Christophe himself, and offered diplomatic, economic, and social advice, including black settlement from the United States.[8]

Clarkson suggested that Christophe should request that the American government purchase from Spain the Spanish part of the island, now the Dominican Republic, and settle free blacks there. He indicated that Wilberforce supported the idea, and advised Christophe of Saunders's work in Boston, New York, and Philadelphia.[9]

Saunders visited Christophe in 1820, acting, he claimed, with the "full authority" of the people of color in Philadelphia. He and Christophe agreed to a settlement plan, which called for a Haitian government contribution of $25,000 and a vessel. Before the agreement could be signed, Boyer's troops invaded Christophe's kingdom, a revolution ensued, and Christophe was killed. While Christophe had toyed with the idea, blacks in the southern republic, first under Alexandre Petion and later under Jean Boyer, also sought to find American black emigrants. Petion issued an invitation to all blacks "who groan under the dominion of barbarous prejudice." Specifically, artisans were invited and promised wages three times that of farmers. Citizenship would be granted after a year's residence. The prohibition of slavery in Petion's republic was held out as an inducement.[10]

After the death of Christophe and the unification of the island under

Jean Boyer, Saunders again visited Haiti. In early 1823 Saunders reported to Clarkson that[11]

... there were 14000 free people of colour in [North Carolina], who were desirous of going to Hayti with all possible dispatch, in case I would give them encouragement. ... There are many thousands in Philadelphia. ... and in different sections of the United States, who were upon the eve of going to Hayti under very favorable circumstances, when the death of the king took place and blasted all their prospects. These same persons are awaiting, anxiously awaiting. ...

A further impetus to Haitian emigration grew out of contacts initiated in 1824 by Loring Dewey, a New York agent for the ACS. Dewey, disillusioned by the difficulty of raising funds for the Colonization Society, and by public opposition and misunderstanding of the Society's proposals, wrote to inquire whether Haiti would still welcome immigrants. Boyer assumed Dewey was writing on behalf of the ACS and replied with a warm invitation to prospective emigrants. He indicated that his government would cooperate with the Society in providing transportation and homesteads. Within a few days an agent appointed by Boyer, Citizen Jonathan Granville, arrived in the United States with instructions to cooperate with American philanthropy in finding emigrants. He had several thousand dollars for chartering ships and sought to recruit six thousand emigrants. Granville announced that he would give each emigrant $40 for passage, and that free land and provisions would be supplied on arrival in Haiti. He spread publicity through newspapers, and by August, 1824, he had sent thirty black families from Philadelphia.[12]

In response to charges that the Haitian emigration scheme was intended to force diplomatic recognition of Haiti, Granville stated that his sole purpose was recruitment. Boyer's objective seems to have been recruitment of skilled craftsmen, sorely lacking in Haiti.[13]

General Robert Harper of the ACS advised Dewey to form a separate colonization and emigration society for Haiti, and he proceeded to do so. Dewey's group, called the Society for Promoting the Emigration of Free Persons of Colour to Hayti, drew its strength and support largely from the New York City affiliate of the ACS. Also a black group formed in New York, and in Philadelphia Richard Allen served as president of a cooperating Haytian Emigration Society. Quakers in North Carolina who had previously supported the ACS now donated funds to the Haitian effort, and the Yearly Meeting of Friends there endorsed the project. Understandably, the ACS came to regard the Haitian effort as competitive, and sent out speakers to offset its appeal. However, in both New York City and Philadelphia the Haitian appeal was too strong to effectively counter, and

the ACS concentrated its appeal in rural areas of the middle states temporarily.

Within a year of Granville's recruiting drive, the Haitian proposal ran into
difficulties. Boyer accused some Haitian emigration agents of mishandling
funds, and the Haitian government dismissed several. Migrants to Haiti
began to encounter settlement problems and some drifted back with complaints.[14] But, despite difficulties, large numbers made the migration. Reliable estimates are difficult to obtain, and modern research on the movement is scattered. One contemporary source indicated that in four years of
migration, roughly 1824–28, about thirteen thousand free blacks went to
Haiti, and that most ended up working at the lowest wages.[15]

One group of sixty migrants from North Carolina, sponsored by Quakers,
left in 1825. Eight months later they were visited by the British consul,
who found them working on a plantation owned by a local official near
Cayes. The settlers spoke freely to the consul, reporting an overwhelming
list of complaints.[16]

Their lodgings were bad, in a sort of barrack; but upon the whole they were
tolerably well treated, being fed and clothed by the proprietors, whether to
be eventually repaid or not was uncertain; they complained however of
want of medical attention and many were afflected with ulcers in their legs
... but most loud were their denunciations of their Haitian neighbors. ...

Two years later the settlers sent out by North Carolina Quakers were
visited by an agent to determine the justice of the complaints. The settlers
told him "that they would rather be slaves in North Carolina, than to remain
there under the treatment they had received since their arrival."[17]

Secretary Ralph Gurley of the ACS suggested that the Haitian emigration
plan was in fact a scheme to smuggle fugitive slaves, not freemen, out of the
United States. That view is supported by the record of a colony which
ended up in the eastern end of the island. In 1824 Philadelphia Quakers
chartered three ships to take escaped slaves from Pennsylvania and New
York to Haiti. One of the three ships of the fleet, the *Turtle Dove,* was
blown off course and landed its passengers on the Samana peninsula, separated from the Dominican mainland by an extensive bay. While the area
was under Haitian rule in 1822–44, it was largely Spanish-speaking. The
small group settled down in isolation and preserved their English speech,
their Protestantism, their American surnames, and place names for their
villages to the present time. The current population of descendants of the
colony is reported at 6,000.[18]

Among American antislavery whites the idea of Haitian emigration for
freed blacks had considerable popularity in the 1820s. Benjamin Lundy,

editor of the *Genius of Universal Emancipation* and the man who introduced abolition as a life work to William Lloyd Garrison, developed an interest in emigration at an 1823 convention held in Philadelphia. Lundy voted with the convention majority to investigate the idea. He sent a file of his newspaper to officials in Haiti, and soon a correspondence between Lundy and the Haitian secretary of state on the question of emigration was published.[19]

Lundy gave publicity to the proposals and to support for developments of separate black settlements elsewhere. One such development was the effort of George Flower to settle blacks in a small community in Illinois and to establish a communitarian society with the goal of freeing the blacks and giving them employment. In 1823 he privately arranged that they be sent to Haiti. About a year later Flower was to work with Frances Wright and to help convince her to attempt the similar program at Nashoba.[20]

Lundy continued to support the Haitian idea even after the Haitian government removed financial support for further emigration in 1825, and he continued to provide information to prospective emigrants and to owners wishing to send their slaves there. Lundy presented a plan in full detail which bore close resemblance to the work of Flower and Wright. Slaves would produce cotton on the basis of a cooperative system which included education on the Lancastrian plan. The slaves were to earn their purchase price, and at the end of five years they would migrate to Haiti or to the Texas province of Mexico. In 1826 Lundy accompanied a group of North Carolina Quaker-sponsored blacks to Haiti, and he tried to open negotiations to renew the Haitian financial assistance to emigrants. He visited some of the settlers and reported that they worked diligently and contentedly in their new lives.[21]

With the decline of support from the Haitian government, the difficulties encountered by the emigrants, rumors of landlord exploitation, and the drop in both philanthropic and planter support for the ACS, Lundy continued to search for alternate solutions.

Mexico

In 1832 Lundy developed a plan for settling freed blacks in Mexico, either in the Texas territory or further to the south. In the late summer of that year, he visited Nacogdoches in Texas, briefly inspecting the land and meeting local notables. He petitioned the governor of Coahuila and Texas to be allowed to settle four hundred black families in the territory. Over the next two years Lundy travelled in the United States raising funds for his project, and he returned to Mexico to make final arrangements. He found that blacks who had already settled in Mexico were interested in joining his proposed colony. He finally obtained a grant totalling 138,000 acres between the Nueces and the Rio Grande, and permission to settle 250 black families within two years. The Mexican governor insisted, however, that Lundy bring some settlers before the land be handed over, and that the settlement must be two-thirds complete within two years. Lundy's title lapsed before he could bring the required numbers.[22]

Lundy's proposal received publicity through his own newspaper and his lectures, and through Garrison's *Liberator*. In addition, blacks considering the ACS plans and other alternatives at meetings frequently debated the Lundy proposal, occasionally endorsing it while condemning the others. Unlike the ACS plan, Lundy's proposal did not support slavery but was designed to provide a refuge for liberated slaves, and its location suggested that it might provide a refuge for escaped and fugitive slaves as well. Among those intrigued by the Lundy proposal in the early 1830s was Martin Delany, whose interest in emigration was to take him to a position of black nationalist leadership twenty years later.[23]

While Lundy's plans for a Texas settlement never came to fruition, his several trips there and his discussions with black American settlers and with Mexican officials proved of crucial importance in the Congressional debates over the Texas question in the next few years. He supplied Congressman John Q. Adams with detailed information which convinced Adams and other northern politicians that the Texas secession and application for admission was intended and would lead to the increase of slaveholder territory and power.

Canada

Prior to his visits to Mexico Lundy had visited a settlement of blacks that attracted increased attention in 1831–32, the Canadian settlement of Wilberforce. This community had its origins in 1829 when free blacks in Cincinnati explored the possibility of emigration to escape increased enforcement of the onerous Ohio black codes. In the summer of that year a committee of Cincinnati blacks sent agents to make inquiry; the agents arranged to purchase four thousand acres. The governor general of Canada approved the proposal by which the Cincinnati group undertook to purchase and resell the land in small farms, using the funds to purchase more lands. The planned revolving fund would eventually allow for the purchase of about a million acres to become a major black settlement. The plans fell far short of the goal and the group purchased only eight hundred acres. In May, 1830, black settlers at the colony organized the Wilberforce settlement, appointing a group of agents and a board of managers. An estimated eight hundred to one thousand blacks moved to Wilberforce; but soon the great majority moved on to other settlements in Canada.[24]

Reports as to the prosperity and well-being of the colony varied from the glowing reports of proemigration visitors like Lundy and agents appointed by the colony like Nathaniel Paul, to the more gloomy observations of independent visitors. Nevertheless, the colony remained intact until going into a decline in the 1850s.

Wilberforce attracted international attention in the first years of its existence, when a college and manual training school, advocated at the First Annual Convention of People of Color, was planned for the community. The plans led to fund raising, particularly in Britain. Israel Lewis, one of the agents, clearly absconded with funds he collected in the name of the school; Nathaniel Paul collected several thousand dollars and offered an accounting of the funds, showing that he had expended them all in travel expenses and his own wages; even William Lloyd Garrison obtained some of the collection for his own use in Britain. No school or college at Wilberforce received any of the funds, and only temporary day schools for children operated from time to time.

While Paul and Lewis used the school proposal to finance their British tours, another leader, Austin Steward, worked for several years to hold the colony together. However, he became disillusioned, returning to New York State in 1836. The failure of the community to resolve its difficulties and to live up to its promise appears to have delayed other Canadian experimental black communities for several years.[25]

The idea of a manual-labor school for freedmen again took shape in 1842 at the British American Institute outside of London, Ontario. The early leaders of the institute included Josiah Henson, an escaped slave who had settled in Canada to preach and assist other fugitives, as well as antislavery missionaries and philanthropists. Around the school the community of Dawn eventually grew, with Henson as its leader. More in the nature of a college town than an organized community, Dawn remained fairly cohesive. Several of the economic activities of the town, such as a lumber mill, grist mill, and brickyard, provided training and financing for the school and its students.[26]

A British antislavery worker, John Scoble, became the manager of the school in 1852, and his administration was characterized by widespread criticism and controversy over mismanagement of funds. When Scoble allowed whites to settle in Dawn, some settlers charged that the original purpose of the community had been perverted. Scoble entered Canadian politics in the late 1850s, and he and Henson continued a public fight over a land mortgage for years.

The difficulties of the colony were in the nature of personality and managerial troubles, and did not grow out of any flaw in the central idea of a training school. Despite its problems, the British American Institute and the town of Dawn remained active and a point of interest internationally for over a quarter of a century. By 1868 the land was divided and sold.[27]

Relatively few of the estimated sixty thousand American blacks who settled in Canada between 1818 and 1861 lived in these planned and organized communities. The major settlement was in the area across from Detroit, in the Windsor-Amherstburg area. In 1846 Isaac Rice, a black leader of Amherstburg, helped organize a convention to provide a program for the incoming fugitives and migrants from the United States. The convention proposed to buy lands about ten miles from Amherstburg at a spot to be called the Sandwich Mission. In 1850 a convention at Sandwich reorganized the effort under a Benevolent Association. Prominent in the leadership of this group were Josiah Henson from Dawn, and Henry Bibb, editor and publisher of *Voice of the Fugitive*. By 1852 the group had reorganized again, with the name Refugee Home Society, and its leaders included Bibb and Henson, a number of antislavery leaders from Detroit, and several white missionaries. During the early 1850s, after repeated shifts in administration, the Refugee Home Society succeeded in buying and reselling land to at least 150 settlers. The land transactions were scattered about the area rather than concentrated in a single settlement.[28] Samuel R. Ward and Mary Shadd, editors of the *Provincial Freeman*, argued that the Society was nothing more than a real estate operation. Ward and Shadd accused the managers of the society with making off with most of the settlers' money; land could be readily purchased from the government without the so-called assistance of the society. Bibb, the writers for the *Freeman* charged, was a tool in the hands of Detroit speculators. Meetings of blacks in Windsor complained that funds raised in the name of all black settlers in Canada were funnelled to the narrow group of leaders in the Refugee Home Society. Other settlers rallied to the defense of Bibb and Henson, including James T. Holly.[29]

The polemics between the *Provincial Freeman* and the *Voice of the Fugitive* over personalities and plans showed that the large Canadian community of free black people produced competing factions and leaders. The groups seemed to be aligned along the lines of fugitives versus free-born blacks. Leaders from both factions including Bibb and Holly, Shadd and Ward, were to play a role in the developing dialogues over black nationalism in the 1850s in the United States.

Summary

The experiments in migration and in the establishment of colonies in North America and the Caribbean had several lasting effects on the development of nationalism. The philanthropic and communitarian settlements had the goal of preparing slaves for a transition to an integrated and free life as citizens. They often incorporated schools devoted to manual training and elementary education as essential to the transition to freedom. The models established by the planters in Ohio and philanthropic settlements like those of Wright or Flower incorporated ideas which were repeated by the organizers of Wilberforce, Dawn, and the Refugee Home Society. All these communities saw education in a separate setting, coupled with individual home and farm ownership, as keys to individual full emancipation. Similar ideas recurred in the later development of black colleges. The close relationship of school and community seemed well established by 1850, as a component idea in diverse plans for black freedom.

The colonial plans in the Western Hemisphere were scattered over four countries—United States, Haiti, Canada, and Mexico—but their founders were in touch with each other. Lundy had a hand in colonial settlements in all four countries, while Frances Wright visited Canada and Haiti as well as the United States. Other individuals, particularly the Canadian leaders, were in contact with each other and with black leadership in the United States. The work of Saunders, who had been associated with Cuffe, and of Loring Dewey, who had worked with the ACS, showed that Haitian colonization attracted some individuals away from plans for African colonization.

The Haitian emigration idea, although apparently moribund by 1829, would be revived in the 1850s by James T. Holly, when it would be expressed in more explicitly nationalistic language. The early Haitian settlements had been established as refuges, and when the Fugitive Slave Act of 1850 made refuge a crucial issue, Haiti received new attention and the earlier groundwork and settlement made a later emigration possible. A similar pattern occurred in Canada. The settlements of the 1830s and 1840s prepared the way for a wave of interest in the 1850s, and produced a cadre of leadership.[30]

The Canadian settlement was by far the largest of all the emigration settlements. Since return from Canada was simple, individuals who went there were not lost to the American scene, as repeated visits by Bibb, Holly, and Ward would show. When emigration took on new respectability in the 1850s, and as the nationalist faction began to emerge in the United States, the Canadian leaders played a central role.

7

EMIGRATIONISM

Black nationalism developed as an "ism," a doctrine with its adherents, its opponents, and an emerging set of principles in the period from the late 1840s through the eve of the Civil War. Although the idea had its precursors in Haiti and earlier maroon activities, and in the formation of Sierra Leone, its pioneers in men like Cuffe, Kizell, Carey, and Russwurm, and its training grounds in Liberia and Canada, black nationalism did not emerge as a faction of similarly opinioned men in black leadership circles until the period 1849–53. After that period black nationalist thinkers and activists were no longer separated individuals who worked out principles of nationalism and took action on their own, with only limited impact on a few disciples. By the mid-1850s the leaders met and knew each other, exchanged ideas and arguments, and initiated a set of associations and contacts. They formed a political faction within the free black leadership which represented a challenge to Frederick Douglass, and which created a living political force.[1]

The decade of the 1850s is a crucial one in the development of the doctrine of black nationalism as well as of the faction. The new leadership group added several new elements to the body of nationalist ideas, such as a literature of black-nationalist-oriented history and a carefully thought-out rejection of American nationality and its claim to loyalty. Development of these theoretical concerns did not preclude black nationalists from following up practical and organizational concerns. Like the Jewish Zionists at the end of the century, black Zionists in the 1850s very practically analyzed the question of where a black homeland should be located, and set up groups to explore and consider locations already developed in Liberia, Haiti, and Canada, and to find others in both Africa and Latin America.

Among the factors influencing blacks was the change in thinking of whites on the topic of colonization. Most white abolitionists continued to reject colonization on the same grounds that the 1817 Philadelphia mass meeting had used when rejecting it, that it was a slaveholders' scheme to insure the safety of slavery by removing black free men. A split in white abolitionist ranks between moral suasionists and political activists became more pronounced in the 1840s. Men like Garrison believed slavery would be conquered by winning converts to justice, while men like Theodore Weld came to accept political action in the form of petitions and campaigns. The question of whether it was practical to reject colonization purely on moralistic grounds that slaveholders supported it out of hostile motives could be discussed by the politically inclined wing of abolition.[2]

By the 1840s many slaveholders had grown suspicious of the ACS and its program. As slaveholders found themselves on the defensive, the notion of emancipating slaves for any reason, even to send them to Africa, began to seem inconsistent with the new arguments that slavery was a positive good for the slaves and for society as a whole, and that it was the natural condition of the black man. Senator Robert Walker stated that contributions to the Mississippi Colonization Society fell off because of the activities of abolitionists. Emancipation, even by will and testament, smacked of religion and guilt, and the Mississippi legislature outlawed it in 1842. Despite such handicaps, the Mississippi Colonization Society had succeeded in sending about 570 settlers to its colony on the Sinoe River before it gave up. The colonization effort, for practical purposes, was dead in Mississippi by 1842.[3]

By the mid-1840s white opinion had changed in at least two important respects. Some abolitionists would discuss emigration, either in conjunction with the ACS or apart from it; most slaveholders were disenchanted with the ACS, and their withdrawal of support produced a domination by the philanthropic and clerical wing of the movement. The antislavery activities of governors Thomas Buchanan and J.J. Roberts in Liberia could proceed without board interference.

Other factors had more direct bearing on the changes in black attitudes towards emigration. One was the rise of a new generation of free blacks. The sons of early black opponents of emigration found the old arguments a bit dated twenty-five years after the establishment of the Society. Several sons of prominent leaders personally visited Caribbean and African points of emigration and reported favorably on them. Other young men approached the question of emigration with an open mind and found in it a practical solution to the lack of rights in America. The backsliding in civil rights, rather than progress, gave reason to consider all forms of direct action, even violence. Further, the sheer survival of settlements in Africa, Canada, and Haiti showed that they were not experiments destined to collapse, but solid, going enterprises.[4]

While these developments created an atmosphere that allowéd the topic of emigration to be talked about, the subject might have remained theoretical had it not been for the impact of several events which gave the idea added urgency. The 1847 Declaration of Independence in Liberia established a self-governing republic; by 1857 consolidation of independent Maryland and Mississippi colonies, as well as purchase and conquest of contiguous territory, expanded the small state. The stigma of the ACS and white control was reduced, and Liberia could at last be honorably considered by those whose emigration sprang from a search for sovereignty and from racial pride, rather than simply from refuge. Immigration to Liberia went up sharply in 1848, from 51 emigrants the year before, to 441; the rate remained high over the next decade. The political independence of Liberia figured in further discussions of possible locations for a black state, although its origin in white deportationism and its continued reliance on the ACS for aid gave cause for some continued suspicion.[5]

In 1850, as part of the Congressional compromise between North and South of that year, the Fugitive Slave Law was enacted. It denied black men accused of being escaped slaves the right to testify in their own defense, and it offered a higher payment to commissioners who ordered the surrender of accused fugitives to the claimed owner than they would receive if the accused were declared free. This aspect of the law seemed to the majority of free blacks and to white abolitionists a means to legalize, institutionalize, and reward the practice of kidnapping free men for sale as slaves in the South. For black men who were in fact fugitives, the law was even more ominous. Since many fugitives had settled, married, and raised families among the free black population in the North, tens of thousands found their way of life directly threatened. Within months of the passage of the law, several thousand blacks fled to Canada. The number of free blacks and fugitives emigrating to Canada in the period 1850–61 has been estimated at forty thousand and represents the largest single emigration from the United States.[6]

With these events as a backdrop to the exchange of ideas and plans among black leaders, the nationalist faction developed in several stages. First, previously taboo topics were raised: emigration, separate institutions, violent direct action, and black identity as distinct from white identity. The older, anticolonization black abolitionists attempted to prevent even the discussion of some of these ideas, but open debate both in black newspapers and in conventions developed in the period 1849–53, and by 1859 the nationalists had organized several groups of their own.

Individual proponents

In 1841 a call for a national convention of blacks was published in Philadelphia. Although the convention did not meet as planned, the issuers of the call wanted to include on the agenda the subjects of emigration, the creation of separate black institutions, and a grant of land from the government. At a New York State convention in 1843, Samuel Davis opened the meeting with a speech which hinted at other than peaceful means to achieve recognition of black men's rights. These individual statements of separatism and indications that revolutionary rhetoric might find an audience appeared at the same time as a growing body of literature which sought to develop racial pride out of the materials of black history.[7]

In the period 1837–44 Hosea Easton, James W.C. Pennington, and R.B. Lewis, all prominent in the convention movement of the early 1830s, published works of black history and pseudohistory with racial pride as the central motif. The themes and illustrations were repeated from one work to another. Beginning with the Bible, the authors showed that blacks, as descendants of Ham, included most of the great civilized peoples of the ancient world: Egyptians, Babylonians, and Phoenicians. Some argued the case that Jesus had a black ancestor. Claimed as black heroes were Augustine, Plato, Caesar, and Hannibal. The lives of eighteenth-and nineteenth-century black men of ability were detailed, including the leading generals of the Haitian revolution. While much of the material was speculative, other parts of the works were strictly factual; all tended to offset preconceptions of black inferiority and to build a sense of pride and identification with the race. Whatever the sentiments of the authors on the topic of emigration, and some opposed it, such works of black history contributed to a sense of black solidarity. Like their European counterparts, black nationalists needed to generate a sense of identification with the group in order to develop any political following.[8]

A statement which united expressions of identity, separatism, and the rhetoric of violence, and probably the most important black nationalist document of the 1840s, is found in Henry Highland Garnet's 1843 *Address to the Slaves,* given at the National Negro Convention in Buffalo. The speech was too fiery for many of the delegates, and a committee attempted to rewrite it for possible adoption by the convention. Even the edited version was voted down, although by a narrow margin. Five years later the speech was printed by a more militant convention. Garnet, a Presbyterian minister in Troy, New York, believed rebellion more likely and possible than emigration:[9]

If you must bleed, let it all come at once—rather die freemen, than live to be slaves. It is impossible like the children of Israel, to make a grand exodus from the land of bondage. The·Pharaohs are on both sides of the blood-red waters! You cannot move en masse, to the dominions of the British Queen, nor can you pass through Florida and overrun Texas, and at last find peace in Mexico.

Borrowing from the black history genre, Garnet reminded his listeners of the exploits of Vesey, Turner, Cinque, and the *Creole* mutineers. His line "Rather die freemen, than live to be slaves" became a slogan, printed or embroidered for framing, and was hung in parlors as far away as Monrovia.[10]

While Garnet's speech can be viewed as an individual statement of nationalist sentiments calling for rebellion instead of emigration, and an isolated outburst not part of any developed movement, the debate over its adoption as a resolution in the 1843 and 1848 conventions is an illustration of how such individual ideas became transformed into political issues and produced factional alignments. Over the next years the debates at conventions on a variety of resolutions revealed a growing rift betweeen separatists who despaired of gaining citizenship and recognition of rights in white-dominated America, and abolitionists who felt that concentration on emigration would distract from the crucial work to be done in the United States.

Growth of the nationalist faction

In 1847 a convention at Troy, New York, reflected efforts to maintain a consensus while considering some issues likely to reveal divisions. A plan for a commercial venture to involve blacks from the United States and Jamaica in a legitimate triangular trade with Africa was peacefully considered. But a split in the convention paralleled the division among white abolitionists. Moral suasionists, led by Frederick Douglass, debated with those favoring political action, led by Garnet. While the activists appeared to be in a majority, Douglass displayed superior debating and convention tactics for the suasionist camp. Gerrit Smith had donated land in upstate New York to be granted to blacks in order that they might meet the property-holding qualification for the vote retained for blacks in that state. Garnet and Douglass agreed that the land should be settled as well as held for voting eligibility. A plan for organized communities to which a token number of whites would be admitted was approved. A division over the issue of whether to establish a black national press reflected personal issues: Douglass voted against the plan, Garnet suggested, because he intended to start his own newspaper and wanted neither competition nor control from a national organization.[11]

However, Garnet continued the debate in Douglass's paper the *North Star*. In early 1848 he wrote, "I hesitate not to say that my mind of late has greatly changed in regard to the American Colonization scheme. I would rather see a man free in Liberia than a slave in the United States."[12]

At this time practicing emigrationists noted increasing support for their ideas among prospective emigrants. S. Wesley Jones, a black businessman in Tuscaloosa, Alabama, wrote in June, 1848: "There are many in the state that are willing to go to Liberia and all they wait for, is to see certain ones of their friends make the move. I candidly believe if all were ready at this time to go, I could easily raise a company of an hundred or more." The increase in interest reflected the news of Liberian independence.[13]

Garnet's changing stand on Liberian emigration also seemed to reflect the changed status of Liberia from colony to nation. In a pamphlet published early in 1848, he claimed "America is my home, my country, and I have no other," reflecting one of the classic antiemigration lines of argument. He had explicitly favored revolution over emigration in the famous 1843 address. But in speeches and published statements in 1848 and 1849 he showed a change of heart about Liberia. He drew on the black history theme in an early 1848 speech in which he detailed a number of important black women of antiquity, including Moses' wife, King Solomon's mistress, and Cleopatra. He discussed the African origins of Terence, Euclid, Cyprian, and Augustine. By contrast, whites came off poorly:[14]

At this time when these representatives of our race were filling the world with amazement, the ancestors of the now proud and boasting Anglo-Saxons were among the most degraded of the human family. They abode in caves underground, either naked or covered with the skins of wild beasts. Night was made hideous by their wild shouts, and day was darkened by the smoke which arose from bloody altars, upon which they offered human sacrifice. . .

After Liberian independence Garnet did not accept the argument that white financing, support, and antiblack motives condemned Liberia as a possible homeland. His interest in Africa continued, and in 1849 he predicted that Liberia would become the Empire State of Africa, and stated that he favored colonization to any country that promised freedom and the vote to the black man.[15]

By 1849 some of the black conventions became acrimonious, and proemigrationists who differed on other questions found themselves thrown together as allies. In a period of several conventions and heightened interest in the issue of emigration, men who had previously only read of each other's positions now appeared together as platform speakers. In January, 1849, a convention in Columbus, Ohio, resolved "once and for all" that "we will never submit to the system of Colonization to any part of the world in or out of the United States." Yet this resolution came after a spirited defense of emigration by David Jenkins, who advocated that all blacks emigrate, and John Mercer Langston, who stated that he loved freedom more than his country. The question was referred to committee, which issued a majority report favoring emigration after the end of slavery, and a minority report condemning emigration. The majority floor vote for the committee's minority report, despite its tone of finality, came only after severe factional division. It was this convention which voted to print and circulate Garnet's 1843 *Address to the Slaves,* along with a more fiery call to rebellion, David Walker's *Appeal.* While accepting radical rhetoric, the convention's anti-emigrationists used Garnet's own earlier statement of preference for rebellion over exodus to attack his current position of support for emigration.[16]

Later in the year Garnet argued on the same side of a debate with two other proemigrationists, Henry Bibb, who moved to Canada, and Samuel R. Ward, who went first to Canada and then on to Jamaica. Bibb, Ward, and Garnet heatedly attacked the position of Charles L. Remond and Frederick Douglass over the issue of sending Bibles to slaves. The emigrationists wished to emphasize solidarity between free blacks and slaves, while the moral suasionist abolitionists felt the project would be a waste of resources.[17]

The increased emigration to Liberia after independence, and the rush to emigrate in 1850-51 as a result of the Fugitive Slave Law, strengthened the arguments of the proemigrationists. But so many of the emigrationists left the country themselves at this time that they weakened the ranks of those fighting the leadership of Douglass. Young Edward Wilmot Blyden, recently arrived from the Danish West Indies, after attempting to enter Rutgers Theological Seminary and two other colleges, went on to Liberia. Garnet, Alexander Crummell, James W.C. Pennington, William Wells Brown, and Ellen and William Craft were lecturing in England. Both Ward and Bibb went to Canada in 1851.

Some more obscure spokesmen remained. One, Lewis H. Putnam, organized a United African Republic Emigration Society in 1851. His enemies claimed he was in the emigration business because it paid well. The influential black clergy and spokesmen in New York became alarmed when Governor Washington Hunt endorsed the Putnam emigration plan. A delegation visited the governor with assurances that blacks did not wish to leave the United States. Putnam charged that such men, members of the black middle class, opposed emigration out of direct self-interest, "for the purpose of keeping full churches and school-houses, a plenty of patients, waiters and other assistants."[18]

The New York activities were noted by Wesley Jones in Alabama, and he gave a clear statement of the nationalist sentiments in defense of emigration:[19]

I trust my brethren will think of this matter and arouse themselves, and let national pride be kindled up in their hearts and go to and make us a great nation of our own, build our own cities and towns, make our own laws, collect our own revenues, command our own vessels, army and navy, elect our own governors and law makers, have our own schools and colleges, our own lawyers and doctors, in a word, cease to be hewers of wood and drawers of water, and be men.

Others considering emigration showed in their correspondence that even if their motives were admittedly economic or based on a desire for personal freedom and security, they now stated those motives in the rhetoric of nationalism. The public debates and the increasing quantity of published literature discussing the nationalist ideas publicized a range of arguments for potential emigrants. Augustus Washington wrote to the ACS in 1851, stating that the hostility of the American government and people had led him to favor emigration and the establishment of a black state. The force of prejudice, he assumed was permanent.[20]

... hence we are driven to the conclusion that the friendly and mutual separation of the two races is not only necessary to preserve the peace, happiness and prosperity of both, but indispensable to the preservation of the one and the glory of the other. While we would thus promote the interests of two great continents and build up another powerful Republic, as an asylum to the oppressed, we would at the same time gratify national prejudices.

Augustus Washington was somewhat unique in explicitly accepting the prejudiced motives of white sponsors of emigration and at the same time accepting that sponsorship in the name of black pride. He did in fact emigrate, stating his faith that Liberia would serve the mission and destiny of showing the capacity of the black man and would help redeem Africa.

A convention of black delegates met in Canada to discuss nationalist and emigrationist projects at this time. James T. Holly, who sent his proposal from Vermont, suggested a North American and West Indian Federal Agricultural Union. This organization would cooperatively purchase lands in Canada and the West Indies, and then resell the land to individual settlers for cash or on credit.[21]

The flood of black emigrants in the years immediately following the passage of the Fugitive Slave Act did not necessarily reflect the triumph of nationalist ideas. The emigrants to Canada who were fugitive slaves were no doubt motivated by their own safety and not by ideology. Some towns in Ohio and Pennsylvania were nearly evacuated by blacks, including both fugitives and freemen. Within two weeks of the enactment of the law, one Pittsburgh correspondent of Garrison's *Liberator* noted almost peevishly,

"Nearly all of the waiters in the hotels have fled to Canada." At a state convention in Cincinnati John Langston spoke out on the natural animosity of the races and argued that blacks would lose their identity as a people if they stayed in America. Yet a vote on emigration at that convention lost by a vote of four to one. It is unlikely that such a convention was particularly representative of the free black population, since, like other conventions of the period, it was heavily weighted on the side of clergy and self-appointed spokesmen. Frederick Douglass may have had the report of the Cincinnati convention in mind when he stated a year later that about one-quarter of the free blacks in Ohio favored emigration. As an opponent of emigration, Douglass would choose his evidence and draw his conclusions for polemic reasons, overlooking the implications of conventions in which the division over emigration would be closer.[22]

A convention in 1852 in Baltimore began by favoring emigration; anti-emigrationists threatened some of the convention officers with bodily harm, and they sought police protection. Finally a rather quiet endorsement of Liberian emigration was issued, with a call to investigate other locations for suitability. As emigrationists of a variety of persuasions worked together, discussions and debates over the relative merits of various prospective homelands grew more common, particularly during and after 1852.[23]

In that year Martin R. Delany published *The Condition, Elevation, Emigration and Destiny of the Colored People of the United States, Politically Considered*, which elaborated the idea that black people were in fact a nation like various stateless minorities and groups within the nations of Europe, and that as a national group blacks should seek a territory. Delany was quite conscious of the parallels between his own ideas and those of contemporary nationalist movements in Europe. In all periods, he claimed, there has[24]

existed a nation within a nation—a people who although forming a part and parcel of the population, yet were from force of circumstance, known by the peculiar position which they occupied, forming in fact, by the deprivation of political equality with others, no part, and if any, but a restricted part of the body politic of such nations. . . . Such then are the Poles in Russia, the Hungarians in Austria, the Scotch, Irish and Welsh in the United Kingdom and such also are the Jews. . . .

Delany recounted the opposition of free blacks to colonization, and reiterated his own opposition to colonization under white sponsorship. But when he turned to practical means of "elevating" the condition of blacks, he found few opportunities opened for young men. Even the abolitionist press, he noted, hired few blacks, and even those held menial positions. In order to refute the assertion of black incapacity for professional jobs, he recounted the history of black achievements. To demonstrate that the laws and customs of the United States were devoted to the oppression of the black man, he included the text of the Fugitive Slave Law. Despairing of the chance to achieve rights in America, he considered the question of emigration. He dismissed Liberia with objections as to climate and lack of true independence from white control. Instead of turning to Africa, he suggested, the black man should seek refuge in the Western Hemisphere. Canada he considered too likely to come into the American union, and he preferred Mexico, Central America, the West Indies, and New Granada in South America. He mentioned that he had argued in favor of Mexican migration as early as 1835, supporting the Lundy proposal, and had been laughed at. Despite his rejection of Africa in the body of the text, Delany added an "Appendix" which suggested that men of adventure should consider settling in East Africa. The essay was a coherent and well-integrated statement of several black nationalist ideas that had developed since Paul Cuffe, and struck a practical, hardheaded note in its cool assessment of emigration sites.[25]

A similar analysis of sites was found in the 1852 *Address to the Free Colored People* by the white James G. Birney. Birney had once supported the ACS, but had been converted to opposition by Theodore Weld. Originally a slaveholding lawyer in Alabama, Birney as an abolitionist had been a convincing convert. But the loss of even limited freedom brought about by the Fugitive Slave Law brought him to reconsider emigration as a reasonable course for the black man. In the 1852 *Address* Birney noted that the Irish and Germans who emigrated away from oppression were more admired in the United States than those who had remained at home to suffer. Free blacks, he pointed out, were currently being invited to emigrate to three areas: Canada, the West Indies, and Liberia. He argued that Canada, dominated by whites, would allow blacks only the most undesirable pieces of land. Canada's independence from America, he believed, like Delany, might be temporary. At the least, he feared, Canada might allow the Fugitive Slave Law to operate within its boundaries. The West Indies would expose black settlers to economic exploitation. Liberia, the most satisfactory of the three possible destinations, would require hard work. He noted that two classes would be unmoved by any desire to emigrate to Liberia—the wealthy and those without ambition. Although Birney was white, his thinking evolved in a pattern parallel to that of men like Delany, and his advice, although gratuitous, was part of the debate over whether and where to emigrate.[26]

White interest in the revival of black emigration was further reflected in Harriet Beecher Stowe's *Uncle Tom's Cabin*. George Harris, a leading figure in the novel, gave nationalistic and separatist justifications for his decision to emigrate to Liberia.

A convention called by Bibb and Holly was held in Amherstburg, Canada, in 1853. It declared that free blacks in the United States owed no loyalty to the country. Consequently, if blacks did not emigrate, they were likely to start a revolution. Canada could serve as a haven for emigrants, but if it proved unsatisfactory then Haiti remained as a possibility. The resolution neatly combined the ideas of both callers of the convention—Bibb's decision to live in Canada and Holly's interest in Haiti.[27]

This frankly proemigration convention stimulated the leaders of the anti-emigrationists to counter with a show of force. The largest national convention of blacks held to that date convened in Rochester immediately after the Amherstburg meeting. The division over emigration generated open discussion, and the convention accepted an explicit set of resolutions directed at whites and opposed to emigration:[28]

We are Americans and as Americans, we would speak to Americans. We address you not as aliens nor as exiles, humbly asking to be permitted to dwell among you in peace; but we address you as American citizens asserting their rights on their own native soil. ... We ask that no appropriations whatever, state or national, shall be granted to the colonization scheme, and we would have our right to leave or to remain in the United States placed above legislative interference.

However, the separatist and nationalist sentiments of the delegates found expression in a far-reaching plan for national organization of blacks in a scheme that seemed to be black nationalism without a territory. A system of elections and representatives was to be established, to send delegates to a national governing body. The central group would have administrative control of a black college, an employment agency, a consumers' union, a library, and a public relations bureau. The convention strove to find a formula which would provide self-determination and some of the power of a state without the establishment of a self-governing territory.

The emigrationists convene

Immediately after the Rochester convention emigrationist leaders decided to organize separately. Holly, Delany, Bibb, and James Whitfield issued a call for a convention to be held the next year in Cleveland, from which anti-emigrationists and Liberian advocates would be excluded. By limiting the call in this fashion, the emigrationists distinguished themselves from the ACS and also guaranteed that the convention would not be taken up in a debate with abolitionists. Frederick Douglass declared that such a limitation on the call was improper, and a debate over that issue and the larger question of emigration itself developed in the columns of his paper late in 1853.[29]

The planned convention met, August 24 through August 26, 1854, in Cleveland, with 102 delegates attending. Although Bibb had died, his widow attended and served on the business committee chaired by Delany. Holly served as secretary to the convention, William Monroe as president. John Langston had changed his mind about emigration and gave a traditional antiemigration speech. He was sarcastically criticized by Henry Ford Douglass, who declared: "Is not the history of the world, the history of emigration? The coming and going out of nations is a natural and necessary result." On the question of whether emigration implied disloyalty, he noted:

I can hate this government without being disloyal, because it has stricken down my manhood, and treated me as a saleable commodity. I can join a foreign enemy and fight against it, without being a traitor, because it treats me as an alien and a stranger. . . .

Nationalism and emigration grew out of disfranchisement and discrimination, leaving H.F. Douglass with a sense of being pushed to his decision reluctantly:[30]

When I remember that . . . I am an alien and an outcast, unprotected by law, proscribed and persecuted by cruel prejudice, I am willing to forget the endearing name of home and country, and as an unwilling exile seek on other shores the freedom which has been denied me in the land of my birth.

Delany read a speech, "The Political Destiny of the Colored Race," which incorporated many ideas and some phrases from his recently published book. He called for the creation of a black empire in the New World, where "the inherent traits, attributes . . . and native characteristics peculiar to our race could be cultivated and developed." The concept of ethnic characteristics as justification for political separatism was in tune with current ideas, as white Americans spoke of Manifest Destiny and Europeans repeated the slogans of the 1848 revolutions. Echoing his earlier work, Delany asserted

We must make an issue, create an event, and establish for ourselves a position. This is essentially necessary for our effective elevation as a people, in shaping our national development, directing our destiny, and redeeming ourselves as a race.[31]

The plan adopted by the convention followed suggestions by Delany, officially declaring that emigration to Central America, South America, and the West Indies, and in the last resort, Canada, was recommended. In Canada, the convention resolved, "when worst comes to worst, we may be found, not as a scattered, weak and impotent people . . . but a united and powerful body of freemen." The tone suggested that in Canada blacks would resist with force any attempts to reenslave.

Delany later reported that the convention held secret sessions which "made Africa, with its inexhaustible productions, and the great facilities for checking the abominable slave trade, its most important point of dependence. . . ." He claimed a careful strategy had been planned: ". . . though our first gun was levelled, and the first shell thrown at the American continent, driving the slaveholding faction into despair . . . Africa was held in reserve." The existence of secret sessions was denied by the other major participants at the convention; Delany later attempted to establish some organized endorsement for his interest in Africa, despite the convention's explicit limitation to Western Hemisphere sites. A National Emigration Board was set up, and Delany began negotiations with Jamaica, Cuba, and a number of republics in Central and South America.[32]

Explorations and organizations—Central America and Haiti

The 1854 Emigration Convention gave a commission to James Whitfield to explore Central America for possible sites and to Holly to make contact with Haiti. Whitfield died in San Francisco on his way to his destination. But Holly visited Haiti in 1855, where he met the minister of the interior and the emperor, Faustin I. He returned to the United States and Canada to lecture on the history of Haiti and its prospects as a possible site for black émigrés.

In 1857 Holly published his lecture, which for the most part was a piece of the new genre of black history; he was explicit in his statement of motives: "to cast back the vile aspersions and foul calumnies that have been heaped upon my race for the last four centuries by our unprincipled oppressors." As a conclusion to the historical coverage, Holly added a brief appeal for emigration to Haiti. He regarded Haiti as provided by Providence, and better than "any man-made and utopian schemes to send us across the ocean, to rummage the graves of our ancestors in fruitless and ill-directed efforts at the wrong end of human progress. . . ." The proper direction of human progress, he believed with Horace Greeley, lay to the west. His peroration is remarkable in that it contained most of the elements of nationalist rhetoric in use at the time—pride in black history, duty to live up to the past, identification of destiny with a heroic heritage, escape from proscription to achieve manhood, the prospect of national sovereignty and even grandeur, and escape from a variety of oppressive practices. Holly concluded by urging his listeners to "boldly enlist in this high pathway of duty."[34]

The emigration convention met again in 1856, and the delegates agreed to further explorations and contacts with foreign powers. Interest in a wide variety of emigration sites spread in the free black community. From Liberia Edward Blyden published his first pamphlet, defending Liberia as a homeland against the criticisms of Delany and Holly.[35]

At the 1856 convention the emigrationists further organized. They created a North American and West Indian Trading Association, based on the idea Holly had introduced several years before, and centered it in his home town of New Haven. They established a Board of Publications which was to issue a quarterly magazine, *Afric-American Repository*, which included among its editors and correspondents most of the leading emigrationists and nationalists at the time: Whitfield, Delany, Holly, Monroe, and Mary Ann Shadd. Shadd's weekly, the *Provincial Freeman*, was also to serve as an official organ of the emigrationists' National Board of Commissioners. All the officers of the National Board lived within a sixty-mile radius of Chatham, Canada.

Delany himself moved to Chatham. Over the next two years he and other commissioners raised funds and continued public advocacy of emigration. John Brown, in an effort to enlist black participation and financial support for his planned raid on Harper's Ferry, met Delany at Chatham in May of 1858. William Monroe, Harriet Tubman, and about thirty other black leaders listened to Brown's appeal. He apparently won few converts, but the meeting did issue a provisional constitution for a free black state to be created in Kansas, which would receive fugitives on a "Subterranean Passage Way" rather than route them to Canada on the Underground Railroad. Although Delany was writing an apocalyptic novel, *Blake*, which described a slave uprising, he continued to prefer exodus to rebellion in this period. In August of 1858, at the Emigration Convention meeting in Chatham, Delany presented and won acceptance for plans to explore the Niger region in Africa.[36]

In the same period, 1855–58, other efforts were under way to further organize nationalist leadership. Henry Highland Garnet returned from lecturing in England in 1855 and formed the African Civilization Society. The main point of disagreement between Delany and Garnet was Garnet's willingness to work with white supporters and financiers. The central purpose of Garnet's new society was not emigration itself, but the "civilization and christianization of Africa, and of the descendants of African ancestors in any portion of the earth, wherever dispersed." The religious orientation brought influential black clergy into the organization, including several AME bishops. The society proposed to send some emigrants to Africa to begin cotton planting there, with a view to threatening the southern cotton planters and offering a legitimate competition to the slave trade. Garnet believed that a practical commercial enterprise such as a black shipping line "would do more for the overthrowing of slavery, in creating a respect for ourselves, than fifty thousand lectures of the most eloquent men of this land." On the eve of the Civil War, the organization of Garnet's African Civilization Society marked the end of slaveholder identification with emigration. The establishment of an organization incorporating black conservatives and black radicals revealed the wide appeal of emigrationism and nationalist ideas.[37]

All was not unity in the nationalist camp, however. Delany's disagreement with Garnet over the acceptance of white financing, and disagreements within the National Commission, came to the surface in such publications as the *Provincial Freeman,* the *Chatham Planet,* and a new magazine published by Robert Hamilton, the *Weekly Anglo-African.* Hamilton printed *Blake,* Delany's novel, in serialized form. Hamilton believed that black people should "set themselves zealously to work to create a position of their own—an empire which shall challenge the admiration of the world, rivalling the glory of their historic ancestors."[38]

Abeokuta

Delany and his associate Robert Campbell, a Jamaican chemist, sailed separately for Africa in 1859. While Delany had secured his own funding as a member of the National Board of Commissioners, Campbell received some aid from the African Civilization Society. Campbell went to the Niger valley by way of London and Sierra Leone. On his arrival in Lagos he made contact with the *alake* (chief of state) of Abeokuta. Campbell discovered that there was already a black émigré colony in the chief's dominion—a group of free blacks returned from Cuba, Brazil, and Sierra Leone over the previous twenty years. Campbell was disdainful of the degree of "civilization," but excited by the precedent which they had established. He proposed that American blacks should found cities which would cooperate with the native Africans in the formation of a national government. He proposed that the native monarchs remain as heads of state, with the emigrants attempting "to lift them up to the proper standard" rather than trying to overthrow or push them aside.[39]

Delany sailed by way of Monrovia, where he met Blyden for the first time. Both men were impressed. Delany's opinion of Liberia improved after he accepted several speaking engagements, honorary dinners, and some guided tours of the settlements. He was loudly cheered by a Liberian audience when he told them that "a desire for African nationality has brought me to these shores." His expedition was approved by Liberian leaders, and

Blyden called Delany a "Moses" to "lead the exodus of his people from the house of bondage." The "Moses" image would recur many times among black nationalists. Delany also met with Alexander Crummell at Cape Palmas. William Monroe, an associate of Delany at the emigration conventions, sailed to Liberia with Delany and stayed on as a permanent settler.[40]

Arriving in Abeokuta after Campbell, Delany and his partner spent six weeks exploring the Yoruba country. On December 27, 1859, Campbell and Delany signed a treaty with the alake, the *ibashorun* (prime minister), three *balaguns* (military commanders), and three lesser officials. The treaty was witnessed by the black missionary Samuel Crowther. Under the treaty Delany and Campbell received the privilege "as commissioners in behalf of the African race in America" to settle "in common with the Egba people, on any part of the territory belonging to Abeokuta, not otherwise occupied." But Delany's settlers would have stepped into a political fray at Abeokuta. Westernizers, including the Saro, or Sierra Leonean, recaptives who had returned were vying for influence, and the multiple signatures on the treaty reflected the unstable authority of the newly chosen alake. But no settlers came under Delany's treaty.[41]

The two explorers returned by way of England, where their trip received public attention. There the African Aid Society, organized for the purpose of providing financial assistance for black emigrants from the United States to raise cotton and other crops suitable to Africa, took an interest in Delany's efforts. Acutely conscious of the Liberian situation, and still suspicious of white financing, Delany made clear to the leaders of the African Aid Society that any emigrants he might bring over should be free to handle their own affairs, and any funds would be arranged as strictly business.[42]

On their return both Delany and Campbell gave lectures on West African life and culture, sometimes in African costume. Delany published his *Official Report,* and Campbell printed a narrative of the trip, *A Pilgrimage to My Motherland.* Both documents reflected nationalist considerations and ideas, and both dealt with practical details of the trip. Delany stated his basic principles in a statement later to become a slogan for black nationalists:[43]

Without this design and feeling, there would be a great deficiency of self-respect, pride of race, and love of country, and we might never expect to challenge the respect of nations—*Africa for the African race, and black men to rule them.* By black men I mean, men of African descent who claim an identity with the race.

Redpath and Haiti

Delany's energies in working out practical arrangements for emigrants were rivalled by Holly. In 1859 James Redpath, a white associate of John Brown, obtained a commission from the Haitian government to work with Holly in stimulating emigration to that country. Redpath first visited Haiti in January, 1859, and returned again in July, 1859, and July, 1860. President Nicolas Geffrard, who had led the overthrow of Faustin, grew interested in acting on the contacts of Holly and in reviving the idea of free black immigration from the United States. Redpath suggested a number of guarantees that he believed should be extended to induce settlement. Geffrard commissioned Redpath to serve as immigration agent. Redpath opened an office in Boston, had at least ten thousand copies of a *Guide Book* for emigrants published, and sent sixteen hundred to two thousand settlers to Haiti over the period 1860-61. Redpath frankly utilized the growing nationalist orientation to stimulate emigration. To the black man Haiti "offers a home and a distinctive nationality," he claimed.[44]

However, the government invitation to migrants, while emphasizing black solidarity, played down the nationalist appeal and emphasized the element of flight from oppression. "Men of our race, dispersed in the United States! Your fate, your social position, instead of ameliorating, daily becomes worse .... Come then to us! The doors of Hayti are open to you. ... Come and together with us, advance our own common country in prosperity."[45]

Redpath's appeal was slightly more nationalist in tone, although he too argued for emigration as an attack on slavery. He suggested that emigrants could raise such crops as tobacco, cotton, hemp, and sugar in order to compete with southern staples and attack the slavocracy. His most eloquent appeals and his rhetoric could compete with those of Delany: "She [Haiti] offers you a home, a nationality, a future. She presents to you the opportunity of not only exhibiting the capacity of your race, but of creating a new Eden in the most fertile of the Antilles. ..."[46] Redpath spelled out the practical and specific details of emigration and settlement. In brief, the Haitian government agreed to: pay passage, provide a week's board and lodging, guide settlers to employers, offer citizenship after a year, protect freedom of worship, exempt settlers from military duty, allow for group settlement, and guarantee the right to leave.[47]

By 1860 black nationalism and emigration had achieved a degree of respectability and organization which it had not had since the days of Cuffe's African Institutions. Even Frederick Douglass wavered in his opposition, accepting an invitation from the Haitian government to visit the island. However, the election of Lincoln and the secession of the southern states interrupted his plans.[48]

The appeals to Haiti, Liberia, Abeokuta, and Canada were couched in explicitly nationalist language. The appeal to racial pride, to black history, to potential racial destiny, the argument that increased manhood would result from sovereignty and calls to duty, recurred again and again. Garnet's slogan, "Rather die freemen, than live to be slaves," and Delany's phrase, "Africa for the African race," along with Holly's appeals to pride, would remain as themes and concepts in later nationalist rhetoric and principles.

Despite the effect of the Civil War in dispersing black organizations and energies, and in apparently vindicating the position of Frederick Douglass who had consistently argued for black alliance with antislavery whites and for remaining in the United States, the ideas and some of the individuals from these peak years of antebellum black nationalism survived through the Civil War and into the Reconstruction era to contribute to later black nationalist proposals and ideas. The roots of nationalism were firmly implanted.

8

BLYDEN AND CRUMMELL

Liberian nationalism as it developed in the years immediately after independence was not entirely foreign to the American scene, since in the 1850s and 1860s Liberian leaders were all Afro-American or West Indian and derived many of their ideas from both black American sources and the philanthropic rhetoric of the ACS. Yet, Liberian self-determination in the colonial period had proceeded in a degree of isolation from events in America, and the development of the republic might have had little impact in the United States had it not been for the fact that the ideas and the political considerations of early independence were formulated into a well-thought-out ideology by two men prominent in Liberia who exported it to the United States. Under pressures of the Liberian situation in the first decades of independence, Edward Wilmot Blyden (1832–1912) developed a form of pan-Negro nationalism which included a romantic vision of the destiny of the black race, the idea of a distinctive African personality, an awareness of the values of African culture, and an awakening of interest in Islam as an alternative to Christianity. Alexander Crummell (1819–98), who worked with Blyden, shared his concept of pan-Negro nationalism and of African personality. He developed a keen sense of the obligation of the individual to the Liberian state; he later applied the idea to the American context and developed what he called the "social principle," approximating what is meant today by a sense of ethnic identity.

The Liberian situation

As already discussed, the development of Liberian independence in 1847 had been preceded by years of effective self-government and the articulation of some nationalist ideas such as the value of sovereignty and self-determination and the protection of the nation against American missionary power, European commercial incursions, and native military encroachments. However, those ideas had not matured into a nationalist ideology in the sense of a doctrine which would justify the existence of the nation, make explicit its destiny, or establish a set of national goals against which policy and personal actions could be judged and measured. The ideas of Kizell, Coker, Carey, and Devany, although containing strongly nationalist elements, for the most part had been committed to print by others, and their concepts were buried in a mass of narrative and correspondence not intended to serve as nationalist polemics. The writings of John Russwurm and Hilary Teague as editors of the *Liberia Herald* did contain some clear-cut nationalist ideas; however, their positions and arguments were largely unknown outside of Liberia.

The new republic suffered several institutional and physical difficulties of a seriously divisive nature. The talents of Blyden and Crummell were needed to deal with very concrete economic, institutional, and international problems. The two intellectuals formulated ideas and arguments to deal with the specific difficulties they encountered and to express their views of solutions; the ideology developed as a by-product of their efforts to respond to immediate problems.

Perhaps the most serious set of problems grew out of the nation's social structure. An elite stratum, which was largely made up of mulattoes and blacks who had been free men before emigration to Liberia, sought to continue the control of commerce and government which they had developed during the colonial period. A farm worker class, which included black settlers previously slaves, liberated slaves from captured and grounded slave ships (collectively called "Congoes," although rarely from the Congo region), and "civilized native farmers," eked out a living on the plantations and congregated when unemployed in Monrovia. Indigenous groups were divided by ethnic and religious differences and varied in their relations with the Americo-Liberians. The coastal Kru had a long heritage of contact with the Europeans and Liberians; other tribes sent members to serve as domestics in Liberian homes or missions; some distant tribes had amicable trading relations with Liberian merchants, although others fought a series of battles ranging from plunder raids to full-scale wars. The evident conflict between the mulatto-dominated commercial elite and the black worker class sprang from divergent economic interests; elements of racism persisted as the elite sought to "marry lighter" and to emulate European and American clothing styles, customs, and standards of beauty. In such a context, any doctrine conceived to unify the nation would of necessity be "pan-African" in that it would incorporate mulattoes and free-born blacks, recaptives and freedmen, assimilated and unassimilated natives, and the children of parents from different groups.

The new nation's constitution had several features likely to produce instability. In an attempt to prevent the domination of government for an extended period by one-man rule, the term of office of the president was set at two years; members of the House of Representatives and half the senators were also elected every two years. The franchise effectively excluded indigenous people. The frequent elections and the varied economic and ethnic make-up of the voting population contributed to intense politization. Despite the frequent and heated campaigns, from 1848 through 1871 the results of presidential elections were not challenged by unconstitutional means.

International diplomatic recognition was of little help. Slaveholding interests in the United States prevented diplomatic recognition of both Haiti and Liberia until the Civil War. Both Britain and France, although recognizing Liberian sovereignty, gradually encroached on the borders.

The problems of economic development were severe. The major sources of wealth were trade for native-produced commodities, particularly palm oil, in exchange for European goods, and coffee plantations developed by the settlers. Monrovia itself appeared poverty-stricken, with muddy or grassgrown streets, small homes, and a tendency to conspicuous consumption in clothing. Illiteracy was high, and few citizens received more than primary schooling through the missions.

Despite such difficulties, Liberia had several strengths. As noted, Liberian independence had partially freed the country from the stigma of the Colonization Society, and immigration increased in the decade after independence. The new immigrants tended to include more free-born blacks, with more education and economic resources than earlier arrivals. As the only black republic in Africa and the only independent English-speaking black nation in the world, Liberia was clearly in a good position to develop trade and contact with the rest of black Africa, particularly nearby West African regions. Interest in and good wishes for the new nation came from American and Caribbean blacks, and to an extent from British and American philanthropy. The ACS, state societies, and churches continued to finance schools, immigration, and the maintenance of an agent in the republic. Of course, such aid was a mixed blessing, for with funding went outside control.[1]

Blyden's preparation for leadership

Born in 1832, Blyden was raised in the Danish West Indies and in Venezuela before briefly emigrating to the United States in 1850. There he met several whites active in the ACS. During his few months stay his application to Rutgers Theological School was rejected, and he witnessed the impact of the newly passed Fugitive Slave Act. He decided to emigrate to Liberia. Blyden consciously set out to educate himself for a leadership role in independent Liberia. He attended Alexander High School for five years and took over the principalship of the school in 1858. He corresponded with British and American leaders, obtaining books and journals. He wrote for the *Liberia Herald* and served briefly in the militia. His view of Africans evolved from an uncritical acceptance of settler hostility and prejudices to a respect for village planning and military skills.[2]

Blyden followed the developing debates in the United States over emigration sites, and he defended Liberia against the criticisms of both Gerrit Smith and Martin Delany. In articles as early as 1852, when he was twenty years of age, he argued emigration from the United States to Africa rather than to Canada. In his first pamphlet, *Voice from Bleeding Africa* (1856), he combined his defense of Liberia with themes from black history, presenting a list of twenty-seven blacks who had made achievements in scholarship, science, and military action in Europe, America, and the Caribbean.

Blyden did not simply praise black virtues, however. He developed a critical attack on the problems confronting Liberia, based on an idealistic vision of what the nation should achieve. But throughout his career he offended potential allies and followers with a self-righteous tone. In *A Vindication of the Negro Race* (1857) he urged the youth of the country to educate themselves; in a eulogy on the death of John Day, an early settler, he asked Liberia's leaders to emulate the pioneer's self-denial.[3]

Blyden's nationalism

Blyden's romantic nationalism was based on an ambitious view of Liberia's potentiality and destiny. In 1857 he decried greed, extravagance, and dependence on foreigners for schools, churches, and funding. He attacked the missionary societies for drawing talent away from civil service. He wanted economic surplus channelled from consumption into investment, and he urged national control of the educational system. He did not spell out the means, such as taxes and tariffs, which could accomplish these ends, but his meaning was clear. He attacked the dependence on commerce between natives and foreign manufacturers as an "evanescent" prosperity.[4]

His attack on this type of commerce was an attack on the way of life of the elite merchant class. Any taxation to support his plans would hit this class most heavily. He saw the commerce as incongruous with a state of liberty, since it fed upon and perpetuated dependence on outsiders. As an alternative, he asked Liberians to turn their energies to education, the extension of religion and moral influence to the native people, and local industry and agriculture. He attacked "partyism" and all political factionalism in favor of national unity—a slightly veiled attack on the group dominated by J.J. Roberts and his followers.

In 1861 Blyden and Crummell visited the United States under a Liberian government commission to seek funds for education. In the United States the two commissioners drew encouragement from the seeming growth of emigrationism. Delany's National Emigration Board joined forces with Garnet's African Civilization Society in 1861, and a united front of American black nationalists seemed to be emerging.

On the return of Blyden and Crummell to Liberia, they urged an appropriation of funds to seize the opportunity presented by the emigration mood among American blacks. They were successful, and with J.D. Johnson returned as emigration agents to the United States. But Blyden and Crummell's tour won almost no converts to the Liberian cause. Blyden adopted a bitter tone when confronted with the lack of enthusiasm among Afro-Americans. They seemed to feel, he noted, "that they owe no special duty to the land of their forefathers." He tried to demonstrate that Providence called descendants of Africa in America to a duty to build up a nationality in their homeland, to assist in the development of indigenous society, and to establish an asylum of liberty. He argued, not altogether candidly, that Americo-Liberians had no antipathy to Africans but were dedicated to their uplift, and he predicted an assimilation of Africans with settlers.[5]

Over the years 1862-71 Blyden developed his nationalist ideas further. In writing of a distinctive African personality, both Blyden and Crummell accepted the prevalent European view of Africans as pliable and non-domineering, but they expressed the concept in positive terms, suggesting that Africans were more spiritual and religious than Europeans, and less competitive, individualistic, and combative. Blyden visualized Africans as the eventual peacemakers and consolers when European war machines would bring civilization to the brink of disaster.[6]

Blyden found much in African culture worth preserving, particularly communal property and cooperative effort, and in this line of thought he laid the groundwork for the justification of African socialism a century later. He claimed that aspects of African culture usually criticized by Europeans as uncivilized, savage, or primitive embodied virtues: secret societies served an educational function; native religions and polygamy were integral parts of the social whole. He clearly liberated himself from white European conceptions on such issues, and in questioning the utility for Africa of Christianity he went much further than many other western-trained Africans of either his or succeeding generations.[7]

Blyden's opinions on Islam grew from a defense of African culture, from his study of Arabic, and from visits he made to Lebanon, Egypt, and the Moslem regions of the interior of Sierra Leone. In the period 1871–76 he published a series of articles which argued that while Christianity had worked against the progress of the black race by attacking African customs and disrupting the totality of African society, Islam was not antagonistic to the African personality, served to reduce some of the more inhumane aspects of African customs, and helped to preserve that which was good. By overlooking ethnic and tribal differences, it had helped unite Africans. He approached the comparative merits of Christianity and Islam on a practical and social rather than theological level, and he defended his thinking with historical and literary evidence. A furor created by this challenge to European thinking spread through the British scholarly and religious press, and his articles were reprinted in a widely read and controversial collection of his works, *Christianity, Islam, and the Negro Race* (1887).

But it was his more locally controversial views on mulattoes, his views on relations between Americo-Liberians and Africans, and his own haughty personality which lay behind his flight and exile from Liberia. The party division between blacks and mulattoes in Liberia, brewing for years, reached a violent pitch in 1870–71. Edward J. Roye, elected president in 1870, sought to implement some of the ideas of Blyden and Crummell, including development and exploration of the interior, public education, a national banking system, and the introduction of railroads. Such a program could break the power of the merchants by bringing new groups into competition as suppliers of products, and it would undermine the influence of the missionaries by breaking the religious monopoly on education. Seeking funds for the program, Roye floated a loan at a severe discount in England, thus providing a ready political issue by overcommitting the nation to high repayments. The supporters of Roberts arrested Roye in a small-scale coi p d'état, and he was later killed during an "attempted escape."[8]

A group of Roberts's supporters then attacked Blyden, and he fled the country. Moving to Sierra Leone, he founded the *Negro*, a newspaper with a pan-African news and editorial policy, and for two years worked as its editor. He later returned to Liberia to serve as ambassador to Great Britain, president of Liberia College, and minister of the interior for a two-year term. In 1885 he unsuccessfully ran for the presidency, ironically as the candidate for the Republican party which had supported his enemies earlier. He con-

tinued to hold diplomatic and educational posts in Liberia and in Sierra
Leone in his later years. But it was through his writings, rather than his
statesmanship, that he remained an international influence. In addition, his
short tour of the United States in 1889-90 served as a stimulus to revived
interest in African emigration.[9]

Alexander Crummell

Alexander Crummell attended several of the few schools available to blacks
in the United States at the time of his youth, and his education exposed him
to the currents of both abolitionist and emigrationist thought. Born in
1819, he attended a primary school operated by Peter Williams, and later
Noyes Academy in New Hampshire with Henry Highland Garnet. Crummell
went on to Oneida Institute, then directed by Beriah Green, who had been
converted to abolitionism by Theodore Weld. As a youth, Crummell was
active in the New Hampshire and New York antislavery societies. He was
denied admission to New York General Theological Seminary, apparently
not because he was black but because he was a black antislavery activist. In
1842 he became deacon and later a priest of the Boston Episcopal Church,
but he grew discouraged at the lack of response to his dry sermons, and at
his ebbing financial resources. In 1847, under the patronage of John Jay,
he went to England to raise funds for a new church. In Britain he was
widely acclaimed and was offered funds to attend Oxford. While a student,
he went to British antislavery rallies and conventions, keeping in touch with
other black abolitionists and with the development of emigrationist and
nationalist thought in the United States.[10]

While in England, well before his meetings with Blyden, Crummell conceived the idea of Africa as the proper field of endeavor for American black
men, and developed an interest in black homelands. In an 1852 address,
"Hope for Africa," he listed Haiti, Sierra Leone, and Liberia as evidence of
progress, along with acts of British and Latin American abolition. He noted
the settlement of colonies by Barbadian blacks in the Gold Coast and of
recaptives from Sierra Leone at Abeokuta, which had been under way since
1839. He coupled his practical political interest with a belief in an African
personality, particularly susceptible to Christianization and modernization
because of its "plastic" nature.[11]

Crummell's nationalism

Crummell was appointed to St. Sylvan's Church on the St. Paul River in
Liberia after receiving his A.B. from Oxford, and soon after his arrival he
delivered a sermon in which he urged his listeners to aim at high personal
ethics, to renounce self-interest, and to develop the character of their children along Christian lines, all in order to serve the nation. Because Liberia
was Protestant, unlike Haiti, it had a unique opportunity to become the
leading black state in the world, and it was up to its citizens to rise to the
challenge. Crummell avoided politics scrupulously, but he disapproved of
some of the habits of the merchant elite such as ostentation, immodesty of
dress, and the search for wealth for its own sake.[12]

As the individual had a duty to the state, so the nation had an obligation
to the commonwealth of mankind, Crummell said, following a recurrent
theme in European nationalist thought. Liberia's destiny was to "raise on
these shores a race of men" which would "confuse and mystify all the past
chronicles of time pertaining to our race." The practical means for achieving
the goal included exploration of the interior, and the building of roads and
missions to open new native groups to Western commerce and Christianity.
He believed Liberia's advantages of the English language and Protestant
Christianity would assist in the first long-range goal of economic and missionary opening of the interior. He echoed a current American phrase quite
appropriately: "To make all this reality, seems the plain duty and the manifest destiny of Liberia."[13]

Crummell, like Blyden, believed that Liberians should turn their attention
to intellectual matters, but he hoped that commerce, particularly between
the United States and Africa, could assist in Africa's progress. In a preface
to an essay by Blyden, Crummell argued that writers and jurists, scholars and
ministers should receive as much recognition as men of wealth, and he decried excessive admiration for the wealthy of Liberia. On the other hand, in
an open letter to the free black men of America, Crummell urged them to
support any activity which would assist Africa, including missionary, emigrationist, or commercial enterprises. He sought to tap "the material interests of adventurous, enterprising colored men," and he appealed to men who
had a "thirst for wealth, position, honor and power" since they would prove
a "handmaiden of religion, and will serve the great purposes of civilization."
He specified the natural products of Liberia and the profits to be made in
shipping. He urged the development of a black fleet, captained by men like
Cuffe, manned by black seamen drawn from the coastal and river shipping
of the United States, and financed by the same capital that flowed to the
construction of black churches in the United States. This attempt to appeal
to "black Yankees" in the early 1860s developed after his contact with

Delany and was expressed on his tour of the United States. His studied appeal to practical self-interest and the profit motive contrasted with Blyden's romantic idealism and appeal to racial solidarity.[14]

Crummell's pan-Africanism, like Blyden's, had roots in the arguments for an ethnically and linguistically uniform Liberia. Such a view could run counter to the goals of the merchant class, who were disdainful of pure black ancestry and who preferred to maintain the exploitative status quo with the natives. Crummell's view of national unity was nicely exemplified in his program for recaptives. He saw in them certain advantages for Liberia: they provided a labor force needed for coffee or sugar production, they rapidly learned English, and joined churches. However, he warned they must have education provided for them, and missionaries should work among them before spending resources in the interior. Bachelor recaptives should marry the surplus settler daughters, he believed, and this recommendation challenged the elite's propensity to "marry light." He proposed a similar assimilation of black Barbadian immigrants, and reflected a goal of an ethnically pan-African, rather than Americo-Liberian, state.[15]

Although he usually avoided political statements, Crummell's arguments for African and recaptive assimilation and public education aligned him rather directly with Roye, Blyden, and the "black" rather than "mulatto" faction. In an address entitled "Our National Mistakes and the Remedy for Them" he decried the neglect of the native population, and the fact that Americo-Liberians forgot "our own humbling antecedents." Recognizing the decline of immigration from the United States during and after the Civil War, he recommended that Liberia set about incorporating the native population politically and culturally.[16]

Liberian nationalism exported to the United States

Crummell returned to the United States in 1873 and joined the Episcopal ministry in Washington, D.C. His particular and specific contribution to American black nationalism was a statement of the duty of the black elite towards the masses, and a sense of racial solidarity which he called the "social principle." "The principle of growth and mastery in a race, a nation or people, are the same all over the globe," he asserted. He recommended that blacks "strive for footing and superiority in this land, on the line of race, as a temporary but needed expedient. . . . " He continued to call for a two-pronged approach, of intellect and commerce, and called for "industrial cooperation" like that of white capital and white labor.[17]

In his last years Crummell retained his suspicion of mulattoes and his sense of pan-African identity; he worked to implement his concept of racial solidarity of the elite with the masses. In his private correspondence he saw mulattoes as a "fanatical and conceited junto" and warned some of his associates against particular mulatto spokesmen. In 1896–97 Crummell helped found the American Negro Academy and delivered its inaugural address. The Academy brought together black scholars, teachers, newspapermen, and clergy with the goal of advancing the "civilization of the Negro race." W. E. B. DuBois, one of Crummell's younger associates in the founding of the Academy, was the best-known of his successors in carrying on the effort of enlisting the black elite in the cause of racial advance.[18]

Although Crummell was older than Blyden by about thirteen years, and his maturity was reflected in a sometimes more diplomatic style, Blyden often took the lead in developing ideas in the period 1856–70 when they were associated in Liberia. Both men were clearly impressed by Delany's visit in 1860, and each referred to the Abeokuta idea thereafter. Both believed in development of the interior, in assimilation of Africans in Liberia, and in Christianizing and civilizing Africa. Both developed a strong suspicion of the motives of mulattoes. While Blyden moved in the direction of respect for Islam and African culture, Crummell moved to a stronger regard fot the beneficial effect of commerce, and after his departure from Liberia he took up the work of black advance in America with the ideological tools he had shaped in Africa.

Together Blyden and Crummell had developed an ideology well adapted to the Liberian situation, which they exported to the United States. Educated black men should provide leadership for a racially oriented state which would be pan-African in its makeup. Mulatto emulation of white values should be rejected. In exporting such ideas to the United States, Crummell continued to fight mulatto spokesmen and continued to work for elite-led racial solidarity. The "social principle" of Crummell was Liberianism without Liberia; the idea of emigration would not solve American black problems, as Crummell saw it. But the principles of racial unity, self-determination, racial pride, and the obligation of the educated to the masses did apply. A generation of young intellectuals exposed to Crummell's ideas through the Academy and through his writings would work for them in the early years of the twentieth century. Crummell and Blyden's earlier advocacy of Liberian emigration would be taken up by other figures, and Crummell's interest in the possibility of an international black-owned shipping line and commerce would continue to be carried on long after he had dropped the idea himself.

9

CIVIL WAR EXPERIMENTS

During the Civil War the Union government attempted several programs to resolve the question of the postwar status of the slave which bore resemblance to earlier separatist ideas, including deportation and settlement in enclaves. Although they were white-directed and conceived, the mass black support for some aspects of the plans demonstrated the continued appeal of a separatist approach. But several prominent black spokesmen either actively opposed such projects or ignored their potential as separatist developments. Martin Delany served as an army recruiting officer, and in the Reconstruction period could be regarded as a "black carpetbagger" in South Carolina. Frederick Douglass's abolitionism had aimed at the incorporation of black people in the body politic and the extension of full rights of citizenship; his doctrine and that of white Radicals did not aim at the creation of a separate black national entity. But the masses of freedmen, many of whom had lived in relative isolation from whites imposed by large plantation conditions, found little in the authority and condescension of white officers, soldiers, and administrators that would encourage them to expect citizenship on an equal footing. Freedman support of separatist plans, particularly those which involved land ownership, stood in contrast to the indifference and opposition of most of the black leadership of the war and Reconstruction period.

Some experimental plans were put forward by white real estate promoters; their failure was due to justified government skepticism. The scheme of Ambrose Thompson to set up a black settlement of freedmen in the Chiriqui privince of Colombia, near what is now the Panama–Costa Rica border, is a case in point. Thompson had tried to promote a government contract for a coaling station on his lands prior to the Civil War. When his freedmen resettlement plan was presented to Lincoln's cabinet, all except the secretary of the interior disapproved. The State Department encountered opposition from Costa Rica, because of fears of a Colombian plan to use the settlers in filibustering expeditions in the disputed border region. Yet, by October of 1862, when the plan was cancelled, Thompson claimed he had fourteen thousand applications for emigration.[1]

Deportation

Congressional leaders and the president himself favored the deportation idea early in the Civil War as the preferred "solution" to the problem of the freedmen. In debates over the recognition of Haiti and Liberia and over emancipation in the District of Columbia, congressmen from border states clearly favored deportation. In April and July, 1862, colonization was specifically mentioned in Congressional acts. The first bill included an appropriation of $100,000 to be spent for the colonization of free blacks from Washington, D.C. The July, 1862, Confiscation Act appropriated $500,000 for deportation without mention of any specific destination. Senator James R. Doolittle of Wisconsin, a spokesman for colonization, was intrigued by the logistical aspects of deportation, and calculated various rates of removal: 150,000 a year would remove the total black population by 1907; 350,000 would complete the project by 1877. He estimated the cost of transportation at $50 per person and calculated the gross cost as feasible.[2]

Another plan, which had the earmarks of a moneymaking promotion, was the Île à Vache plan. A "merchant," Bernard Kock, had arranged early in 1862 a ten-year contract with the Haitian government to set up logging operations on a twenty-five-square-mile uninhabited island off the southwest coast of Haiti. In September, 1862, Kock met with Secretary of State Seward and wrote to Lincoln to arrange for black settlers. Despite warnings from some of his advisers, Lincoln signed a contract with Kock December 31 1862, to settle 5,000 freedmen on the offshore island. The contract spelled out provisions for housing, salaries, schooling, and medical services. Kock's company was reorganized by shareholders, and he was sent out as manager with 543 settlers in April, 1863. The emigrants faced smallpox, uncleared forest, and the confiscation of their meager funds by Kock. A government investigator in December of 1863 reported on conditions, and the navy quietly brought the 365 survivors back in March, 1864. The Île à Vache failure was the closest to implementation ever achieved in the whole history of government-sponsored deportation debate.[3]

Other sites were investigated but rejected. An offer came from an Ecuadorian landholder to sell tracts along the Pacific coast. The Netherlands inquired whether free blacks could go to Surinam to take up five-year labor contracts. Denmark offered three-year contracts for the island of St. Croix; the British offered to take ten thousand freedmen a year on five-year indentures for the Caribbean, and also suggested British Honduras. Luckily for the freedmen, all these proposals were rejected by Seward on the grounds of likely exploitation and inadequate protection of freedmen's rights.[4]

A plan which combined elements of deportation with the idea of a territorial enclave was that of Senator James H. Lane of Kansas. He proposed that units of black troops be assigned duty on the southwest frontier; later their families would be sent to join them as the nucleus of a colony. Funds appropriated under the Confiscation Act would be diverted to assist the colony. The territory he proposed reached from the Rio Grande northwards, overlapping the territory of the Lundy grant. He coupled his deportation logic with some nationalist ideas: " . . . by acquiring an undisputed title to the soil, and an independent local organization, they may enjoy the privileges of republican civilization, and there concentrate their whole strength for mutual improvement." His plan was not approved.[5]

Lincoln's tentative attempts to win support among black leaders and spokesmen for deportation ideas were unsuccessful. On August 14, 1862, Lincoln met with a group led by the Reverend Edward Thomas, a supporter of emigration, but which included Frederick Douglass and delegates from several groups opposing colonization. Lincoln asked support from the delegates on the grounds that the two races could never live comfortably together. Meetings held over the next month passed resolutions critical of both deportation and Lincoln's position, and Garrison's *Liberator* reprinted anticolonization resolutions in the same style Garrison had used thirty years before in response to the ACS. A group of Philadelphia freemen in response to Lincoln suggested land reform within the United States and full citizenship as the proper course.[6]

Land reform

On the question of land reform and redistribution, white radicals and black freedmen could agree. Freedmen saw land ownership in an immediate and nonideological way. Wherever opportunities were presented for freedmen to acquire land, the response was enthusiastic. As far as white Republicans were concerned, the idea of confiscation and redistribution of plantations seemed logical enough. While the question of property rights stood in the way, legal mechanisms existed in the seizure of rebel lands as punishment for rebellion, or in some locales for failure to pay taxes. The vision of the mass of freedmen in the role of small farmers seemed appropriate. Western antislavery whites preferred to see the slave remain where he was, supplanting the plantation owner in the economy and not challenging northern or western white labor or commodity producers. New England abolitionists supported the idea on the grounds that the slave, if he proved himself as a small farmer, would vindicate the economic, humanitarian, and egalitarian arguments they had used against slavery.

The most successful of the land redistribution plans was the Port Royal experiment. After Union forces seized the islands around Beaufort, South Carolina, in 1862, the government faced an unusual problem. The white planters had fled, but the slaves remained. Under Treasury Department control, a group of selected ministers and teachers, many with abolitionist background, went to act as supervisors of the cotton plantations. The operation was soon shifted to army control, under General Rufus Saxton. While Saxton believed the freedmen should take up small plots of land for their own use, the idealistic superintendents believed that the economic units of the plantations should be retained, so that the freedmen could demonstrate that they could produce cotton better as free wage earners than as slaves. One of the superintendents, E. Philbrick, with Boston financing, arranged to purchase several large plantations and to work them as large units with freedmen serving as wage laborers. Saxton, on the other hand, worked to implement smallholding, and urged freedmen to claim lands by preemption. Some lands were sold by the government for overdue taxes, and many freedmen purchased lands at such sales.[7]

General Sherman implemented a more direct form of land redistribution in his Field Order Number 15, but its lack of legal foundation put the black settlers at a disadvantage. Following his March to the Sea came tens of thousands of black refugees from slavery. Sherman ordered that lands along the coast from Savannah to Florida be granted, and that captured steamers be used for protection and for keeping supply lines open. General Saxton warned that such a plan was doomed to failure, and at first balked at helping to arrange the settlements. His fears were well founded, for most of the Sherman field order land was later taken back by the former white owners through court action, despite occasional armed resistance by the black landholders.[8]

The activities in the Sea Islands had several long-range results. In the area around Beaufort and Port Royal, the titles to land, especially those established in the tax sales, were more secure. Although northern abolitionist efforts to establish a model community along New England lines including churches, town meetings, public schools, and militia service, fell short of completion, some of the schools and churches survived, and the area retained the highest percentage of black ownership of land of any region in the country. Much of the local decision making and government proceeded outside formal governmental structure, in the black-controlled churches. Secular law was regarded as "unjust law," church law as the "just law."[9]

The high interest and participation of the freedmen in land redistribution on the Sea Islands demonstrated both land hunger and the freedmen's desire and willingness to control their own destiny independent of whites. At meetings, in letters, at inquiry hearings, and in conversations with officers and agents, freedmen expressed their demands for land. A meeting held by General Sherman and Secretary of War Stanton with twenty representatives of the Sea Island freedmen prior to the issuance of the field order, convinced the military of the desire for ownership. These black demands and the field order itself influenced the final version of the Freedmen's Bureau bill of 1865 which provided for the rental and purchase of forty-acre allotments. President Andrew Johnson's failure to implement this provision of the bill moved Senator Thaddeus Stevens to introduce a bill which would have granted forty acres to each freedman, rather than allowing purchase. The land was to be confiscated from the seventy thousand most prominent rebels, part of it to be redistributed and the rest sold to cover pensions and other government expenses.[10]

Another military experiment also demonstrated that nationalist principles of self-determination had great appeal to the freedman. In Mississippi efforts to lease plantations to northern and loyal southern white agents in 1862 had produced only exploitation of the freedmen. In 1863 General Grant ordered the confiscation of the estates of Jefferson Davis and his family at Davis Bend for the establishment of an all-black settlement under army protection and direction. Five thousand acres were divided into small holdings placed in the hands of individuals, partnerships, and small companies, involving about 1,750 settlers. By the second year of the experiment, the black farmers showed a profit. By contrast to the Port Royal experiment and the field order lands, the Davis Bend settlement incorporated more institutions of local self-government. Lands were set aside for communal use, and black sheriffs and judges were appointed to settle disputes and maintain order. As in the case of the Sherman confiscation, however, the lands were later returned to the former owners, under the Johnson administration.[11]

After the demise of Davis Bend the freedmen settled there established Mound Bayou, which stood for decades as the only example of political black control of a locality in the United States. Isaiah T. Montgomery, son of Benjamin Montgomery, who as a slave had been manager of one of the Davis plantations, established the town in 1887 on a new site on high ground purchased from a railroad. Through the 1890s the town had a minor boom, with the establishment of a farmers' cooperative, a cottonseed mill, and real estate ventures. Booker Washington would come to regard the town as a living example of the principles of civic self-reliance, and the town has maintained its independence to the present.[12]

The government-directed experiments in deportation and land reform had on the whole few such permanent effects. White motives for deportation echoed early arguments of the supporters of the ACS, and Senator Lane's proposal for a Texas settlement paralleled the Lundy plan of a generation earlier. The stir caused by Lincoln's attempt to use the deportationist argument to convince black spokesmen showed that the failure of understanding which had characterized the ACS in 1820 persisted forty years later. Battlefield emancipation and the Emancipation Proclamation suddenly made the speculations and fears of earlier deportationists and abolitionists into immediate and practical concerns. Western antislavery advocates who had sought to prevent the spread of slavery to the frontier and western states now supported plans which either would settle slaves where they had lived or which would deport them. New England abolitionism, tinged with egalitarian arguments, found implementation in plans designed to demonstrate that the freedman could work as a wage earner and make a profit for capital. While black spokesmen from the North opposed deportation in language little changed from earlier opposition to the ACS, they, like the masses of black freedmen would support land reform.

The few land reforms implemented survived only if the freedmen involved could secure unassailable title to the lands, as in the tax sales at Port Royal and the direct purchase of land at Mound Bayou. The failure of the forty-acre plan of the Freedmen's Bureau bill and of Thaddeus Stevens's proposal left an unfilfilled promise which later black spokesmen could revive in arguments for reparations. The limited success of redistribution was due not only to President Andrew Johnson's reluctance to "punish" rebels by confiscation and redistribution, but to the persistence of white planters and white-controlled courts in seizing back lands and striving to keep the black man in the exploitable status of sharecropper or wage earner, rather than independent yeoman farmer. Where land tenure survived, with it went a measure of self-determination which could serve as an example of separatism for those who sought to revive it after Reconstruction.

10

TERRITORIALISM IN KANSAS AND OKLAHOMA

The testimony of the freedmen at Port Royal was explicit enough—they simply wanted to own land and to be left alone. But the clarity of that desire for self-determination was overlooked in the flood of statements, programs, and proposals imposed by white politicians, army officers, and philanthropists. The ideas and reactions of the literate minority of blacks in the North in the post-Reconstruction era are more available to study by the historian than are the sentiments of the mass of the black population, simply because the minority left the kind of public record of ideas that is easy to document. But several developments in the period following 1876 provide an impression of the kind of doctrine which the masses of freedmen preferred. Several migrations under spontaneous leadership and the wide and rapid popularity of a handful of those leaders indicated that the idea of a territorial enclave under black control in the United States continued to have a life of its own.

Kansas exodus

The first mass movement of black freedmen to a new territory was to Kansas in the 1870s. The underlying causes of the exodus from the South were many. The system of credit and crop-lien debt servitude which substituted for slavery was highly exploitative. The political collapse of black Reconstruction governments and of Freedmen's Bureau proposals introduced a skepticism about white promises of incorporation and integration into American life. The man who emerged as the leader of the exodus to Kansas,

Benjamin (Pap) Singleton, believed that he himself was the cause of the movement, rather than social factors, and he was quite proud of his title as the "Moses of the Colored Exodus."

Singleton was born a slave in 1809 and had been sold several times to the deep South. He ran away repeatedly and returned to his native Tennessee. After several foiled attempts he escaped to Canada and joined the émigré colony near Chatham, in western Ontario. He lived in Detroit after 1846, where he maintained lodgings for fugitives on their way to Canada.[1]

After the Civil War Singleton returned to Tennessee and began to preach a self-help doctrine similar to that of the black Canadian leadership. Although suspicious of the value of education, and regarding schools as a means of depriving contributors of funds to support a small idle group, Singleton urged his listeners to buy homes and small farms and reject politics. In 1869 he formed the Tennessee Real Estate and Homestead Association, which helped black families locate land much as had the Refugee Home Settlement in Canada; but Singleton found the Tennessee land available to blacks too worn out or too high-priced. In 1871 Singleton sent several agents to Kansas to investigate the possibility of settlement there, and in 1873 he personally visited Kansas to examine sites. In that year he led a group of three hundred settlers to Cherokee County in southeastern Kansas and founded "Singleton Colony." Over the next six years he shepherded many groups to Kansas and settled them on lands at different points around the state, including Dunlap Colony in Morris and Lyon counties, and Nicodemus Colony on the Solomon River in the northwestern part of the state. An associate of Singleton operated a Topeka headquarters which located lands open to settlement, and another agent in Tennessee helped assemble the migrant parties which Singleton personally guided up the river.[2]

By the end of 1878 Singleton claimed that he had led 7,432 blacks to Kansas. In 1879 a "fever" for emigration to Kansas swept through the South and a true mass migration got under way. The group of 1879, known as "Exodusters," flooded into Kansas to the dismay of local white officials. The town of Wyandotte, Kansas, first stop in that state on the steamboat journey up the Mississippi, saw 1000 migrants arrive in less than two weeks in the spring of 1879. By mid-June of that year some 5,100 migrants had arrived.[3]

Singleton and his organization tried to keep up with the rush of new migrants from Mississippi, Louisiana, and Arkansas. A group of black residents of St. Louis commissioned Singleton to assist in moving along the crowds of settlers stranded in that city.

Black leaders in both North and South were highly critical of the exodus, including Frederick Douglass, P. B. S. Pinchback, and Blanche K. Bruce. Singleton regarded them as unrepresentative: "They had good luck and now are listening to false prophets; they have boosted up and got their heads a whirlin', and now they think they must judge things from where they stand, when the fact is the possum is lower down the tree—down nigh to the roots."[4]

In 1880 charges by Democrats that Republicans were encouraging black migration to Kansas in order to strengthen their control led to a senatorial investigation of the exodus. Singleton was questioned, and he brought his scrapbook of clippings to the hearing. He regarded the political explanation of the migration as an attempt to cheat him of the credit for the movement: "I am the father of the exodus . . . the whole cause of the Kansas migration," he said. Yet he recognized that deeper causes were at work, and he talked of economic and social conditions in the South. The only way to "bring the South to her senses" was for blacks to leave and force an improvement in conditions for those who stayed behind.[5]

The opposition of both blacks and whites in Kansas to further migration helped to convince Singleton to try to work against the flood by warning paupers not to come, and by 1881 the migrations tapered off. The black settlers in Kansas attempted to consolidate their position in politics. Singleton remained active, organizing the Links and the United Links, which for a period in the 1880s, worked with the Greenback party.[6]

As Jim Crow practices became common in Kansas and many of the migrants moved into slums in the larger towns rather than take up small farms, Singleton grew disillusioned. In September, 1883, he was arguing for Canadian emigration, and he suggested Liberia as an alternative. After a brief interest in Cyprus as a possible destination for black emigrants, Singleton formed the United Transatlantic Society with the purpose of African emigration. The inauguration of Cleveland in 1885, the first Democratic president since before the Civil War, generated rumors that slavery would be reintroduced; white observers speculated that such fears contributed to the appeal of Singleton's new organization. Singleton used emigrationist-nationalist ideas in appealing for membership. He claimed that freedmen could expect no opportunities in the United States, and should seek a "national existence" apart from the white race. His society held several conventions endorsing Liberia, but sent no emigrants.[7]

Other groups of blacks in Kansas itself developed an interest in moving to a new homeland in the 1880s. At a convention held in Parsons, Kansas, in 1882, the delegates petitioned Congress to set aside every third section of land in Oklahoma to be open to black settlement only.[8]

Oklahoma settlements

The interest in Oklahoma soon took the form of founding communities, which combined elements of real estate promotion, utopianism, and spontaneous boom towns. The most prominent leader to emerge in the movement to Oklahoma was Edwin P. McCabe.[9]

McCabe and his friend A. T. Hall were young black immigrants to Pap Singleton's prairie settlement at Nicodemus in 1878, and formed part of the active leadership there in the 1880s. Hall was from Chicago and McCabe had met him there after moving from New York. Hall had been editor on the Chicago *Conservator* and McCabe was working as a clerk in the Cook County courthouse when they met and planned to migrate together to Kansas. At Nicodemus their skills were in great demand. They soon set themselves up as attorneys and land agents helping settlers to locate claims and run surveys.[10]

McCabe became secretary of the Nicodemus Town Company which preceded the formal incorporation of the town. As three other local towns competed for the role of county seat, the Nicodemus leaders carefully bargained with the voting strength of their town, which had about 12 percent of the county's voters. Nicodemus successfully supported an integrated slate of candidates for county officers put up by one of the contending towns, and Nicodemus men received some of the patronage. Hall was appointed to conduct the county census, and McCabe served as temporary county clerk for a period in 1880.[11]

In 1881 McCabe was elected county clerk; in 1882 he won the office of state auditor of Kansas, apparently the highest elective office held by a black man in a northern state until that time. Hall sold out his partnership in the land business and moved to St. Louis, where he became city editor of the *National Tribune.* He later returned to Chicago.[12]

McCabe was reelected to office in 1884, but was denied the Republican nomination for a third term. Whether his personal disappointment at the party's rejection of him soured him on integrated politics, as suggested by contemporary journalists, or whether he simply sought new opportunities, he grew interested in plans like the one put forward by S. H. Scott, a black lawyer in Fort Smith, Arkansas, in 1885, to develop Oklahoma as a separate black state.[13]

Discussion of Oklahoma as a black refuge and black self-governing area had been going on for several years. Four to five thousand blacks who had lived among the Creeks, Cherokees, and Chickasaw Indians in Oklahoma as slaves in the antebellum period were freed in 1866. Another thousand lived in separate villages and hamlets among the Seminoles, with a role of "vassals and allies." One Creek freedmen's village, founded in 1872, later became the large town of Muskogee. These black settlements provided the core of the Oklahoma black population prior to 1889. Proud of their Indian association, these groups tended to resent outside blacks who came to settle with them. However, in 1881 a Freedmen's Oklahoma Association formed to advocate the migration of outside freedmen into Oklahoma to settle lands which had been set aside in 1866 for the Indian freed slaves. But the secretary of the interior ruled that the use of the term "freedmen" in the 1866 treaties with the Oklahoma Indian tribes referred only to blacks freed by the Indians, not to migrants. In 1884 President Arthur recommended to Congress that black freedmen among the Indians be settled in a single district, but Congress did not act on the proposal.[14]

Whites anxious to settle the fertile lands in the Indian territory agitated and illegally moved to settle lands throughout the period 1879-89. The much-publicized availability of the land and the shadow of a black claim to the lands through the freedmen provisions of the 1866 treaties, stimulated the discussion of the idea of black migration there through Arkansas, Kansas, and states of the Deep South.

With the planned opening of surplus Indian lands to legal settlement under the Dawes Act of 1887, and the availability of some land under that act by individual sales in 1889, McCabe moved to promote a townsite. He purchased a number of lots from a white resident of Guthrie and set up the McCabe Town Company. Agents of the company sold the lots throughout the South to blacks—the price included a railroad ticket to Guthrie, about ten miles from the site, and a choice of one lot. A restrictive covenant was included in the title: no lot could ever pass to any white man, and no white could reside or do business on the lots.[15]

McCabe named his new town Langston, after J. M. Langston, the black attorney and educator who had spoken in favor of emigration in Ohio in 1849. Langston had had a distinguished career during Reconstruction with the Freedmen's Bureau and had served as dean and president of Howard University and as consul general to Haiti. When McCabe named the town after him, Langston had just been elected to Congress from Virginia. By 1890 McCabe had drawn about two thousand settlers to Langston, but the 1891 opening of nearby Sac and Fox lands attracted many away. By 1900 the town's population was down to less than a thousand. McCabe published a paper, the *Langston Herald*, which his agents could use to help publicize the town, and the paper brought national attention to McCabe's work.[16]

McCabe's efforts at Langston were viewed as a threat by white settlers, and the idea of a "black state" may have been partly the creation of white propaganda. Several local papers which opposed black settlement gave the idea a bad press, including the *Norman Transcript* and the *Vinita Indian Chieftain.* Later the *New York Times* and the *New York Post* took up the issue, suggesting that McCabe was the leader of a plan to create a black state, or at least guarantee a black settlement in each Congressional representative district. While McCabe did not advocate the plan in such a specific form, his actions suggest that as a politician he wanted to keep his options open. In 1891 the idea of a black state might appear realizable if enough migrants could be attracted. As McCabe's *Herald* and his Afro-American Colonization Company recruited settlers, the rumor of a proposed black state, however frightening to local whites, could help attract settlers. Indeed, over twenty-five black towns were established, and several thrived for decades. But if black settlement did not reach a sufficient proportion, McCabe could continue to play the role of a black politician in an essentially white-dominated political machine, delivering votes as leader and spokesman. The black proportion of the population of Oklahoma fell from 8.4 percent in 1890 to 7 percent in 1900. While pockets of blacks might have a chance for local political clout, the mass migration of blacks was simply flooded out by white Sooners. But the black population in Oklahoma had increased considerably in absolute terms, from 22,000 in 1890 to 56,000; a good proportion of the increase could be attributed to McCabe's efforts. By 1897 McCabe was using the political strength he represented to gain certain benefits for the black population and for himself personally in the form of political appointments.[17]

In 1897 McCabe received appointment as auditor in the Oklahoma Territorial government and held the post until 1907. After statehood, under Democratic party control, he served as assistant deputy auditor for a year, and left the state in 1908 to return to Chicago. The Colored Agricultural and Normal University of Oklahoma (later Langston University) was located on town land donated by McCabe. The continued survival of the town is due largely to business and payroll associated with the college.[18]

McCabe, like Singleton, received credit for a movement which grew spontaneously and which had many sources. His own town of Langston was only one of many all-black communities in Oklahoma that derived from other efforts. Taft was founded by freedmen from the Creek nation after the Civil War, and in 1909 became the location for a state orphans' home for black children and a state school for Negro girls. Another settlement near Muldrow, west of Fort Smith, Arkansas, was founded by Cherokee freedmen. The large black settlement at Okmulgee had Indian origins. Smaller black settlements at Rentiesville, Tatums, Summit, Vernon, Redbird Clearview, and Wybark were established in the 1890s.[19]

Boley

Better known than any of these settlements was the town of Boley, established in 1903–1904. Boley, like Langston, was the result of a combination of utopian ideas, townsite promotion, and spontaneous boom. According to local legend, Boley was founded on a bet between two whites on the question of whether the black man could govern himself. Land was purchased from a Creek freedwoman, and black settlers were invited. A black railroad worker was appointed townsite manager, and the town was widely advertised. By 1905 it had a newspaper, the *Progress,* and by 1908 some 2500 inhabitants, two banks, two cotton gins, a hotel, and a Creek-Seminole college and agricultural institute. Later the State Training School for Negro Boys was established a few miles from Boley, equivalent to the girls' school outside of Taft. Booker Washington said of Boley, after a visit in 1905, that it "represents a dawning race consciousness." He hoped it would "demonstrate the right of the Negro, not merely as an individual, but as a race, to have a worthy and permanent place" in America.[20]

Whites who saw in the all-Negro town a parallel to their own conceptions of segregation approved Boley's development as long as it posed no immediate political threat. Boley received further national publicity from an item in the *St. Louis Globe Democrat,* which endorsed it from a segregationist point of view. "Boley is what is known in Oklahoma as a 'nigger town' . . . . Here at last I was to find the negro question solved."[21]

The *Boley Progress,* like the *Langston Herald,* published editorials which represented a mixture of town promotion and black separatist ideas: "Come and help prove to the caucasian race and not only the caucasian race but the world that the Negro is a law-making and law abiding citizen, and help us solve the great racial problem that is now before us."[22]

Despite the high hopes of Boley promoters, when the choice of a county seat in Okfuskee County came up, two white towns, Weleetka and Okemah, vied for the honor. In a move similar to the successful manipulation in Nicodemus, Kansas, Boley joined in supporting an integrated ticket. But the Oklahoma situation differed considerably from that in Kansas. While the governor of the Oklahoma Territory, Abraham J. Seay, was a Republican appointed by President Harrison, white Democrats from Arkansas and Texas made up the majority of the new population flooding into the territory. Republicans had been dominant in Kansas, and there the struggle within the local party machinery for control of county conventions had determined the eventual outcome. In that political situation the settlers at Nicodemus could maneuver successfully for alliances within the Republican party. But in the bipartisan Okfuskee County setting Democrats controlled the county election commission which refused to certify duly nominated

blacks on the Republican slate. Furthermore, the commission gerryman-
dered the voting districts to make black voting nearly impossible. Boley
was denied even a voting precinct, although as a gesture to gain black support the Okemah county seat advocates temporarily allowed two voting
stations at Boley. In later elections the precinct was eliminated and black
votes were simply not counted.[23]

Black men in Boley and throughout Oklahoma were effectively disfran-
chised in 1910 when the voters of the state passed an amendment to the
state constitution imposing a literacy test and grandfather clause. In effect,
the amendment allowed the local registrar to impose arbitrary literacy tests,
to score them himself, and to deny blacks the vote, while not requiring a
test of whites and many Indians.

Early statehood saw a number of physical attacks on Boley residents and
other black residents in Oklahoma. White sheriffs and deputies descended
on the town, brandishing their weapons and arresting groups from the local
pool halls and card rooms. Black owners of outlying farms were threatened
by white groups who wanted to force land sales. In 1911 at nearby Okemah
a thirteen-year-old boy and his mother were lynched. Such terror, combined
with disfranchisement, Jim Crow facilities in white market towns and county
seats, police methods, and finally a cotton market collapse in 1913 left the
dreams of a racial haven at Boley shattered.[24]

Summary

The events in Kansas and Oklahoma in the period 1879–1913 followed a
pattern. The first migrations away from the conditions of Reconstruction
had been spontaneous, finding leadership in local figures like Singleton and
McCabe. These spokesmen developed a separatist doctrine reflecting elements of the nationalist tradition. Singleton's ideas of homesteading and
directed settlement may have derived from his contacts in the antebellum
Canadian settlement; McCabe combined some of Singleton's ideas of settlement with party political methods learned in Chicago and Kansas.

In Oklahoma the pre-existing black communities among the Indians, and
the provisions of the 1866 treaties with the Indians setting aside freedmen's
lands, provided a base for later expansion. Langston, Taft, and Boley, on
lands acquired under the Dawes Act, survived the political attack after statehood, at least in part because nearby segregated black educational institutions provided payroll. But the eventual triumph of Jim Crow in the form
of disfranchisement, racist terror, and harassment prepared the way for an
African emigration appeal.

The very ordinary backgrounds of Singleton and McCabe, and the masses who moved to Kansas and Oklahoma, are convincing evidences of the genuineness of the movements. The ideas and plans of the black settlements in those states were grassroots examples of the racial solidarity advocated by Crummell. The failure to achieve any lasting political hegemony in either region was due to the tenacious and sometimes corrupt white control of the political process. Prior to World War I blacks did not migrate in great numbers to the northern cities, and the experience of the black settlers in the two western migrations demonstrated a cycle of mass movement, hastily erected popular leadership, idealistic and utopian hopes, and crushing disillusionment which would be repeated in the later migrations to New York, Chicago, and even later, the west coast cities. The nationalist and separatist aspirations of the masses cried out for articulation by spokesmen.

11

AFRICAN EXODUS REVIVED

In the years after Reconstruction the appeal of Liberia as a possible destination for black emigrants revived. Like the territorial plans, this form of black nationalist planning caught on among the new audience of freedmen. What had been a concern of a limited number of black intellectuals and of slaves liberated through the efforts of the ACS, now became a mass movement. In the revived Liberian exodus plans the idea introduced by Alexander Crummell that blacks should own the shipping which would carry them to Africa was also revived, and in a few instances, was implemented.

Black-owned shipping

The idea of purchasing ships, which was later to be taken up by Marcus Garvey, had deep roots in the concerns of American black nationalists, and its recurrence as a theme is a feature of black nationalism in America which is not found to a similar extent in other nationalisms. As we have noted, Paul Cuffe, the leading pioneer of black nationalist ideas in America, was most famous as a ship captain and shipowner. In the early days of the Liberian colony, Francis Devany and other settlers believed that the colony needed a flag of its own, in order to protect the infant coastal fleet. In the colonial governments governors Thomas Buchanan and J. J. Roberts of Liberia and Russwurm of Maryland had made efforts to develop a navy and merchant fleet. Thus, when Crummell wrote of black-owned shipping in 1860, and developed the concept of a black-owned and black-manned fleet as an expression of the international solidarity of the race, he did so in the context of an already long-standing black interest in the idea.

Crummell had spelled out his proposal in "The Relations and Duties of Free Colored Men in America to Africa," a letter published as a pamphlet late in 1860, and reprinted in 1862 during his tour of the United States as a colonization agent, with Blyden.

At an early day, whole fleets of vessels, manned and officered by black men from the United States and Liberia would outrival all the other agencies for grasping West African commerce. Large and important houses would spring into existence among you through the states. Wealth would flow into your coffers.

BD: want American dream of wealth and success but... I

But the financial motive should remain secondary to the more crucial "moral and philanthropic" considerations, he believed.[1]

The kings and tradesmen of Africa, having the demonstration of negro capacity before them, would hail the presence of their black kinsmen from America, and would be stimulated to a generous emulation. To the farthest interior, leagues and combinations would be formed with men of commerce; and thus civilization, enlightenment and Christianity would be carried to every state, town and village of interior Africa.

Even before Crummell returned to live permanently in the United States, his ideas and concerns had impact. He had met with Delany in 1859, and Delany published a summary of their conversation in the narrative of his African trip in 1861. In 1862 Crummell's tour, addresses, and published writings disseminated his proposals.

Among Crummell's auditors on this trip was the young AME minister Henry McNeal Turner, twenty-eight years old at the time. Turner was born of free ancestry in South Carolina in 1834 and joined the Methodist church as a youth. During the Civil War he served as a chaplain in the Union Army, and at the end of the war became an itinerant preacher for the AME church. Settling in Georgia, he worked in the Republican party, was elected to a term in the Georgia legislature, and secured a postmaster appointment under Grant.[2]

Again a religious link.

Liberian exodus from South Carolina

religious

Turner was to cross paths with Martin Delany in one of the first post–Civil War emigration efforts, the Liberian Exodus Joint Stock Steamship Company, formed in Charleston in 1877–78. The movement began spontaneously during the first four months of 1877 when the Democratic "Redeemer" government fought for ascendancy over the "Black Reconstruction" Republicans of South Carolina. A number of rural counties which reported interest in emigration were the very counties dominated by "straightout" white supremacy groups. Interest in Liberia grew, and the Liberian Independence Day, July 26, was celebrated with festivities. At the celebration the Reverend B. F. Porter called for formation of a stock company, which was immediately organized. The new emigration group wrote to the ACS for advice, assistance, and information, hoping to cope with the growing surge of interest. Prospective migrants began arriving in Charleston, and in January, 1878, Porter purchased a 412-ton clipper, the *Azor*, in Boston.[3]

At a consecration service for the ship, Martin Delany, who was serving as a trial justice in Charleston, was presented with a Liberian flag in honor of his pre–Civil War pioneering work in African emigration. The Reverend Turner conveyed the Crummell message to the assembled group. The ship would "not only . . . bear a load of humanity, but . . . take back the culture, education and religion acquired here. The work inaugurated then would never stop until the blaze of Gospel truth should glitter over the whole broad African continent."[4]

In April, 1878, the *Azor* sailed with 206 emigrants. The group did not fare well; twenty-three died before reaching Africa. After a stopover in Sierra Leone the survivors finally reached Monrovia in June. Expenses incurred on the voyage and for pilotage and towage at Sierra Leone ran the company into debt, and a planned second trip never materialized. The settlers from the *Azor* sent back conflicting reports as to their success. Eventually a few of the settlers from South Carolina entered Liberian public service: David Frazier became a senator and C. L. Parsons became a supreme court justice. But the difficulties of those searching for funds to return received more publicity.[5]

Henry McNeal Turner

As an AME minister, Turner continued to influence masses of freedmen to consider emigration. As editor of the *Christian Recorder* and later as bishop, he travelled throughout the South and frequently gave guest sermons. He constantly reiterated the themes of redemption of Africa through the return of Christians from the United States, and the control of the effort by black-owned shipping lines, which would serve as proof of black ability and as a source of pride.

Turner argued for the development of Liberia and discussed the concept of emigration and shipping as both a national and a racial concept. He expected that Liberia, as a black state, would eventually receive world recognition. He hoped that "our children's children can rest securely under [Liberia's] aegis, whether in Africa, Europe, Asia, America or upon the high seas." He frequently returned to the practical and hardheaded calculations of shipping, reflecting the same reasoning utilized by Crummell. The enthusiastic support Turner received as he lectured convinced him that willing investors and passengers could be located. "If a line of steamers were started from New Orleans, Mobile, Savannah or Charleston, they would be crowded to density every trip they made to Africa."[6]

Did Turner stimulate an emigration interest that otherwise would not have developed, or did he simply give expression to an existing mass desire? Whichever view one takes about the relationship between leaders and mass movements, it is clear that Turner's ideas did have a wide following. Time and again in the 1880s and 1890s, a rumor would sweep through a particular county or state that a ship had been prepared to carry emigrants back to Africa. Hustlers and fraudulent fund raisers took advantage of the widespread interest. Stock was sold in nonexistent companies, and such schemes helped discredit the authentic efforts of black businessmen and preachers who attempted to organize companies for emigration. Several parties of emigrants arrived in port cities and awaited ships which would never appear. The intensity of the desire to believe, even in rumors or in frauds, was testimony to the mass appeal of this nationalist alternative to Jim Crow and to economic exploitation.

The Congo Free State

Among the sources of revived interest in African emigration in the late 1880s was the publicity surrounding the formation of the Congo Free State by Leopold of Belgium. Theoretically self-governing, with Leopold as sovereign and with an international association of European capital interests to provide trade, finance, and shipping, the unique colony attracted the interest of both black and white promoters in the United States. In 1886 the United States and Congo National Emigration Company was organized in Baltimore by three whites, one of whom claimed to represent the Danish government. The group sought black shareholders as well as whites. After attempting to tap unspent colonization funds from the Confiscation Act of 1862 and finding that the funds would not be released without Congressional action, the company was turned over to its black stockholders. The Reverend Benjamin Gaston, who had lived in Liberia in the period 1866-86, secured appointment from the company as general agent, and he toured the Gulf states to raise funds and stir interest in emigration. As a result, groups of prospective emigrants sold their land and marched on Atlanta. Eventually 2500 black people from Atlanta and surrounding country awaited transport at Savannah. Gaston shipped three groups to Liberia, numbering 17, 30, and 42 migrants, in the period 1893-94.[7]

The idea of emigration to the Congo attracted George Washington Williams, who had earned a distinguished reputation as a black historian. Williams visited the Congo in February, 1890, to investigate its suitability as a location for emigrants. In reports to Secretary of State Blaine, and to the president, he denounced the conditions he found in the Congo. His investigation, cut short by his death in August, 1891, was carried on by others, eventually leading to a public outcry in both Britain and America. Another courageous black critic of the Congo was William Henry Sheppard, who had served there as a Presbyterian missionary. The criticisms initiated by Williams and Sheppard were eventually followed by the investigations of Roger Casement, which resulted in British pressure to force Belgium to reorganize the Free State and govern it directly, rather than as a personal colony of Leopold.[8]

Blyden as emigration agent

The influence of Crummell's African associate Blyden clearly played a part in reviving interest in Liberia in the 1890s and the early 1900s. Blyden visited the United States in 1889-90, meeting with white churchmen, newspapermen, and politicians in Chicago, Philadelphia, Washington, and Charleston, and with a variety of southern black leaders. The purpose of Blyden's trip was to raise funds for Liberian repatriation. He came in response to an invitation from the ACS, which through the 1880s had been sending about one hundred colonists a year with its dwindling resources. His first appearance in 1889 was arranged by the ACS, when he attended the convention of the American Missionary Association in Chicago. Although he won no converts there, he urged the Christian missionary effort to support black rather than white missionaries in Africa. His views on the superior record of Islam in winning African converts were well known, and he was given a respectful, if cautious, hearing.

In Charleston Blyden was interviewed by J. C. Hemphill, editor of the *News and Courier;* Blyden gave the full rationale for emigration, which was carried prominently by the paper and then circulated by news service throughout the South. The *News and Courier* was the organ of South Carolina's conservative Democrats in that period, and the followers of the "Redeemer" Wade Hampton welcomed Blyden's approach to the race problem. Indeed, an assistant editor of the paper, Carlyle McKinley, had anonymously published *An Appeal to Pharaoh* shortly before Blyden's arrival, in which he had urged repatriation of blacks to Africa. It was a *News and Courier* reporter, A. B. Williams, who accompanied the *Azor* to Liberia in 1878 and left a record of the operation in a book entitled *The Liberian Exodus.* Blyden wrote an editorial for the paper in which he supported white endorsement of emigration. The convergence, from opposite points of view, of the programs of race control on the part of white supremacists and of race consciousness on the part of black nationalists was clearly exemplified in the *News and Courier* policy over the period 1878–89.[9]

Blyden went on to Jacksonville, Florida, where he was well received by the white conservative press. He then spoke in Washington, D.C., at the annual meeting of the ACS. His timing coincidentally brought him to the nation's capital at the moment that the issue of the black man's situation was under Congressional debate. President Harrison in his address to Congress in 1889 had asked that the federal government enact legislation to protect the right of blacks to vote in the South. The southern white reaction was outrage: specifically, the response included the invention in Mississippi of the literacy test as a means of disfranchising blacks, a system soon duplicated in other states, and as we have seen, eventually used in Oklahoma. Another aspect of the southern response was the introduction in Congress of bills calling for the federal financing of black deportation. The most important of these bills and the one which became the center of a national debate was introduced by Senator Matthew Butler of South Carolina, co-leader with Hampton of the state's "redeeming" conservative Democrats. Butler's bill asked an appropriation of five million dollars to support the emigration of every black person who promised to become a citizen of the country to which he emigrated. Another bill by Senator John Morgan of Alabama sought support for trade with the Congo Free State. Morgan had earlier introduced a resolution resulting in United States recognition of the Free State, and Morgan apparently believed Leopold's claim that the Congo would represent a federation of self-governing black states. Morgan, like George Washington Williams, had hoped that the Congo would become a chain of Liberias, attracting black American emigrants.[10]

Morgan endorsed the Butler bill, pointing out that the funds could support emigration to the Congo as well as to Liberia. Butler, in advocating his bill, drew upon Blyden's *Christianity, Islam and the Negro Race,* while Wade Hampton used cost estimates from *Appeal to Pharaoh.* When Blyden addressed the convention of the ACS, he referred to the Senate debate and to the national interest in the Butler bill, rightly predicting that the partisan nature of the bill would bring its defeat. However, he welcomed the concept of white support, even from avowed segregationists like Hampton, Butler, and Morgan.

Also active in support of the Butler bill was Bishop Turner, although he disagreed that all blacks were fit to emigrate. The black press, particularly T. Thomas Fortune's *New York Age* and the *Christian Recorder,* then under the editorship of Benjamin Lee, opposed the bill. The opening convention of the Afro-American League, led by Fortune, rejected and ridiculed the Butler bill. Instead, the new organization endorsed the idea of self-help and remaining in the United States. Turner wrote an open letter challenging such opposition to the bill. After the death of the bill in committee, Blyden sailed back to Africa. Bishop Turner saw him off at the dock.[11]

Emigration efforts 1890–1905

The debate of 1889–90 on the Butler bill drew national attention to both Blyden and Turner, and brought the emigration concept to the notice of millions who sought escape from the increased proscription, segregation, and racial terror of the period. A wide variety of organizations demonstrated that the idea of black-owned shipping coupled with African emigration had taken on a life of its own. The International Migration Society, set up by Daniel J. Flummer, sent the small steamer *Horsa,* a Caribbean fruit-trade vessel, with about 200 passengers in 1895 from Savannah. On March 2, 1896, the same organization chartered the *Laurada* and sent another 321 emigrants. Flummer went on to found another group, the Liberian Colonization Society, but succeeded in sending out only 16 emigrants under its aegis. In the period 1890–1905 there were at least ten other organizations formed around the concept of steamship purchase and emigration. One company, established by Ernest W. Lyon, a protégé of Booker Washington and American minister to Liberia 1903–10, was strictly devoted to shipping, for Lyon discouraged emigration, particularly after witnessing the plight of about fifty self-financed emigrants from Georgia in Liberia. His New York–Liberian Steamship Line, formed in 1905, like an earlier company he had participated in, the West African Steamship Company of New Orleans, failed to acquire enough capital to purchase ships.[12]

With all the frauds, false starts, and black opposition in the emigration business, it might seem surprising that followers could be found when a genuine and serious effort was made to organize emigration. The development of mass support for exodus movements from Oklahoma demonstrated the idea's profound appeal and the gravity of the social conditions from which the emigrants sought escape.

Some of the Oklahoma proposals, like those elsewhere, had abortive beginnings. Blacks from the settlements near Muldrow and Muskogee reacted to local conditions with Liberian interest. The problem at Muldrow was that the local Cherokee blacks, although intermarried with Indians, found themselves more discriminated against by Indians as "state Negroes" from Arkansas came to settle among them. In 1891 Indian freedmen were swept by an emigration "fever," sold their farms, some at less than 10 percent of their value, and left for Africa. About 200 hopeful migrants, including 122 children, left by train for New York in midwinter early in 1892, only to find that the expected ship never arrived. Other groups from Arkansas joined the Oklahoma group, creating a crisis for the ACS in New York.[13]

In 1897 another group in Muldrow organized Liberian Emigration Clubs, which planned to buy a ship, fill it with emigrants, and cross to Africa. Like the earlier group, many sold out their farms and took a train for New York. Eventually three families of this group were able to finance their own passage to Liberia.[14]

In nearby Arkansas and Texas several schemes in the 1890s were either fraudulent or mismanaged. In 1893 a black minister was lynched when his three thousand followers discovered he had sold them worthless $3 tickets to Africa. Two confidence men collected thousands of dollars, and then chartered a train to send their victims to Brunswick, Georgia, supposedly to meet an Africa-bound ship. A more serious effort was organized by the Reverend Daniel Johnson of San Antonio, Texas, who planned an all-black joint stock company along the lines of the Crummell-Turner proposals, which would enter into commerce and carry emigrants to Africa. His Afro-American Steamship Company, like others, failed to raise sufficient funds and soon collapsed.[15]

African emigration from Oklahoma

As the hopes of racial autonomy or at least self-government within the American system were shattered in Oklahoma, the Liberian idea won more and more converts. In 1908 a convention projected by George Washington, an "aged Negro of Okmulgee," was to deal exclusively with the question of Liberian emigration. Washington had reputedly lived in Liberia for two years, and saw in that country "the salvation of his race."[16]

The Liberian emigration doctrine caught on in Boley, as in other black communities in Oklahoma, but might have been no more than another passing flurry had it not been for the energy and compelling drive of an obscure African businessman, Alfred Charles Sam. Sam was born at Appasu, Gold Coast, the grandson of a chief in West Akim. He had been educated at a German missionary school, and succeeded his grandfather and his uncle to the chieftainship of Obosse and Appasu. Sam engaged in the rubber export trade, and by 1911 had formed the Akim Trading Company,

Incorporated, in New York. The company held lands in the Gold Coast, and conducted commerce successfully in late 1912. In 1913 Sam formed a second company with wider ambitions, including African emigration from the United States, calling it Akim Trading Company, Limited, incorporated under South Dakota law. He was authorized to sell up to forty thousand shares at a par value of $25 each.[17]

The fact that Sam had been preceded by confidence men and impractical visionaries did make his task difficult. Both the black and white press suspected he was a fraud. As his movement continued to recruit an Oklahoma following, his repeated explanations and quiet pursuit of his goals were met with sheer disbelief, hostility, criticism, legal obstruction, and harassment. But his followers suffered few doubts, and their faith was to a great extent well founded. Sam was in fact an African chief, as he claimed; his corporation was in fact legally empowered to sell shares; he did in fact eventually buy a ship and take emigrants to Africa.

Through 1913 Sam sold shares in Oklahoma. J. P. Lidell, a black teacher from Boley, became his treasurer and later the president of a federation of clubs formed to support Sam's proposal. Within a year Sam had collected over $70,000, enabling him to buy a ship in New York, the *Curityba,* and to have it outfitted for the trip. After painful delays and some emergency fund raising in New England, Sam set forth from Galveston, Texas, in his ship, rechristened the *Liberia,* on August 20, 1914. The ship carried sixty emigrants, or "delegates" as he called them, who were to examine the possibilities for settlement in the Gold Coast and to report back to those who had to stay behind. Some five hundred hopeful emigrants waved goodbye from the dock; another five hundred were encamped at Weleetka, not far from Boley.[18]

On the arrival of the *Liberia* off the African coast, it was impounded by the British authorities. Although the settlers were allowed to debark, the costs of maintaining the ship and the refusal of the British to allow Sam to purchase fuel forced a court-ordered sale of the ship against port charges. The delegates moved inland to the village of Akim Swedru. There they found that they could settle on the tribal lands, but that conditions were vastly different from what they had dreamed and hoped. The natives practiced rotating agriculture that required clearing land, working it for a few seasons, and then moving to another location. No family held title to a specific plot, and the tribe as a whole held the land. As Christians, and as nonmembers of the village, the settlers' presence would be by sufferance. Even though many settlers had pioneered in Okfuskee County, they had built log, sod, and frame houses there, not temporary brush lean-tos. Insects, tropical fevers, and homesickness prevailed, and most of the party wrote home to relatives attempting to get passage money for their return.

A few families stayed on, and the rest trickled away. Sam himself went into business again, and eventually moved to Liberia to work in the cocoa export business, which was enjoying a boom in West Africa at the time.[19]

Summary

What Alexander Crummell had proposed as an aspect of the interrelationship between Africa and America was developed into a set of specific ideas by Turner. Those ideas had the potential for wide appeal among discontented black people at specific times and at specific locations. Both Turner and Delany, active in Reconstruction politics, turned to emigration just after the Democratic party takeover. The specific moments of organization around the Turner idea are particularly striking: Charleston, 1877; Muldrow, 1891 and 1897; Boley, 1913. In each location particular disappointments and tensions contributed to the appeal of the idea. At the end of Reconstruction South Carolina's straightout, "redeeming" white supremacists were victorious. In 1891 Cherokee freedmen were pressured by new migrants from outside Oklahoma, and that pressure continued through the decade. By 1913 bad crops, depression, and political disfranchisement following statehood helped propel Chief Sam and his ideas to the forefront.

White support for emigration was far more limited in the post-Reconstruction era than it had been in the antebellum decade, and was primarily found among the most outspoken white supremacists of the Hampton-Butler group. The ACS struggled along on a reduced budget through the 1890s. Around the turn of the century such white support evaporated. It was not that the belief in the United States as "white man's country" had declined among whites, but that other, more direct means of insuring white control had more practical appeal than did deportation—the new methods of segregation, disfranchisement, and lynching.

The increase in white supremacy in itself had the effect of making emigration appeal to black people even more, particularly in a place like Oklahoma, where hopes had been raised for some degree of self-determination. Other black spokesmen reacted in other ways to the increase in segregation, political proscription, and terror. Both Booker Washington and W. E. B. DuBois, who opposed each other on a variety of issues, drew on elements of the developing black nationalist tradition that did not involve emigration in their responses to the black man's plight at the turn of the twentieth century.

12

WASHINGTON, Du BOIS, AND PAN-AFRICANISM

Booker T. Washington (1856-1915) and William E. B. DuBois (1868-1963) are well known as black spokesmen and as representatives of often opposing views. Neither of the men's views are simply characterized. They engaged in many controversies, took a variety of positions, and like other prominent and long-lived leaders on occasion appeared to contradict themselves. The recent revival of interest in black nationalism has contributed to a tendency by scholars and biographers to revise earlier estimates of the two men and to see them as figures in the black nationalist tradition. Such a view can be supported by a variety of statements and positions from the lives of each of the two, but to argue that either was a black nationalist per se is an exaggeration. Here we will examine their views in relation to black nationalism, looking at the ideas they drew from the tradition and at the elements which they contributed to it.

The two men are often contrasted with respect to their views on higher education and on civil rights. In the interest of a sharpened contrast, Washington is often depicted as an "accommodationist"—cooperating with the developing system of segregation, and DuBois is shown as a "radical" advocate of full equality and higher education to train black youth for the professions. While there is truth in such labelling, each of the men is more complex to the careful student of his life and work.

The paradox of Washington

Booker Washington's life reads like a Horatio Alger novel. Born a slave, he received a rudimentary elementary education in the Reconstruction years, working in salt mines and as a domestic. Admitted to Hampton Institute, he worked his way through; his diligence and talents won him a teaching position at Hampton after graduation. Recommended to the board of trustees of a new institute, Washington took on the job of developing Tuskegee into a major center for industrial education. Under his leadership Tuskegee began to attract attention as a model of practical education. He was projected to national fame by an address at the Atlanta Industrial Exposition in 1895. In that speech he struck a note of conciliation between the races which was enthusiastically endorsed by many whites. Arguing that blacks should train for the work to be done in the South in farming, industry, and commerce, he recommended that blacks abjure political office and cultural aspirations in favor of earning money and building a foundation for future advance. He asked whites, especially employers, to accept blacks as loyal and willing workers.

Washington's fame as an advocate of racial cooperation spread—he was regarded by white officialdom as the spokesman for blacks. Such support was not intangible. Washington carefully manipulated the attention he received, and developed a nationwide following among blacks. T. Thomas Fortune, with his *New York Age,* was solidly in the "Bookerite" camp. White charity funds and the offer of federal appointments were soon channelled through Tuskegee. Washington's control of such resources and his influence in the period 1900–1910 were so effective that his operation came to be called the "Tuskegee machine."

Nothing in Washington's public life and influence contradicts the notion that he was an accommodationist. His recommendation that blacks should avoid agitation on the question of political rights offered no challenge to the disfranchisement of blacks in the era. His view that blacks should seek vocational training did indeed accommodate to the segregation of job opportunities which, through this period, relegated blacks to poorer economic situations year after year. Even his manipulation of patronage and charity did not threaten white control—his advice was sought and he gave it, generally directing resources to men of his own views.

Yet Washington had another side to his ideology. He was, like many politicians, an adept manipulator of his public image in order to gain resources. In a careful analysis of Washington's correspondence and private activities, August Meier demonstrated that Washington did indeed have a keen sense of racial justice and did a great deal to fight for black rights behind the scenes. While he let the public believe he accepted constitutional disfranchisement of the black man through manipulated literacy tests, he was quietly marshalling funds to back court challenges to the laws. He resorted to corresponding in code when he raised funds for such purposes. Meier argued that Washington's manipulation of patronage under Theodore Roosevelt showed Washington's deep involvement in politics. He was involved in a series of court actions assisting blacks in securing integrated juries, and worked privately in the Alonzo Bailey peonage case. In short, Meier concluded, Washington presented an ingratiating mask, but he was in reality a powerful politician. Meier, writing in the era of legal victories in civil rights, the late 1950s, saw Washington as an early precursor of such an approach.[1]

Harold Cruse, writing in the late 1960s, suggested that Washington could be viewed as an early example of an "economic nationalist." The evidence for Cruse's point is also rather convincing. Boley, Oklahoma, and Mound Bayou, Mississippi, both attracted Washington's interest and support. In an article in *Outlook* in 1908, Washington described Boley in glowing terms. He used his influence to raise funds for that effort. Washington knew and supported Isaiah Montgomery at Mound Bayou; and Charles Banks, cotton-gin owner at Mound Bayou, was an associate of Washington and an officer in the Washington-founded National Negro Business League. Other Washington associates, particularly T. Thomas Fortune, were active in the development of Harlem as a black residential neighborhood, founding the Afro-American Realty Company. If black separatism in the form of local control and black-owned business enterprise is to be regarded as an expression of black nationalism, then clearly Washington worked within the tradition and made contributions to its institutional development.[2]

In a more general sense, some of Washington's ideas can be seen in the black nationalist tradition. The National Negro Business League, which he founded, and later the Urban League, which he supported but did not actively participate in establishing, represented his approach to the economic situation of blacks. Suggesting that black people should work together to improve themselves, Washington's arguments sounded in part like those of Crummell. Washington argued that blacks should patronize each other's businesses; they should harbor resources which would be invested back in the community. Harold Cruse, August Meier, John Bracey, and Elliot Rudwick classify Washington's views on these questions as "bourgeois economic nationalism."[3]

Washington's complex activities and positions certainly provide parallels between his ideas and those of earlier nationalists like Delany and Crummell. Tuskegee itself reflected principles developed by earlier advocates of black separatism. Tuskegee Institute was to be the center of a community, and as a school it was concerned with training for both job skills and "citizenship." In these respects it followed the logic of the schools established by communitarian utopian experiments and the Canadian settlers. In a more general way the nineteenth-century philosophies of education advanced by Pestalozzi and the Lancastrian system, forerunners of vocational and "progressive" education of the twentieth century, influenced both the early experiments and Tuskegee. But the emphasis on racial advance, separate development, and black solidarity gave Tuskegee a unique and prominent place. Washington's ability to win white financial assistance by maintaining a cooperative and accommodating facade, and his ability to manipulate publicity, drew national and worldwide attention to his efforts.

Confronted with disfranchisement and proscription in the 1890s and early 1900s, Washington reacted to those developments in ways similar to Crummell, Montgomery, and McCabe. What set Washington apart from these leaders and spokesmen, who might more properly be regarded as black nationalists, is the fact that Washington was careful not to jeopardize his role as the white-recognized black spokesman by being either too active in his advocacy of civil rights or too explicitly separatist. So his separatism remained cloaked in a careful and polite form of acceptance of segregation, and his conservative political style concealed the implications for national liberation which others might draw from his self-help doctrines.

Others, less conservative in style, developed Washington's ideas in sometimes more militant language, and through them Washington's impact, both in the United States and abroad, was immense. African and Latin American students attended Tuskegee and carried his ideas home with them. Washington was consulted in the formation of the Pan-African Conference of 1900 in London, although he did not attend. Washington's interest in Africa was remarked by Blyden in an article in the *AME Church Review.* In 1912 Washington called a conference at Tuskegee on Africa, and in the period 1913–15 worked to develop business relations with Africa through the Africa Union Company. A number of African and colonial educators sought to model African education on the Tuskegee example. J. H. Oldham, an Englishman active in missionary and colonial office planning, specifically hoped to utilize ideas from Tuskegee to foster accommodation rather than political activism among educated Africans. On the other hand, Marcus Garvey wrote to Washington from Jamaica in 1915 and was attracted by some of the principles exemplified by Tuskegee. Despite his radical reputation, Garvey incorporated several Washingtonian ideas into his program, particularly the principle of black-owned business. *influence each other*

By the period 1890–1915 many black leaders and spokesmen drawing on black nationalism had developed a healthy skepticism about the advantages of working with whites. Figures like Turner and Chief Sam preferred black support and black financing. Many of their statements would alienate
→ hostile to opposition

potential sources of white support. Washington's willingness to maintain a "responsible," that is, a noncritical, attitude towards financially powerful white interests had its rewards. It should be remembered that Paul Cuffe and John Russwurm, among early nationalist figures, had no hesitation in working with whites and accepting white philanthropy. Their collaboration was for specific practical objectives, as was Washington's. Even Crummell and Blyden, who had far less accommodationist reputations than did Washington, cooperated with white supporters such as the ACS, white clergy, and conservative and openly racist politicians. But Washington's style was far more conciliatory than that of those prominent contemporaries, and for that reason his direct impact on young black intellectuals of his time was limited.

The nationalist ideas of W. E. B. DuBois

Like Washington, W. E. B. DuBois presents a conflict in his positions. Although usually thought of as an advocate of civil rights and socialism, the nationalist ideas which he accepted and developed were a recurrent minor theme in his writings. DuBois, by contrast to Washington, had a comfortable early life. He was born of mixed white and black ancestry and raised in a small town in Massachusetts. His first encounter with large numbers of other black people came as he attended Fisk University. He later attended Harvard, and in 1895 became the first black Ph.D. in the United States. He spent the period 1893–94 studying in Berlin, and when he sought to enter college teaching in the United States he was clearly the best-educated black man in the country. He worked briefly on a research grant from the University of Pennsylvania, studying the history of black people in Philadelphia, and then taught at Wilberforce and at Atlanta University.

In the period 1895–1903 his views on self-help were close to those of Washington. In 1899, for example, DuBois published *The Negro in Business,* in which he urged the development of more black-owned businesses. He suggested, as had Crummell, that blacks should exclusively patronize black businesses, where possible. When Washington's Afro-American Council considered establishing a businessman's league, the post of director was offered to DuBois, but he did not accept. In 1900, when Washington established the National Negro Business League, he did not credit the previous work of DuBois, although he was probably aware of it. In later years members of the Business League worked closely with DuBois in several organizations.[5]

DuBois served as a founding member of the Crummell-led American Negro Academy, and grew increasingly disenchanted with Washington's opposition to higher education in favor of vocational education. DuBois developed Crummell's concept of a black elite whose duty was to lead the race, and he planned that the "talented tenth" of black men should take advantage of educational opportunities and move into the professions of law, scholarship, teaching, journalism, and politics, using such positions to advance the race.[6]

After 1905 DuBois came to be regarded as the leader of the anti-Bookerites, and the " radicals" among younger black intellectuals admired him as their spokesman. DuBois was a founder of the short-lived Niagara Movement, which by 1909 was in disarray. Devoted to pursuit of civil rights by court action, and to the use of the black vote, the movement suffered from both internal and external problems. One of DuBois's cofounders, the self-styled radical editor of the *Boston Guardian*, William Monroe Trotter, displayed an egocentrism which made working with him difficult. The general elitism of the organization, its lack of a wide base of support, Washington's opposition, and the antagonism of potential white philanthropic sources to Niagara platform planks also contributed to the movement's break-up.[7]

DuBois joined with a group of white reformers in founding the National Association for the Advancement of Colored People (NAACP) in 1910, and for several years he was the only black member of the national board of the organization. As editor of the NAACP organ, the *Crisis*, he demanded and received a free hand in editorial policy.

In his autobiography DuBois remembered his own position in this period as that of a civil rights advocate, slowly evolving towards a socialist outlook. Others have found in his writings of the period traces of "Negro chauvinism," that is to say, black nationalist ideas, which ran counter to his interest in civil rights within the total American society. DuBois's opposition to Washington and his reputation as a radical leader have partially obscured this tendency in his thought. But through the first three decades of the twentieth century DuBois maintained a nationalist orientation in several important respects.[8]

The sources of such an orientation are difficult to attribute, precisely because DuBois was so well trained and so broad in his experiences. He was so widely read and well informed that rival claims of influence by particular prior thinkers must be assessed cautiously. It is noteworthy that DuBois himself particularly credited Alexander Crummell as contributing to his thinking. He also explicitly credited Heinrich von Treitschke, under whom he had taken a course while in Berlin, with having shaped his ideas on race. Von Treitschke had defined a nation as genealogically related, an extended family, and DuBois clearly adopted the same approach in 1897 in "The Conservation of Races," published by the American Negro Academy. The fact that von Treitschke was regarded as an early advocate of pan-Germanism

117

is notable, since DuBois later was viewed as a pioneer of pan-Africanism.[9]

DuBois attended the first pan-African conference in London in 1900. The conference achieved little; it served more as a social gathering of the black community in London than as a constructive foundation of an organization. DuBois was elected vice president of the group.[10]

During the First World War DuBois hoped that the postwar world would see the development of a socialized economy in the United States, with black people in a separate status. He envisioned a socialist African state, to be formed by the merger of Belgian and German colonies there, with additions from other colonies. DuBois was the leader of what he called the "First" Pan-African Conference in Paris, February, 1919, overlooking the 1900 meeting as a significant step in pan-Africanism. The 1919 conference tried to influence the Versailles Peace Conference to formulate a legal code for the protection of Africans to guarantee social and political gains. The conference did not demand an end to colonies, and it was severely split between delegates from the Belgian and French colonies and the Anglo-American black delegates. The conference had little impact, and both black and white press gave it only limited coverage. DuBois did not organize support for the goals of the conference in the United States, even within the NAACP. He later cooperated in a second conference in 1921, a third in 1923, and a fourth in 1927. These conferences attracted little American support and tended to represent gatherings of intellectuals who did not speak as delegates of any sizable groups. Nevertheless, the resolutions and positions of the conferences demonstrated the vitality of the idea of international black solidarity.[11]

Although DuBois did little organizational work which could contribute to the development of black-controlled territory or which would represent political black nationalism, his activities in the less tangible area of developing a sense of national identity were numerous. As editor of the *Crisis,* DuBois took an active role in "cultural nationalism," that is, the development of an identifiable black culture and of pride in that culture. The *Crisis* became an outlet for black writers, and served for more than two decades as the leading intellectual black publication in the United States. DuBois, in editorials, called for pride in things black, including black standards of personal beauty. The *Crisis* led in the fight to capitalize the *n* in "Negro" in print through the 1920s.

In 1934 DuBois resigned from the NAACP in the middle of a controversy which reflected the fact that he continued to regard black separatism as a viable alternative to integration and civil rights within the American system. The dispute also reflected a long-standing debate between DuBois and the NAACP board over *Crisis* management, circulation, and financing. Whether the ideological or the managerial issues were more fundamental, the public impression created was that the root of the split was over separatism versus integration. DuBois suggested that blacks should form all-black communities and cooperative organizations and directly receive federal assistance under New Deal plans. Only in this manner, he believed, could blacks guarantee that they received a fair share of resources. The Resettlement Administration, for example, funded a number of small new towns for sharecroppers and agricultural workers displaced by drought and depression. Such communities were all-white, and without corresponding communities of their own blacks would receive no assistance whatsoever under this particular program. The NAACP board regarded such a position as directly counter to their own approach, which required a fight against segregation in all forms.[12]

DuBois's thinking on social and economic issues did in fact evolve towards socialism, and in the post–World War II period he supported the American Communist party, officially joining in 1961. When he wrote in retrospect about himself, he did not give the same role to his nationalistic ideas that they may in fact have had. He "edited" his life in several other respects in his autobiography, to the dismay of later biographers. He did not mention, for example, his attendance at the 1900 Pan-African Conference, nor the convergence of his views with those of Washington in the late 1890s.

Washington and DuBois as contributors to black nationalism

The influence of both Washington and DuBois on African leaders was profound. Many individual Africans, either as students in black American colleges or as visitors to the United States after developing as leaders, expressed their solidarity with the struggle for black American liberation and their admiration for particular black leaders. Casely Hayford, J. E. K. Aggrey, and Kwame Nkrumah of the Gold Coast, John Chilembwe and Hastings Kamuzu Banda of Nyasaland, Nnamdi Azikiwe of Nigeria, and Peter Abrahams of South Africa, among others, all emphasized the influence of black American nationalist ideas on the formation of their own outlooks.[13]

The impact of Washington and DuBois on the development of black nationalist thinking in America is also considerable. In the case of Washington, however, his accommodation style offended many younger black intellectuals. But he directly engaged, for the Business League, for the African Conference, and for the establishment of Tuskegee, in activities which some viewed as separatist in orientation. His associates, admirers, and imitators sometimes gave expression to the nationalist implications of his work, although the organizations which Washington himself established tended to mute that message in the interest of conciliation.

In DuBois's case, his influence was that of an independent intellectual rather than an organizer. His work with the *Crisis,* his support of the pan-African movements, and his advocacy of separate black funding were his most specifically nationalist activities. His editorship of the *Crisis* gave a forum to young creative writers, and his claim that all the figures of the Harlem Renaissance of the 1920s were first published in his magazine seems well founded. In this respect, he served to implement the objective of both Crummell and himself to enlist the elite in the task of the race struggle, and the race consciousness displayed by that generation of writers could be construed as the fulfillment of that aspect of Crummell's ideas.

DuBois's debate with the NAACP leadership over the issue of separatism had no long-lasting institutional consequences. While the pan-African conferences organized by DuBois were criticized as ineffectual discussions and debates of intellectuals isolated from any mass support, their impact in the long run was considerable. Through the conferences European, Caribbean, and American black leadership met, exchanged ideas, and developed a sense of common objectives in fighting against colonial oppression and the excesses of white racism in the United States. When pan-Africanism entered its so-called second phase, during which an active international movement for African independence emerged, the contacts, ideas, and influences of the first phase took on more importance. When the Fifth Pan-African Congress met in 1945 in Manchester, England, organized by Kwame Nkrumah and George Padmore, DuBois was elected international president and honored as the "father of pan-Africanism." Although he took no active role in the organization, the recognition of his early work served a purpose. Through DuBois the movements for black self-determination and rights within the United States were symbolically, if not organizationally, linked with the international effort to decolonize Africa and the Caribbean.[14]

Each of the two men coupled ideas from the nationalist tradition with sometimes contradictory views. Booker Washington's economic nationalism was couched in language which did not challenge white supremacy. W. E. B. DuBois's pan-Africanism, his cultural nationalism, and his interest in separate black institutions were minor by comparison with his energetic advocacy of civil rights and socialism. Therefore, the effect of both leaders as contributors to the black nationalist tradition within the United States, although significant, was diffused by their activities and commitments to other causes.

13

MARCUS GARVEY

While the nationalism of both DuBois and Washington was a minor theme
in their approaches to the situation of the black man in the United States,
it was the central theme and the life work of Marcus Moziah Garvey (1887
-1940). More than any other early twentieth-century figure, Garvey
brought together the separate streams of black nationalist thought, organized a mass movement around a coherent nationalist ideology, and left a
legacy of influence and impact. His methods and mass following earned him
many black and white enemies, most of whom depicted him as a demagogue
and a fraud. Despite such criticisms his movement, which reached its peak
strength in the period 1919-24, must be recognized for its success in giving
clear expression to black nationalist ideas, as well as for its success in attracting a following.

Garvey's background

Garvey was born in Jamaica, and on his father's side, could claim descent
from the maroons. Marcus Garvey's father was a moody, bookish man, who
lost his property in a series of lawsuits. After dropping out of school at
about the age of fourteen, Garvey started to work as apprentice printer. By
age twenty he was a master printer and a foreman in Kingston. In 1907 he
took active part in a printers' strike, the only foreman to do so. Finding
himself blacklisted after the failure of the strike, Garvey engaged in local
political activities, then spent several months in Costa Rica and Panama.[1]
In both countries Garvey was disturbed at the plight of blacks from the

British Caribbean, and found his complaints to the British consul ignored. He then visited Ecuador, Nicaragua, Honduras, Colombia, and Venezuela. In 1912 he went to London and secured a job as messenger for the *Africa Times and Orient Review.* The paper was edited by an Egyptian black man, Duse Muhammad Ali, an advocate of Egyptian self-rule. He had written *In the Land of the Pharaohs,* and through the *Africa Times* he advocated the rights of nonwhite, non-European peoples. Duse maintained a wide correspondence, and among those he associated with were several figures later to be important in Garvey's movement. Garvey's later emphasis on black identity with other oppressed nonwhites echoed the Duse position.

While in London, Garvey read Booker Washington's autobiography, *Up from Slavery,* and later gave it credit for awakening in him the desire to be a race leader and to develop a self-governing black state. In 1914 he returned to Jamaica and established the Universal Negro Improvement and Conservation Association and African Communities League. He later shortened the name to the Universal Negro Improvement Association (UNIA). Through 1914 and 1915 he worked to enlist a Jamaican following in this self-help-oriented group. His central objective at this time was to set up industrial and vocational colleges patterned on Tuskegee. Like Washington, he found local white support for the plan, including the governor of the island. Garvey opened correspondence with Washington and indicated that he intended to visit the United States. While he later emphasized his connection with Washington, he may have exaggerated the influence, hoping to inherit some of Washington's prestige or following. Garvey's interest in the betterment of black people predated his reading of Washington, and was perhaps as much influenced by his labor struggles, by his visits to Central America, and by Duse Muhammad Ali as by Booker Washington. Nevertheless, it is clear that Garvey consciously adopted parts of Washington's program, and hoped to meet the boss of the Tuskegee "machine" on a visit to the United States. Washington politely responded to Garvey's inquiries, but he died before Garvey's arrival in the United States. Garvey was particularly interested in one of Washington's plans, which echoed the earlier Crummell proposal, a trading company to operate between Africa and the United States.[3]

The urban context

When Garvey arrived in the United States in March, 1916, he found the black population in northern cities disrupted and disturbed by a range of severe problems, some new, some old. European immigration to the United States had fallen off because of the war conditions, and the northern factories' demand for labor was filled by both West Indian and southern blacks. For such migrants the North had seemed a land of promise—employment in the booming industries supplying war material to the Allies attracted both groups. The southern black man hoped to escape increasingly rigid segregation and the sharecropping, farm tenancy, and low wages that plagued his life. The employment recruiters' general and sometimes specific promises received black endorsement by the efforts of several northern black newspapers, particularly the *Chicago Defender.*

Migrants and immigrants found conditions in New York, Detroit, Chicago, and Philadelphia far from ideal. While many found jobs, they could get housing only in the most decrepit and poorly serviced sections. Coupled with the disruption facing all migrants from small towns or rural areas to major cities were several hostilities peculiar to their own situation. Not only were West Indians segregated as blacks, but American blacks found them alien, and they, like other foreign settlers, were often forced into even further isolation. The old-timers, the blacks who had settled in northern cities before the turn of the century, resented the newcomers, both southern and Caribbean, regarding them as unsophisticated, superstitious, illiterate, and likely to disrupt established relations with whites. The newcomers found the old-timers aloof, resentful, and hostile. Coupled with such divisions in the black population, which were exacerbated by the influx of migrants in the war period, there were several other long-standing divisions which persisted. The small elite of educated blacks lived in a world apart from the mass—DuBois's so-called talented tenth was closer to a talented 1 percent. Furthermore, as Crummell and Blyden had pointed out, the hostility between black and mulatto was severe—blacks believed mulattoes tried to curry favor with whites at the expense of the race. The distinction between lighter and darker, often ignored by whites in that both groups would suffer from discrimination, paralleled the other divisions. Many of the elite and the old-timers in the North had some white ancestry, while most of the newcomers were dark.

Like other West Indians, Jamaicans made explicit and open distinctions between mulattoes and blacks. The islands had what amounted to a three-caste system of whites, mulattoes, and blacks, while the United States, at least from the white point of view, had a two-caste system of whites and blacks with all people of obvious mixed ancestry classed with blacks. Garvey, as a dark black man from Jamaica, had been raised in a society which openly recognized the three-way distinction, and in which blacks resented the snobbery of the mulatto. Garvey explicitly attacked mulatto leadership, and his angry tone gave expression to the feelings of literally tens of thousands of followers.

In 1916 Garvey lectured through the United States, with the initial purpose of rallying support for the Jamaican UNIA. His audiences of new migrants had been exposed to a generation of the preaching of Henry McNeal Turner, so that Garvey's appeals to race pride and to African identification were not particularly foreign. But his oratory attracted crowds, and his ideas won immediate support in the very cities most crowded with new migrants. The total northern migration of black people in the decade 1910-20 represented about 500,000. Approximately 260,000 of the migrants were concentrated in Chicago, New York, Philadelphia, Detroit, Cleveland, and St. Louis. Garvey lectured in all these cities in his first year in the United States.[4]

Garvey's organization

Garvey established the first American branch of the UNIA in 1916, and over the next three years established some twenty more. While membership figures were always a matter of debate, since Garvey would list supporters as "members" in public statements, it was clear that Garvey's was the first true mass movement among blacks in the United States, attracting hundreds of thousands of followers. He established a newspaper, the *Negro World,* which he edited himself through 1920. Despite the impressive structure and membership, the organization's true headquarters was wherever Garvey happened to be.[5]

Garvey showed his flair for promotion in the methods he used to attract followers. At mass conventions held in 1920, 1921, 1922, 1924, and 1926, Garvey aroused interest by parades, publicity, and organizational detail. His followers formed marching groups including the African Legion with military dress uniforms, and the Black Cross Nurses. Bands, choruses, and the widely displayed flag adopted by the UNIA in red, green, and black, added color and excitement. Intellectual black men, critical of Garvey, attributed all his success to such showmanship, often overlooking the fact that Garvey was an effective manipulator of ideas as well as of spectacles.

If the diverse appeals of Garvey had any one element in common, it was the call to race pride and race solidarity. The African Legion and Black Cross Nurses were gratifying to identify with, as were the titles of nobility that he bestowed on the officers of his organization. Garvey's newspaper gave free promotion to black dolls for children. In speeches, poetry, and columns for his paper, Garvey glorified black history, pointing to African, American, and Caribbean black heroes. The Reverend George Alexander McGuire, a black Episcopal priest, joined the UNIA in 1920 to become the chaplain of the organization. In 1921 McGuire was consecrated bishop in the American Catholic church and founded a new African Orthodox church.

By 1924 McGuire urged blacks to worship Christ as a black man and depicted the Madonna as black. While McGuire maintained the African Orthodox church independently of the UNIA, most contemporary outsiders
assumed the membership of the two organizations was identical.[6]

Garvey's contribution was not in the originality of his ideas and plans
but in his ability to arouse a mass of followers to a whole range of existing
black nationalist ideas. The publicity and attention which he drew from
both the black and white press brought a general awareness of most of the
ideas to a wide audience for the first time. He advocated black-owned businesses, and established the Negro Factories Corporation. In this idea he had
been preceded by the writings and activities of Crummell, DuBois, and
Washington. Garvey advocated an end to white rule in Africa, and in this
aspect of his nationalism he had been preceded by Duse Muhammed Ali
while DuBois had earlier organized and attended pan-African conferences.
Garvey's interest in black shipping and in Liberia had a rich set of precedents, as we have seen, in the whole development of Liberian emigrationism,
Turner's appeal, and the intense interest in black-owned shipping of Crummell, Delany, Turner, Chief Sam, and lesser leaders in the period 1890–1915.
A back-to-Africa plan that involved a territorial grant but which never
attracted a large following had been put forward as early as 1896 by a Barbadian, J. Albert Thorne. Thorne sought a land grant from the British in
Nyasaland, and corresponded with the consul general there. In 1922 Thorne
resented Garvey's success and accused him of imitation.[7]

Garvey's crises

Garvey's personality itself was a source of great controversy; while his followers saw him as charismatic, his opponents and critics saw him as vain,
bombastic, and egotistical. He demanded personal loyalty in his associates,
and in picking out those associates he may have been excessively concerned
with finding admirers rather than independent men of talent. It was his
associates who ruined him, just as Harding's appointees ruined the president
in the same era.

Garvey gave his opponents ammunition when he met with Edward Young
Clarke, the Imperial Giant of the Ku Klux Klan, in 1922. In a number of
statements Garvey indicated that his ideas of racial purity coincided with
those of the Klan. Probably more crucial in earning the enmity of the black
elite and of other race leaders were his attacks on specific individuals such
as DuBois in the most hostile terms. His intemperate statements, while
attracting the support of those who shared his dislike of the elite, landed
him in lawsuits and helped solidify most of the leadership of the NAACP,

125

black journalism, and the black educational establishment against him.

Garvey would probably have survived the enmity of the black elite, but his very success with the black masses attracted the attention of the essentially conservative white Justice Department. Operating under the mistaken assumption that Garvey's movement was radical in a socialist sense, the Justice Department kept a close eye on his activities. Actually, Garvey was as opposed to Marxists as was Attorney General Palmer, for Garvey had expelled Cyril Briggs from the UNIA, and Briggs's organization, the large West Indian immigrant African Blood Brotherhood, was the only left-leaning political group with any number of black members. A smaller group of black intellectual radicals, those associated with A. Philip Randolph and Chandler Owen in publishing the socialist-oriented *Messenger,* also vehemently opposed Garvey.[8]

Garvey provided the legal establishment with an excuse to investigate his activities early in 1919. In an address at Pittsburgh in May, Garvey suggested in passing that one enterprise blacks could support would be a black-owned trading company, reiterating the earlier interest he had expressed in the company planned by Booker Washington. The audience response was overwhelming. Just as Chief Sam had been swept up by support in 1914, Garvey found five years later that the idea had instant appeal. Money for stock in such a line, as well as for tickets to Africa, began to flood his offices. After the New York district attorney warned Garvey that acceptance of funds for investment without first incorporating properly was illegal, Garvey incorporated the Black Star Line in the state of Delaware. The shipping line proved to be Garvey's most spectacular activity, and to be his nemesis.[9]

Like most of his other programs, this one was not original with him, but the intense publicity he gave it brought it to the notice of both blacks and whites who had never heard of his predecessors. The corporation, through $5 stock sales, raised about $750,000. While these resources were considerable, the highly risky shipping business was in a postwar slump. Merchant shipping in the United States began a decline in that era from which it never fully recovered, and companies with far more resources failed in the business. But Garvey was plagued with further difficulties. His appointees purchased the *Yarmouth,* a 1452-ton steamer, in 1920, and he renamed it the *Frederick Douglass.* He later purchased two smaller ships, the *Shadyside,* a river steamer, and the *Kanawha,* a small steamer-cutter. All three ships were overpriced and cost the corporation hundreds of thousands in repair bills, brokerage kickbacks, and lawsuits.

As these ships lost money, Garvey continued to promote the idea of ship purchase, and to raise funds. Cyril Briggs and others published exposés in 1921 of the difficulties of the line, and on the basis of editorial complaints and stockholders' inquiries Garvey was arrested in February, 1922, on a mail fraud charge, along with three associates. He came to trial in 1923 and defended himself in a long and rambling proceeding. He was convicted and sentenced to five years in prison. The trial involved some obvious injustices. He was convicted on the dubious testimony of one witness who had received Black Star Line promotional literature through the mail, while three officials more directly involved in the stock promotion were acquitted. His sentence of five years was excessive—most white convictions on this charge resulted in a fine or a year in jail. Garvey appealed the case in 1925, but lost. He started his sentence in Atlanta penitentiary, then received a pardon from President Coolidge in 1927. Immediately after the pardon he was deported to Jamaica, again on dubious legal grounds since the provision under which the action was taken specified that aliens convicted of a crime within five years of their arrival were subject to deportation. Garvey had arrived in March, 1916, but his conviction was not until June, 1923, well beyond the five-year period.[10]

While the Black Star Line attracted attention, Garvey had been laying plans for a Liberian settlement, much in the Blyden-Crummell-Turner tradition. He established a branch of the UNIA in Liberia in 1920, bringing into his ranks there a following among both natives and Americo-Liberians. The mayor of Monrovia, Gabriel Johnson, was active in Garvey's movement and was designated by the 1921 convention of the UNIA as Supreme Leader of the Negro People. But President C. D. King of Liberia had reason to be nervous about the growth of Garveyism in Liberia. Garvey's attack on British and French imperialism could arouse those powers to protect their bordering colonies of Sierra Leone, French Guinea, and the Ivory Coast by interfering in any UNIA-sponsored colony in Liberia. Garvey's thinly disguised plans to become a power in internal Liberian politics and to use Liberia as a base for further political adventures offended King. Many of King's political enemies aligned themselves with the Garvey group, including many from the southern Maryland County. Garvey sent delegates to negotiate a grant of land, and they arranged the cession of a large tract in Maryland, on the Ivory Coast border. King, however, secretly negotiated a concession with the Firestone Rubber Company in the very land selected by Garvey's advance agents. When a delegation of the UNIA arrived to prepare for settlement, King refused them permission to land. Garvey's proposals for an organized Back to Africa movement to begin building in Liberia were killed.[11]

Despite Garvey's immense appeal, he had made enemies of several individuals and groups whose opposition contributed to the destruction of his movement. Not only did the United States government deport him, but his troubles with both the executive and the courts prevented the United States

Shipping Board from negotiating the sale of surplus ships wanted by
Garvey's organization. The Liberian government's rejection of his plan for
settlement stemmed from the justifiable fear that Garvey would attempt to
dominate the small nation and alter its internal social structure. Briggs and
Randolph, as radicals, envied Garvey's success in developing a mass base,
but believed his plans were fraudulent and misleading. Their complaints
gave support to government charges of fraud. DuBois, offended by personal
attacks on his loyalty to the race launched by Garvey, and insulted by
charges that he was too white to be a race leader, helped organize black
opposition to Garvey. Garvey had won a following and support among
many prominent black leaders—including James Bruce, Carter Woodson,
and Claude McKay. Yet his alienation of the NAACP circle and the radicals,
as well as the Liberian and American governments, deprived him of needed
support and assistance at crucial points in his career.[12]

Garvey's impact

Garvey's importation to the United States of some ideas developed out of
his West Indian background, and the impact of those ideas in both Africa
and the West Indies after his decline, illustrate what one scholar has called
a "triangular trade" of ideas and politics. Garvey's deportation hardly
ended his influence. Since he had popularized so many elements of the
black nationalist tradition, a whole generation of black leaders received an
exposure to nationalist ideas. Garvey's impact among African and West
Indian leaders aroused the concern of the British Foreign Office, which, like
the United States Department of Justice, viewed Garvey's ideas as radical
and potentially subversive. Since his movement and the press coverage it
received were so widespread, one could argue that practically every black
leader in the 1930s and 1940s was influenced by Garvey. A few specific
connections and lines of impact are noteworthy. Elijah Poole, later to become Elijah Muhammad, was a "corporal" in the UNIA Chicago chapter.
Casely Hayford, a lawyer and nationalist in the Gold Coast, was active in
the UNIA, though he had also worked with DuBois. Rabbi Arnold Ford,
a leader of a black Jewish sect in New York, was for a time a UNIA member,
and his following joined the UNIA en masse. Others, prominent and obscure, who had been active in the UNIA, participated in a variety of religions,
movements, and organizations in the two decades following Garvey's deportation.[13]

While Garvey carried on the UNIA activities from Jamaica, his absence
from the United States created a vacuum in leadership of his own movement
In 1929 he offended several of his most active lieutenants by insisting that

128

the international headquarters of the UNIA be in Jamaica, and the organization split in two. When one of Garvey's followers in British Honduras died, willing his $300,000 estate to the UNIA, both Garvey's own group and the rival UNIA sued for the funds. Again Garvey lost in court. But more crucial than what happened to the treasury was the outcome for the mass following itself. Split between two UNIA organizations, the "Garveyites" were still available in the thousands as potential members in mass organizations.[14]

Several new religious groups in the United States, notably the Moorish Science Temple, the Father Divine Peace Mission Movement, the Nation of Islam (Black Muslims), and the RastafarI in Jamaica increased in growth after 1929. Some writers, including E. Essien-Udom, Theodore Vincent, and Harold Cruse, have repeated the assertion that these later movements drew their following from among ex-Garveyites. The idea is a reasonable one, since the greatest growth of the later movements was in the same cities and among the same social groups as the core of the Garvey movement. But no statistics have been gathered to substantiate the connections. Garvey had united a large number of people with his ability to weave together a nationalist ideology and movement from diverse discontents. When his personal leadership waned and his movement dissolved, other organizers did not simply cut up the Garveyites into smaller units. Rather, each of the later leaders, some of whom had first become nationalists under Garvey, drew a particular following, sometimes from among previous Garvey supporters, often from similar and overlapping social groups whose aspirations and need for political expression were parallel to that of the earlier UNIA rank and file.[15]

After Garvey's personal decline in power many black leaders came to recognize his contributions, including some of his most bitter opponents. W. E. B. DuBois, Cyril Briggs, and newspapers like the Chicago *Defender*, despite their record of opposition to Garvey, praised him after his death. African leaders, including Kwame Nkrumah and Jamaican politicians of various factions, have credited Garvey as the father of nationalism. To an extent, such post-mortem recognition can be viewed as merely ceremonial or symbolic, but his role as a mass leader and as a nationalist is well established among admirers and detractors.[16]

Garvey as a nationalist has been compared to Theodore Herzl. Like the Jewish Zionist, Garvey was raised in an environment relatively free of discrimination, and then, experiencing it, developed a plan to create a new state in which his national group could live free of stigma. Garvey of course was not the first Zionist among blacks, and the concept of Liberia as a black Zion predates Herzl's Zionism by more than fifty years. But the comparison between Herzl and Garvey is apt in that both Garvey's Zionism and Israeli

Zionism are twentieth-century phenomena. In that connection, Garvey has also been compared to Mussolini; indeed, he made the comparison himself. Garvey's techniques—uniformed marchers, titles, the development of an intensely personal loyalty among his followers, bombastic oratory, and an inner elite corps of supporters—are all parallel to the Italian fascistic form of nationalism. Elements of Garvey's ideology as well as of his organization bear out this particular parallel: the concepts of racial purity, race pride, and glorification of ancient history were common to both movements.[1]

Despite the intensely twentieth-century quality of the Garvey movement, most of his program was not new, as we have seen. His contribution was to publicize nationalist ideas and to politicize a vast public. He brought together ideas advocated earlier by others: Martin Delany's motto, "Africa for the Africans"; Crummell's interest in shipping and in Liberia; Blyden's suspicion of mulattoes and of white-dominated Christianity; Turner's call to pride in race; DuBois's interest in African liberation from colonial rule; Washington's black-owned enterprises.

In Garvey the black nationalist tradition was expressed with coherence and with flamboyance. Despite his short-run triumphs and his spectacular failures, his lasting contribution to the black nationalist tradition was to develop the doctrine into a message that was understood by the masses. He gave the nation a flag in both a literal and symbolic sense, for he put together an ideology which could serve as a rallying point for national identity out of ideas which had had an underground existence for a century.

14

MYSTICS, MOVEMENTS, AND STREET AGITATORS

The black church

From its beginnings in the late eighteenth century, the black church in the United States had incorporated several principles of separatism which bear investigation as possible contributing factors in the development of a black nationalist tradition. By their nature as separately organized, separately managed, and separately financed black enterprises, the black churches were crucial to the evolution of black nationalist ideas in a number of ways. First, simply as physical properties under the control of black people they provided meeting houses in which matters relating to blacks only could be discussed free of white interference. Such was the case in the many meetings through the 1820s and 1830s regarding the American Colonization Society, the plans of Benjamin Lundy, and emigration to Liberia. When the national conventions were organized, representatives were largely chosen by black groups meeting in black-owned and run churches. Second, as the primary enterprise entirely owned and patronized by black people, the church provided a career line for leadership. Several of the figures important in early black nationalist thinking had their beginnings as leaders of a congregation, including Lott Carey, Daniel Coker, Elijah Johnson, H. H. Garnet, J. T. Holly, Alexander Crummell, and some of the leaders of the Canadian black community. H. McNeal Turner is perhaps the most striking example of pursuit of leadership by this avenue. Third, a number of black separate enterprises associated with the church grew out of the fact that black people could amass a considerable financial weight cooperatively and communally, through the church. Church-based groups established "burial and sickness" societies which evolved into insurance companies, and schools, mostly at the primary level, in the pre-Civil War period.

Less tangibly, the separate black churches contributed a principle—self-control or self-determination. Since whites condoned and even stimulated the development of black churches, black leaders had a relatively free hand in this one area of life during the antebellum period. Thus, the rise of separate Baptist congregations in Savannah in 1779, in Boston at the African Baptist Church in 1805, and in New York at the Abyssinian Baptist Church in 1809, and the development of the African Methodist Episcopal church as a denomination in 1816 from a mother church in Philadelphia, and the African Methodist Episcopal Zion church in 1822 from New York, were all concrete expressions of a separatist ideology.

These churches followed the doctrinal character of the white churches. A few attempts have been made to read into some of the churches' practices survivals of African culture—in the lyrics and music of black spirituals, in the call-and-response structure of some services, and in the parallels between possession in a holiness evangelical-style church and possession in the Orisha and Vodum rites of West Africa. The difficulty with tracing such survivals in church practices is that many of the factors which parallel African cultural elements also parallel strictly European cultural elements, and there is no clear method for sorting out the major influence in such a situation.

Thus, while early black churches provided a meeting place, a training ground for black leadership, and an ideological model for black self-determination, there was little about the churches' doctrine or theology which in any way directly challenged traditional views of white political control or white-established theology. Even Turner's arguments for Liberian emigration and for black pride in no way challenged established theology.[1]

But with the development of Garvey's organization and the establishment of the African Orthodox church under Bishop McGuire, a clear and rather spectacular departure from accepted theology in America took place. The picturing of a black Christ and black Madonna was not original with McGuire. Devotional cults of the Madonna elsewhere in the world had depicted her as nonwhite, and in some cases the cult had expressed intense nationalist feelings, as in Mexico. In the period when McGuire attracted followers among the Garveyites with this black tone, other new prophets also appeared.

The search for simple solutions

In the period from about 1915 through the 1920s and the depression years of the 1930s, conditions in the northern city were cruel, particularly for the new migrant. The joint effects of economic deprivation and white hostility produced a search for panaceas of every description. At the same time that Garvey used an eclectic nationalist ideology to attract a mass following, literally scores of less succesful individuals developed programs, cults, sects, and whole religions offering spiritual and physical solutions. Indeed, even the growth of the numbers racket, or "policy numbers," in the period reflects the same search for instant relief from poverty and degradation. "Jackleg" preachers—untrained and unordained—set up hundreds of storefront churches. Herbs, oils, incense, charms, teas, fortunes, idols, and ideologies were vended on street corners. While it was tempting for serious observers to pass off such charlatans and fakirs as exploiters of the mass, the reasons for the relatively large appeal and the frequently serious ideas of some of the more successful cult and sect leaders should not be overlooked. While the whole phenomenon of panacea promoters in the black community in the period serves as a commentary on the conditions, a close look at several particular leaders and their programs shows that the appeal to black pride and the ideas of the black nationalist tradition continued to have a lively existence after the Garvey movement broke up. As already indicated, a number of scholars and observers regarded the growth of such movements as the consequence of the UNIA breakdown, believing that the mass organized by Garvey formed into a variety of other smaller groups. The fact that some similar movements were already under way when Garvey arrived in the United States suggests that the significant connection between Garvey and the other leaders is that their appeals were parallel and drew from the same tradition, not that Garvey caused the others to have success. Indeed, if Garvey had not showed up in the United States, the masses that he organized in the UNIA had many alternative organizations available.[2]

Black Jews

Among the more obscure of the religions growing in the period were a variety of black Jewish groups. Prophet F. S. Cherry organized a black Jewish group in Philadelphia called the Church of God; another group, founded in Belleville, Virginia, and Washington, D.C., by Prophet William S. Crowdy (who later turned the organization over to Bishop William H. Plummer, also known as Grandfather Abraham) was called the Church of God and Saints of Christ. These two groups appear to have developed as the products of revelations to their founders. In theology and practice they varied considerably from orthodox Judaism.[3]

In Harlem, however, a more orthodox variety of black Judaism developed under the leadership of Rabbi Wentworth Arthur Matthew, who organized the Commandment Keepers there in 1919. At least eight other black Jewish groups grew up in Harlem in the period 1919–31, some associated with the Matthew-led organization. Matthew's orthodoxy may at least partly arise from the association between Harlem blacks and the white Jewish community. In addition, Matthew plausibly claimed he was born in Lagos, Nigeria, and raised in the West Indies in a Falasha family. The Falashas are descendants of an Ethiopian group whose legends indicate descent from a Jewish colony established there as early as 600 B.C. Augmented over the centuries, and intermarried with other Ethiopian groups, the Falashas have remained an identifiable Jewish group despite persecutions and dispersement.

Matthew's claim to be a Falasha is not accepted by all white Jews; one observer of the movment suggests that Matthew became interested in this particular ancestral line only after hearing of the existence of the Falashas through the organization of an American branch of an international Jewish group set up to aid the Falashas by Jacques Faitlovich in 1922. Matthew claimed to have studied Judaism in Berlin in 1924–27, leaving the Commandment Keepers under the leadership of Rabbi Arnold Joseph Ford, a Barbadian immigrant. Ford later emigrated to Ethiopia. Many of the followers of both Matthew and Ford were West Indians, and while the rabbis did not try to convert new arrivals in Harlem, they did "enlighten" many as to their true, Falasha heritage. While it is conceivable that among the tens of thousands of West Indian migrants to Harlem a few hundred were in fact Falashas, it is also clear that Matthew developed a congregation by conversion.

A number of the precepts of the Commandment Keepers' theology reflected a nationalist orientation. As a non-Christian religion, it moved away from the accepted, dominant religion of white Americans. By claiming that the black man was a Jew, Matthew and his followers rejected the white society's view and estimate of themselves. Accordingly, Matthew advised his followers to reject the term "Negro" in favor of Ethiopian, African, or Afro-American. In economic policies they followed a self-help approach, and by 1943 Commandment Keepers owned over fifty small businesses. Black Jews would patronize stores owned by either black or white Jews, and would hire members of the faith regardless of race, so whether their commercial enterprise was "Washingtonian" or simply a reflection of white Jewish norms and ideas is open to question. The black Jews were quite strict in their maintenance of dietary rules, and in holding to a law-abiding and moral style of life. By joining a lodge, the Royal Order of Ethiopian Hebrews, the Harlem group kept in contact with other small black Jewish communities elsewhere in the United States. For a period in the 1920s, during the leadership of Ford, the whole congregation, numbering some five hundred members, joined the UNIA.[4]

The groups led by Cherry and Plummer in Philadelphia and Washington were far less scrupulous in their adherence to Jewish culture and religion, but like the New York group, they displayed certain nationalist principles. Cherry, for example, believed that Jacob was a black man, and that the black race is the real Jewish race. Furthermore, he held that the original race of man was black, and he contended that Jesus was black. Like the Commandment Keepers, Cherry's followers were admonished to lead a strictly moral life, and while full kosher rules were not followed, the eating of pork was forbidden. The followers of Crowdy and Plummer also agreed that blacks were Jews and observed the Jewish calendar. At Belleville, Virginia, the Washington group maintained a communally owned farm, a school, and several other enterprises.

Moorish Science

Another non-Christian group which expanded in the 1920s was the Moorish-American Science Temple, founded in 1913 in Newark, New Jersey. With branches in Pittsburgh, Detroit, New York, and Chicago, the Moors were well organized and have survived to the present. Their founder, Noble Drew Ali, whose original name was Timothy Drew, rejected not only Christianity but a whole range of white ideas about the black man. He rejected the terms "Negro," "colored," "black," and "Ethiopian," claiming descent from the Moabites. His flag, a star and crescent on a field of red, was posted in the windows of converts. In 1927 Noble Drew Ali held a successful convention, and at one time or another had temples in Philadelphia, Kansas City, Charleston, West Virginia, Lansing, and Youngstown.

His followers who distinguished themselves by wearing fezzes and growing beards, were particularly active in Chicago. Troubled by aggressive members who infuriated white police in Detroit and Chicago, Drew issued orders not to argue with whites. Perhaps to offset charges of un-Americanism, he made the display of American flags an essential complement to the display of his own flag.

Noble Drew Ali referred to Garvey as the John the Baptist of his movement. Drew issued membership cards which showed the holders' corrected name, often altered by the addition of El or Bey to the existing name. Drew's organization developed a large following, and the Chicago chapter had several thousand members. The large revenue from dues, as well as from the sale of a number of products, including oils, cosmetics, and teas, all with a Moorish label, may have contributed to the contest for power which developed in his movement in 1929. Sheik Claude Greene, one of his followers, physically removed the furniture from Drew's headquarters, and an outburst of fights spread through the temples as the two factions sparred for control. Greene was shot and stabbed to death, and Drew was arrested, although he personally was nowhere near the crime. Released on bail, he died soon afterwards under mysterious circumstances. The various temples, racked by division between the Greene and Drew factions, fell under autonomous leadership, and the Moors, as a single organization, broke up. But the New Jersey branch, at least, continued to attract members through the period since 1929, and is still active.[5]

Father Divine

Another religious movement which drew tens of thousands of followers in the interwar period was that of Father Divine. Like other prophets, he had obscure origins. One reliable account states that he was born George Baker, about 1880, in Georgia. In the period 1899–1912 he lived in Baltimore, working as an assistant preacher in a Baptist church and associating with a roving preacher who followed the doctrine of the "in-dwelling God," that is, the principle that God dwells in everyone. In 1912–14 George Baker preached on his own as the Messenger. He was arrested in Valdosta, Georgia, where he was arraigned as John Doe, alias God, and was ordered to leave the state. He arrived in 1915 in New York with about a dozen followers and established a temple in Brooklyn. As Major J. Devine, he slowly built a following. His group practiced sexual abstinence, with married partners living separately. He began serving food to outsiders free of charge and attracted followers through the reputation for hearty meals. In 1919 he purchased a house in the white suburb of Sayville on Long Island. Through the 1920s he attracted few followers; by 1929 he had about ninety, many drawn from the servants of suburban families. Those who joined contributed their whole earnings to Major Devine, and he provided for their physical as well as spiritual needs. In 1930 he attracted a few well-off whites, and changed his name again, to Father Divine.[6]

Late in 1931 Father Divine got in trouble with the law again, and this time it brought him to national attention. During a late-night meeting at the Sayville house, local police entered and arrested Divine as a "public nuisance" on the complaint of neighbors. The arrest drew him public sympathy on two counts, for he seemed a victim of both interference with freedom of religion and racial harassment. Justice Lewis J. Smith, who conducted the trial, displayed hostility to both Divine and his followers, and condemned Divine to a year in jail and a $500 fine. Four days after sentencing Divine, Justice Smith, about fifty years old and in apparent good health, died. Divine was reputed to say from his jail cell, "I hated to do it."[7]

The publicity associated with the trial and with the reputed "Divine retribution" catapulted Divine's career. Within a month he was released on bail pending his appeal; and on the grounds that the earlier trial had been prejudicial, his conviction was reversed. Within a year Divine had opened his first "heaven" in Harlem. Between 1933 and 1937 his followers and organization in New York leased nine private houses converted to dormitories, three apartment houses, and twenty-five restaurants. He opened two groceries, several barber shops, and operated a fleet of vegetable, fish, fruit, and coal wagons. He opened other "extensions" in Newark, Jersey City, Bridgeport, and Baltimore.[8]

In 1941, as the result of a court judgment against him by a disgruntled follower who wanted his money back, Divine moved his headquarters to Philadelphia to avoid process servers. He returned to New York City only on Sundays thereafter. Within two years his Peace Mission Movement had become a large property holder in Philadelphia.[9]

Divine left most of his followers believing he was God. But it was his secular policies and activities that exemplify clearly the survival of the nationalist appeal through this period. Divine's followers were both black and white, although most were black. Divine did not "recognize" color. As in the Moorish Science Temple, followers dropped their names in favor of new ones assigned by the leader, although Divine's choices were not exotic—Mr. Wisdom Smiling or Miss Victory Dove, for example. He engaged in several political and direct-action efforts in the thirties. He set up what he called the Righteous Government Movement, which like much else in his activity combined practical and fantasy elements. He advocated an end to race discrimination, lynching, and segregation, as well as the abolition of capital punishment and an end to war. On a less practical level, he advocated that the United States Constitution be adopted worldwide, and that English be the universal language. He cooperated in the mid-1930s with several Communist party activities and front organizations, including the League against War and Fascism. The most spectacular effort in this regard was a joint parade organized by the Communist party and Father Divine in 1934.[10]

Smaller organizations

In New York Divine came in conflict with two other religious and activist leaders in the mid-1930s, Daddy Grace and Sufi Abdul Hamid. Daddy Grace had founded the United House of Prayer about 1925, and by 1935 had establishments all along the east coast, including the South. While not claiming to be God, the head of the United House of Prayer believed that salvation was "by Grace alone." Sufi Abdul Hamid was a colorful street agitator who had first developed a following in Chicago and then moved to New York. Hamid started a "Don't Buy Where You Can't Work Campaign" in New York City, and his movement was in conflict for leadership with a similar one led by more conservative clergy and union organizers. His opponents charged him with using the boycott method to enrich himself personally through extortion. Hamid added to his fame by living with or marrying a Chinese-black seeress, Madam Fu Fu Tan. Both Grace and Hamid attacked Divine as a charlatan, and he in turn cursed them. Hamid died shortly thereafter in an airplane crash, for which Divine took credit much as he had with the judge. Hamid's reputation, like that of other agitators and prophets of the period, is difficult to assess in ideological terms, but his adoption of an exotic name (he was reputedly born Eugene Brown), his costumes, and his references to the Koran echoed some of the nationalist elements of the Moorish movement.[11]

Among the welter of movements and religions which rose and fell in the 1920s and 1930s were several identified with Ethiopia. In 1920 Grover Cleveland Redding, claiming to be an Ethiopian, organized in Chicago the Abyssinian movement. He achieved national notoriety as the result of an incident during a parade when he burned an American flag. In the resulting street fight a black policeman and two whites were killed. At Redding's trial he gave details of his movement. He asked his followers to identify with Ethiopia as the mother country, to renounce the term "Negro," and to plan emigration to Ethiopia. Redding and a follower were executed. Ethiopia again attracted supporters in 1935 as the result of the Italian invasion. Groups which gave voice to this support included the United Aid to Ethiopia, the Ethiopian World Federation, Incorporated, and the Peace Movement of Ethiopia. The last organization survived some years as a back-to-Africa movement on a small scale in Chicago. Much of the black press supported the Ethiopian cause without reference to any particular organization.[12]

Another temporary group was the National Movement for the Establishment of the Forty-ninth State, which, according to Gunnar Myrdal, was organized among ex-Garveyites. It may have derived its inspiration from the official position of the Comintern towards race relations in the United States in the period 1928–35. The Communist party held that the United States should set aside the black belt counties of the South as a self-determined, autonomous black state. Similar to the Soviet policy towards national minorities within the Soviet Union, this policy would recognize blacks as a "national minority" within the United States and grant self-government. The policy was dropped after 1935 as the Communist party developed techniques of winning support which involved cooperating with existing groups on a local basis.

The nationalist appeal survives

Through the 1930s the NAACP and the black leadership in education and the press loudly opposed separatist, nationalist, and mystical-religious panaceas. The point of view of the integration-oriented leadership dominated the activities of the black protest movement which developed in the post–World War II years. The apparent convergence of the views of black separatists and white segregationists continued to arouse the suspicions of many responsible black leaders, just as a similar convergence between the views of black emigrationists and white supporters of the ACS had troubled men like Martin Delany and Frederick Douglass. In the twentieth century leaders attracted by some elements of the black nationalist tradition, such as W. E. B. DuBois, were repelled by the garish mass-appeal methods of Garvey, Drew, or Hamid. The religious appeal of Divine or Grace, or the assertion of a wholly new identity by the black Jews, held out little attraction to such a black intellectual. On the other hand, support for blacks under Italian attack, or support for the right to work backed up by black solidarity, could attract intellectuals and nonintellectuals alike.

Rather than assuming that every black movement of the period 1929–45 drew upon ex-Garveyites for its support, the careful observer will recognize that Garvey and leaders like Matthew, Cherry, Drew, Divine, and Hamid all developed programs and ideas which came to grips with the nationless feeling of the black masses. The word "alienation" is so overworked as to represent jargon if used loosely, but it applies in a precise sense to the position of blacks treated as aliens in the land of their birth. The more colorful leaders' programs offered alternatives to the condition and sensation of alienation, often reflecting previously established elements of the nationalist tradition. Self-help, financial independence, rejection of names inherited from the slave period, challenge to white conceptions of black people, pride in being black, elevation or creation of elements of heritage—all these had been parts of the nationalist tradition, and all had a healthy survival among the street agitators and prophets of this period.

In the 1930s the Democratic party began to make appeals designed to win and hold black support. Actions of Franklin and Eleanor Roosevelt, the policies of the New Deal, and the beginnings of a labor-black political coalition all held out hope that black leadership would find a hearing in Washington and among white leaders generally. The small gains in Supreme Court decisions and administrative action made in the late 1930s and early 1940s can in retrospect be viewed as the beginnings of the civil rights advances of later decades. With these factors in mind, it is clear why so few black leaders with intellectual training were attracted by the nationalist tradition in the 1930s. Yet among the poor in the cities, cut off from any evidence of social gains, the separatist appeal of the street agitators and cultists would be powerful. The pan-African appeal of support for blacks in Ethiopia and the appeal to black solidarity in the fight for jobs could attract support among both poor and relatively well-off, but in neither movement did a nationally prominent figure emerge. But the black nationalist tradition did not die with the removal of Garvey, nor did the logic of its appeal evaporate in the face of a few minor civil rights gains. The variety of cults with a cumulative membership of several hundred thousand kept alive and demonstrated the continued vitality of nationalist ideas among black people who suffered most from white hostility and from economic deprivation. It was from one of the new religions that the major nationalist leader of the next generation was to emerge.

15

MUSLIMS AND MALCOLM

Muslim origins

The origins of the Black Muslims, the Lost-Found Nation of Islam, are obscure. In 1929 or 1930 a black man by the name of W. D. Fard, who peddled raincoats and silks in Detroit, began holding meetings to discuss Mecca, and to preach a new doctrine. While the Moslem orientation of some of his teachings has led several observers to assume that Fard was the leader of one of the factions of Moors that arose after the death of Drew, there is no solid evidence for such a conclusion. The similarity between one of Fard's aliases, Professor Ford, and the name of Arnold Ford, who had led the Commandment Keepers before removing to Ethiopia, led another writer to the purely speculative and incorrect suggestion that they were the same individual. What can be substantiated is that Fard's doctrine, which developed into a major religious and social force over the forty years since his appearance, paralleled the other nationalist religious developments and surpassed them in organization, membership, and in its ability to weave together elements from the nationalist tradition.[1]

In the period 1929–33 the Nation of Islam could be viewed as merely another cult, one among the many which drew a following in Detroit. While membership rolls were never publicly available for statistical study, several outside scholars have asserted that Moors joined the Nation in this early period. Fard organized his dispersed following well. By 1933 he had established a temple, a ritual of worship, a University of Islam (an elementary and secondary school), a Muslim Girls' Training Class dedicated to teaching domestic arts, and the Fruit of Islam, which served as a bodyguard. He set up a hierarchy, with a minister of Islam and a staff of assistant ministers. Fard chose as his messenger and minister of Islam Elijah (or Robert) Poole, who had migrated to Detroit from Georgia in 1923. Fard had developed the practice, similar to that of Drew, of dropping "slave names" of his followers, and assigning an "original" name. Poole was renamed Elijah Muhammad.[2]

In mid-1934 Fard disappeared, leaving his new religion and its organization in Elijah Muhammad's hands. As in the case of Drew, his disappearance was credited to foul play by either local police or dissident followers. The facts remain obscure.[3]

Under Elijah the organization suffered a factional disturbance, and Elijah moved his headquarters to Chicago, to Temple number 2, in 1934 or 1935. During the depression years the membership increased to the range of 8,000–10,000, but the movement was severely cut back by the effect of World War II. Elijah himself and several others were arrested for draft evasion and for advocating resistance to the draft; he was imprisoned from 1942 to 1946. The FBI assumed that Muhammad was working with the Japanese, but these charges could not be substantiated. By the end of the war the estimated total membership was down to less than 1000. At that time there were four temples: Detroit, Chicago, Milwaukee, and Washington, D.C. In the period 1946–55 the movement grew slowly, and from 1955 to 1960 expanded widely to at least 69 temples. While the Muslims claimed 200,000 members in their peak years, outside observers estimated the high point of membership to be about 100,000.[4]

Expansion of the Nation of Islam

Several factors contributed to the survival and expansion of this obscure cult into a major religion and a major social movement. While part of that success can be attributed to the leadership and superior organizational genius of Elijah and his hand-picked lieutenants, it was the theological doctrine and the social views of the movement which attracted members.

As Elijah developed the principles of the religion, it varied considerably in its premises from orthodox Islam. In its views on race the Nation of Islam was intensely nationalistic, and directly at odds with the views of other Moslems who regard their religion as a world faith open to all mankind. The Nation of Islam did not allow whites to participate in its services; it maintained a separate structure and did not exchange visits with existing orthodox Moslem temples; Muhammad claimed white men are devils, a view scoffed at by the orthodox. Further, Elijah Muhammad developed a body of teaching called Yacub's History, which states that the black race is the original race of man, and that whites were eugenically evolved in a long-range experiment by Yacub conducted on an island in the Aegean. As this race was progressively bred towards lightness, evil traits manifested themselves. Whites eventually were expelled, fleeing to Europe where they lived in caves. Elijah predicted a catastrophic end to white world domination, and advocated physical, economic and political separation of blacks from whites. None of these eschatological or programmatic tenets are found in other branches of Islam.[5]

Whether the Nation of Islam represented a cult or a full-fledged new religion is a question with both theoretical and legal aspects. As members of a private cult without religious standing, it would be difficult for Black Muslim ministers to claim exemption from military service as clergy, and it would be difficult to claim the right to hold religious services in prisons. On both counts, Muslims encountered opposition from the courts. In the eyes of the sociologists of religion, however, the issue is a matter of definition. If a *church* is defined as a religious group seeking to become an integral part of the social order, a *sect* as a religious group dissatisfied with the social order and withdrawing from it or seeking to alter it, and a *cult* as a religious group led by a charismatic figure mystically absorbed and indifferent to the society and its problems, then it seems reasonable to argue, as does C. Eric Lincoln, that the Muslims, while resembling a cult particularly in their early period, developed into a Moslem sect, and are destined to survive in that form.[6]

What characterized the shift from cult to sect was the concern of Muhammad and his ministers with developing teachings that did bear on the plight of dispossessed and oppressed black people in the United States. By coupling black nationalist ideas, many with deep roots in the nationalist tradition, with a religious approach, the Nation of Islam marshalled support in large numbers. Like the Garvey movement, the Nation of Islam's eclectic absorption of nationalist principles helped insure a wide response. Like the less successful black Jews and Moors, the Nation built a following among blacks disillusioned with Christianity and already treated as aliens in America.

One deeply rooted nationalist principle advanced by Muhammad was the economic self-help idea put forward by Cuffe, Delany, Crummell, and Booker Washington. Like Garvey, Drew, and Divine, Muhammad set up separately owned enterprises. The list of businesses has expanded and changed, but it has included restaurants, farms, groceries, dry cleaning plants, dressmaking shops, clothing stores, apartment buildings, barber shops, and gas stations. Like Crummell and Washington, Muhammad has urged his followers to buy from black enterprises, not necessarily those owned by the Nation of Islam. By 1960 the estimated purchasing power of the black population in the United States was $20 billion—more than the gross national product of many nations, and sufficient, in the eyes of Muslims, if properly spent, to bring prosperity to blacks. Muhammad actively sought support among black businessmen, and at least one of his annual conventions offered free display space to privately owned black enterprises.[7]

Another nationalist idea, and one primary to political black nationalism, is the idea of a separately governed nation. Aside from Liberian and Haitian advocates among American black nationalists, only Garvey had given clear voice to this aspiration. Muhammad's references to the principle of self-government did not spell out a clear program for the achievement of a black state, yet he approached the issue. As a "nation," the Nation of Islam in itself represents a government within alien territory. Furthermore, Muhammad spoke both of the idea of territorial nationalism—a grant of land within the boundaries of the United States—and of emigration, but all such references appeared to be deliberately indefinite. E. U. Essien-Udom suggested that Muhammad was vague in order to avoid entanglements with federal authorities over political goals which could be viewed as subversive. Opponents have attributed his vagueness to fraud: attempting to attract and hold followers by voicing a demand which he never intended to realize and which would be doomed to failure. In the late 1950s and early 1960s, the Muslims claimed affinity with Asia, and when speaking of a homeland referred to Mecca, in Saudi Arabia. After visits by Muslim leaders to the Middle East and Africa, and the development of African independence, the Muslims shifted attention to Africa as the homeland.[8]

The emphasis on black history, both factual and mythical, which characterized the work of earlier nationalists like Delany, Holly, Crummell, Blyden, and Garvey, was a major part of the Muslim approach. The most extreme development, Yacub's History, has its parallels in the eschatology of the black Jews and the Moorish Science Temple. But Muslim schools have given emphasis in the curriculum to the achievements of black Americans and to the history of Africa, and Muhammad himself made reference to standard historical works to demonstrate elements of black history that might serve as sources of pride. Facts such as the Moorish control of Spain, the empires of West Africa, the flowering of Moslem scholarship at Timbuktu, and the probability that Aesop was a black man were mixed with the assertions of Yacub's History.

The emphasis on black pride and a self-established identity, common among nationalists since Cuffe, was developed by Muhammad. Muhammad rejected Christianity as a white man's religion. Blacks should reject that religion, he argued, along with whites' image of "Negroes." The dropping of slave names and adoption of revealed names, after a period while the person was designated "X," parallels earlier efforts to symbolically reshape personal identity. The adoption of a high standard of personal morality, the rejection of rich foods and adoption of partial fasting, rejection of pork and some other nonkosher foods, the adoption of conservative clothing for both men and women, are all measures which help reshape personality and give a new sense of identity. Like Garvey and Blyden, Muhammad has called for elevation and respect for the black woman, although the role assigned women has been a conservative, domestic one.

Schisms and opponents

Orthodox Moslems in the United States, as well as leaders of separate Moslem organizations hoping to draw black followings, have been particularly hostile to the Nation of Islam. Included among some of the smaller Islamic black nationalist groups are the Ahmadiyyat movement with a base in Chicago. This organization, comprising followers of a worldwide sect based in Pakistan, had a minuscule following in the United States from 1921. Grover Redding's Abyssinians, mentioned previously, also opposed the Nation of Islam. A more serious threat to Muhammad occurred in the Moslem Brotherhood of America, Incorporated, established in 1950 by a West Indian black man who called himself Imam, or religious leader. Talib Ahmad Dawud, a Moslem since 1940, operated several businesses and established temples in Philadelphia and Harlem. In 1960 Dawud launched a campaign against Muhammad, claiming his deviations from orthodox Islam were at issue. Apparently Dawud hoped to win converts among those who might split away from Muhammad's organization. Newspaper claims that Dawud had 100,000 followers in the United States in that period were unsubstantiated. Another anti-Elijah Muhammad black Moslem organization was led by Jamal Diab, Imam of the Islamic Center in Chicago, which had both white and black American members. Membership figures in all these small groups of Islamic persuasion are impossible to establish, but it was clear that they were in heated competition for a following among groups which overlapped. An example of the competition and overlap was the reputed loss of members of the Ahmadiyyat movement to the Islamic Center. None of the smaller groups could claim success in winning support away from Elijah Muhammad.[9]

Malcolm X

The most serious schism to develop in the ranks of the Nation of Islam came as a result of the departure of Muhammad's New York minister, Malcolm X, in 1964. Malcolm was the best-known Muslim minister, and the one individual who, more than any other, secularized Muhammad's doctrines, revived and spread black nationalist ideas, and reshaped black American thinking in the mid-1960s. Far less obscure to the modern general reader than any of the other figures discussed in this work, his rise to fame, his split with Muhammad, and his last year as an independent racial leader before assassination, have been well recounted. Like both Garvey and Muhammad himself, Malcolm was an eclectic nationalist, drawing together a number of elements in the black nationalist tradition. His uniqueness lay in his charisma and sincerity, and in his ability to bring the central principles of a black nationalist approach to an audience that was wider in its social base than was that of Muhammad or even Garvey.[10]

Born as Malcolm Little in 1925, in Omaha, Nebraska, he was exposed to the terror tactics of the Ku Klux Klan as a child. Malcolm's father, a Baptist minister, was also a Garvey organizer, who, whites charged, spread trouble among the "good Negroes" of Omaha. Malcolm was convinced that his father's death, under mysterious circumstances, was a Klan-ordered murder. After his father's death the family was broken up, and Malcolm was raised by a number of relatives and foster parents.

As a teenager and young man in Boston, he acquired the nickname "Big Red" and a reputation as a hustler, con artist, and burglar. He was arrested and sentenced to a ten-year sentence at the age of twenty, in 1946. While in prison, he was converted to the Nation of Islam by his older brother and other relatives, on visits and by letters. He was released in 1952 and moved to Detroit. He visited Chicago and was enrolled in the movement, changing his name to X. He was appointed assistant minister of Islam in Detroit. After several months training in Chicago, he moved east, organizing a mosque in Philadelphia, and then took the appointment of minister of Islam at Mosque number 7, in New York City, in 1954.

As minister in New York in the period 1954-64, Malcolm was a leading member of the Nation in one of its most thriving locations, and through the dramatic years of the civil rights movement. The ten-year period which began with Malcolm's New York appointment also began with the *Brown v. Topeka School Board* decision of the Supreme Court which has been heralded as ending legal segregation in the United States. However, at the very period when gains were made through the NAACP-sponsored effort of utilizing the courts and legislature to enforce rights, black leaders in increasing numbers became skeptical of that method and the value of desegregation. That increased skepticism may help account for Malcolm X's success in winning support and followers to the Nation of Islam in that period. Another factor in Malcolm's rise to fame was his availability, in New York, to the mass media headquarters in that city. Through a number of televised interviews and magazine articles, Malcolm obtained a vast national audience, both black and white. His clear style of argument and forceful personality disturbed whites and gave expression to ideas shared by millions of blacks.

Malcolm X's break with Muhammad

The frustrations of the civil rights era reveal the issues at stake in the eventual secession of Malcolm from the Nation. Muhammad's stated position was to avoid politics and to stay out of alliances with other black groups, with unions, and with whites engaged in civil rights activities. In a number of situations Malcolm believed that local action could be taken in coordination with other groups, particularly in dealings with the police. As his black audiences demanded practical and programmatic answers to questions, the ultimately unresolved and often deliberately vague aspects of the official doctrine of the Nation of Islam left Malcolm in an awkward position. If a black nation should develop, where should it locate? If whites were to be destroyed in an apocalyptic rain of fire, when and where would it occur? How could blacks insure their own safety? While the answers of a cult, couched in symbolic terms, might satisfy a limited number of true believers, potential supporters and followers turned away in the absence of specific answers to such specific questions.

In 1959 Malcolm visited Mecca, with a trip to Egypt, the Sudan, and Nigeria. In his autobiography he credited his visit and contacts with Middle Eastern Moslems, some of whom were white, with beginning his disillusionment with the doctrine of Muhammad. But the theological reasons for his disagreements were given immediacy by several personal and political factors. He had developed a personal following as the most articulate and well-known of Muhammad's ministers. That following pressured him to give political expression to the nationalist ideas inherent in the doctrine he preached and to violate Muhammad's rule against political action. Furthermore, he was disturbed by rumors of financial and sexual misconduct at the headquarters in Chicago, which would give him an issue around which to launch an internal reform. But the incident which touched off his break with Elijah was a strictly political one.[11]

After the assassination of President John Kennedy in November, 1963, Elijah issued orders for a moratorium on verbal attacks on Kennedy by his ministers. However, Malcolm gave an address on December 4, 1963, entitled "God's Judgment of White America." In response to a question after the address, Malcolm used the sentence, "The chickens are coming home to roost," which reflected the theme of his address that the violence of America as suffered by blacks would be visited on whites as God's judgment. He criticized black civil rights leaders for having allowed themselves to be taken over and manipulated by white liberals, including the late president. Malcolm was summoned to Chicago and was "suspended" for ninety days by Elijah. Before the conclusion of that period he resigned from the movement entirely. Whether the speech was merely an excuse for discipline to be imposed by Elijah or not, Malcolm took this opportunity to leave the Nation of Islam.[12]

During the year from February, 1964, to February, 1965, Malcolm's ideas evolved in public addresses, in speeches at colleges and churches, and in television appearances and interviews. He set up two organizations to marshal support for his new positions, the Organization of Afro-American Unity (OAAU) and the Muslim Mosque, Incorporated. The OAAU was to draw together those interested in his secular program, and the new Mosque was to provide a setting for members from Temple number 7 of the Nation of Islam who might follow him away from Elijah. A fully clear exposition and development of his direction was prevented by his assassination February 21, 1965. The killing was never solved as a crime to the satisfaction of his followers and admirers. Many of the members of the OAAU immediately assumed that Muslims had arranged the killing, but a body of opinion soon grew that the police or other representatives of white power ordered the assassination.

Malcolm X assessed

While his fame and charisma attracted attention, an assessment of the contents of his ideas in his last year has remained a matter of controversy. This much can be said with certainty. Malcolm moved away from Elijah's doctrine of the white man as "devil" and towards an attack on racists as a particular group of whites. He recognized an African identity, and urged black Americans to view themselves as Africans in America. He no longer advocated either a separate black territory or emigration, and to this extent he rejected the political definition of black nationalism.

He maintained most of the nonpolitical elements of the black nationalist tradition, and in his eclectic style he blended together arguments for racial pride, self-help, and faith in Islam, with an indication of solidarity with the world revolution against imperialism. His departure from Muhammad and from the idea of separate political existence, as well as his suggestions of allegiance with white anticolonial revolutionaries and radicals, gave some credence to the claims of a variety of left spokesmen that Malcolm, like DuBois, had evolved in the direction of Marxism. Claims to the ideological "inheritance" of Malcolm have been made by Trotskyists, Muslims, civil rights leaders, several revolutionary black nationalists, and even white liberals. The inheritance was more than an ephemeral or abstract issue, since his considerable personal following represented organizational potential; but within a year the OAAU's strength was dispersed.

Malcolm X's greatest influence was not in establishing a particular organization, or in adding followers and arguments to any particular doctrinal group. Rather, working from what had been an obscure, Islamic-oriented black nationalist sect, he revivified the whole range of black nationalist ideas and brought them before both the black and white public as they had not been since the days of Garvey. The thirty-five or forty-year hiatus in black nationalist thinking, during which the tradition had lived only in small groups and cults, had ended. For a generation black nationalism had only an underground existence; its "rediscovery" effectively shaped the self-image of a generation of black youth, stimulated the growth of many new organizations, and gave a new orientation to the study of black history.

16

BLACK NATIONALISM REVIVED

The social context

In the decade between the death of Malcolm X and the writing of this work, the black nationalist tradition has displayed a new vitality. A wide variety of movements, spokesmen, and groups have given voice to particular black nationalist ideas, most of which first appeared in the nineteenth century. The diversity of the organizations can be viewed as evidence of disunity, but more importantly the diversity serves to prove the continued appeal of different aspects of the tradition. When the doctrine was most popular, its many organizational forms gave room for severe disagreement. The 1850s, 1890s, and 1920s were also decades which saw the development of overlapping and sometimes competing nationalist organizations.

The previous periods of nationalist activity could be partly attributed to outside factors producing a conscious disillusionment on the part of the masses of blacks with the white American pretense of equal citizenship. The Fugitive Slave Act, popular sovereignty in Kansas, and the Dred Scott decision are the landmarks of disillusionment in the 1850s. The 1890s saw disfranchisement by literacy tests, the growth of Jim Crow statutes, greatly increased lynching, and the *Plessy vs. Ferguson* decision instituting the separate-but-equal principle of segregation. The Garvey movement of the 1920s has been attributed to the failure of migration to northern cities to produce an improvement in the conditions of the migrants. Civil rights gains in the decade 1954–64 would seem, however, to violate the pattern. Yet, the widened appeal of black nationalist ideas in this period of political gain also occurred against a background of justified skepticism about the promise of American life.

150

For the civil rights decade was characterized not only by "gains" but by several severe setbacks. The pace of court action in implementing desegregation appeared agonizingly slow. The scale of white resistance was spectacular, with church bombings, assassinations, and white-led riots giving vent to deep-seated hostilities. The need for compulsion to gain compliance with the law demonstrated the necessity of "clout" in American political affairs. The introduction of Gandhian *satyagraha,* or love-force, in the form of passive resistance by James Farmer in the Congress of Racial Equality (CORE) in 1943 and by Martin Luther King, Jr., in 1955 in the Montgomery bus boycott had limited results. The necessity of court orders, the force of financial boycott, the use of federal troops and marshals, all demonstrated that white Americans would not voluntarily respect the rights of blacks even when the courts had explicitly redefined them. The concentration of civil rights activities in the South left the economic and social conditions such as municipal services, residential segregation, and police relations of the northern black man untouched. Within several of the leading civil rights organizations, particularly CORE and NAACP, the question of white liberal participation and its role in directing black energies away from the difficult issues of white racism and economic exploitation towards integration in schools and other public facilities provided another source of skepticism, frustration, and anger.

But as in the earlier eras, the survival and revival of black nationalist ideas was not simply the function of a reaction against the excesses of white racism expressed through white-controlled institutions and activities; to view it so would be to ignore the more fundamental reasons for its continued life. Particular leaders whose personal experience and ideational development gave them the ability to focus aspects of the nationalist ideology and to give expression to the fundamental desire for self-determination felt by the masses of blacks must be credited with the flowering of the doctrine in this period. Malcolm X, as we have seen, was probably the most important and charismatic of these figures. Others, from a variety of backgrounds, gave expression to one or another aspect of the doctrine. Some, like Malcolm, developed their thinking after a period in prison. Several had careers as organizers or workers in relatively conservative civil rights–oriented groups before developing as spokesmen of nationalism. Several came from the ranks of intellectuals—writers, teachers, clergy, critics, and scholars. None, however, had Malcolm X's ability to symbolize in his own life and personality the aspiration for black mastery and self-determination.

Types of nationalist activity

As in earlier periods of black nationalist activity, the decade after 1965 witnessed a bewildering proliferation of groups, often competing in membership and leadership. A number of categories of such activity can be clearly designated. *Left nationalists* include groups which formed alliances with revolutionary and socialist organizations, often interracial, and which blended the language of traditional black nationalism with Marxist and anti-colonial ideas. Another group revived the *territorial nationalist* idea, and emphasized the goal of a geographically defined nation. The goal of self-determination was expressed differently by literally hundreds of *independent black institutions,* with educational, cultural, and community-action orientations. An effort to organize and give direction to such institutions was the goal of the Congress of African People held in 1970. Among independent black institutions are a number whose nationalism is marginal, but whose justifications for separate self-determination echo arguments advanced earlier in the development of black nationalist thought. A number of civil rights advocates adopted nationalist rhetoric and some nationalist ideas. In addition, several nationalist *religious groups* continued to thrive, and some new ones developed. But such a list of categories is based on functional distinctions. Left nationalists, territorial nationalists, the independent black institutions, and the black nationalist religions, while expressing elements of the black nationalist tradition, are not working towards the same goals. Despite efforts to unite the different followings into a single, more effective movement, long-term alliances were made difficult, perhaps impossible, by the very different objectives and views of the different groups. Like nationalists elsewhere in the world, American black nationalists remained divided by questions of economic policy, tactics, religion, leadership, and interests, and united only loosely by a sense of common nationality.

Left nationalists

One of the figures who represents most clearly the departure from conservative, legalistic tactics of the NAACP and who was regarded as the initiator of "revolutionary nationalist" thinking was neither a revolutionary nor very much of a nationalist. Robert F. Williams, as president of the Monroe, North Carolina, NAACP in 1959, made a relatively nonrevolutionary statement that lynching might have to be met with lynching. The national NAACP board suspended him for six months for the statement, which the board regarded as liable to provide arguments to the NAACP's white opponents in the South. Williams continued to be active in a series of demonstrations in Monroe, and as the result of protecting some freedom riders he was arrested on the charge of kidnapping a white couple. While on bond, he fled the United States, first to Canada, then Cuba, and then to the People's Republic of China. In 1969 he returned to the United States, resided in Michigan, and fought extradition to North Carolina. His activities in Monroe, a book he published in 1961, *Negroes with Guns,* and a periodical he published intermittently while abroad, *The Crusader,* gave publicity to the principle of armed self-defense. Harold Cruse later pointed out in a perceptive critique of a variety of black radical positions, *The Crisis of the Negro Intellectual,* that despite interpretations placed on Williams's ideas and actions, what he suggested was not at all revolutionary, in either tactic or objective. Williams advocated that civil rights demonstrators, particularly in the South, should resist white terror tactics and arm themselves against assault. He did not argue for the development of a revolutionary cadre aimed at attacking the state, but for the constitutional and legal right of self-protection. The tactic he suggested was to be used to gain integration, and Williams specifically rejected separatist and nationalist ideas.[1]

Williams did not propose a program which would bear on the situation of blacks in northern cities, where the danger came not from unrestrained independent white terrorists, but from police brutality of an everyday sort and from insidious manifestations of racism. But a variety of white Marxists and black spokesmen seized on Williams's discussion of armed self-defense, and in some cases, coupled it with black nationalist ideas.

Robert Williams's ideas of armed self-defense stood in marked contrast to the unarmed civil disobedience tactics advocated earlier by James Farmer of CORE and Martin Luther King, Jr. When an organization designed to implement armed self-defense, called the Deacons for Defense, was established in Bogalusa, Louisiana, and began providing armed escorts for demonstrators who themselves were unarmed, the contrast between the two tactics was dramatically illustrated. Unarmed civil disobedience, which had been so successful in India under Gandhi's leadership, had been directed against the British government. Incidents of police or military violence against demonstrators had only assisted Gandhi's followers in their goal of discrediting the British. But in the American South, violence against demonstrators tended to come from leaderless white mobs, and incidents of violence rarely served to discredit any responsible authorities. The Deacons' aid was not desired by the civil rights leaders precisely because it gave proof that *satyagraha* was not suited to the American context of angry white resistance.[2]

An organization which attempted to implement a more radical interpretation of Williams's ideas was the Revolutionary Action Movement (RAM) established in 1963 and relatively well destroyed by police action by 1968.

Seeking to establish a "Third Force" "somewhere between the Nation of Islam and SNCC," the group specifically claimed to be black nationalist, although it did engage in supporting civil rights activities. Adopting a Garvey motto, "One purpose, one aim, one destiny," RAM's manifesto and activities echoed several nationalist themes. The organization emphasized black heroes, advocated all-black self-control and self-consciousness, set up classes in black history, freely used analogies to African liberation struggles, and utilized the concept of pan-African identity. In its manifesto RAM distinguished between "reactionary nationalism" and "revolutionary nationalism" and indicated, in a somewhat confusing use of terminology, that "nationalism is really internationalism today." One of the leaders of RAM, Max Sanford, emphasized the analogy between the black situation in America and that of colonies, and he asked for independent black "nationhood" and reparations payments.[3]

The idea of armed self-defense became mixed with several black nationalist ideas in the formation, in 1966, of the Oakland, California-based Black Panthers for Defense. The name chosen by the leaders of this organization reflected two previous organizations, the Black Panther party set up in Lowndes County, Alabama, by Stokely Carmichael, working through the Student Non-Violent Coordinating Committee (SNCC), and the Deacons for Defense in Louisiana. Both Huey Newton and Bobby Seale, students at Merritt College in Oakland, had read and discussed the work of Williams and had followed the career of Malcolm X. The Panthers' ten-point program combined a number of specific civil rights demands with several separatist principles developed in the black nationalist tradition. In brief, the Panther program asked for self-determination, full employment, reparations for previous exploitation, housing, education, exemption from military service, armed self-defense in conformity with the Second Amendment of the Constitution, release of black prisoners on the grounds of unfair trials, and the establishment of black juries for black defendants on the grounds of trial by a jury of peers. In the Panthers' statement of beliefs, the preamble to the Declaration of Independence, which justifies revolution when government becomes destructive of the inalienable rights of man, is fully quoted. The Panthers' rather unique ability to combine fundamental principles of American government, principles of self-determination as exemplified in the black nationalist tradition, and some current ideas of armed self-defense gave them a coherent and flexible doctrine which attracted followers. Their practice of bearing arms, and an armed demonstration at the California State House in Sacramento, produced publicity.[4]

An early member of the Panthers was Eldridge Cleaver, the author of a compelling autobiography, *Soul on Ice,* written while he was in prison. On his release he joined the OAAU, attempting to set up a working chapter of

Malcolm's organization in San Francisco. Among the intellectual influences on Cleaver were the writings of Frantz Fanon, a black Caribbean psychologist who had settled in Algeria. Cleaver interpreted Fanon's arguments for revolution in a colonial situation to apply to the situation of the black man in the United States. Panther literature continued to reflect the colonial analogy.[5]

In the period 1968-70, after rapid expansion to about thirty chapters around the country, the Panthers had a number of conflicts with local police, particularly in Oakland and Chicago. Most of the leadership was arrested, some were killed, and several, including Cleaver in 1969, went into exile. The simultaneous nature of the attacks made quite believable the Panther assertion that the organization was victimized by a police-government conspiracy.

While the Panthers attempted to merge their organization with others and to form alliances, most such effort seemed to bring relatively little success through the mid-1970s. By 1974 the Panthers had evolved into an organization devoted to tactics for ghetto survival and for political action. The persistence of several Marxist and nationalist ideas, and eclectic radicalism, has demonstrated that the black nationalist tradition in America can be utilized in a national liberation front similar to the organizations in the anti-colonial revolutions of Africa and Asia.

A similar effort to reconcile some of the ideas of self-determination and black control with Marxism can be found in the writings of James Boggs in the period 1963-67 and in the development of radical black unions—particularly the Dodge Revolutionary Union Movement (DRUM) and the League of Revolutionary Black Workers. Writing for the independent socialist magazine *Monthly Review,* Boggs, who was himself an auto worker, suggested that white radicals should recognize the need for black self-determination and control of their own radical organizations, but that blacks should face the historical and social differences between their situation as a sector of the working class in a highly industrial society and the situation of colonial peoples elsewhere. In the American situation nationalism is difficult to apply. He saw black nationalism as a progressive force in that it draws the revolutionary potential of blacks together, but he warned that black nationalist revolutionary efforts would be fruitless unless blacks took on the task of revolutionizing the whole social structure.[6]

Black power and separate territory

Several black nationalist ideas received widespread press coverage and attention in 1966 when Stokely Carmichael, who had been active in SNCC, raised the simple slogan "Black Power" while on a protest march in Mississippi. The phrase had been used before, particularly in the summer of 1965 when a group called the Organization of Black Power met in Detroit to attempt to represent Malcolm X's ideas, and earlier in 1966 by Adam Clayton Powell at a commencement address at Howard University. But Carmichael's use of the term raised an outcry in the white press, for as he used it, the concept seemed to represent black rejection of white participation in the civil rights movement. The phrase itself became the subject of debate, and a variety of meanings were proposed by different spokesmen, including Carmichael himself, H. Rap Brown, and Charles Hamilton. Of course, the concepts of power, self-determination, and separately operated black organizations and pressure groups had been present in the United States for over a century. The almost hysterical white press reaction to the use of the term may have represented a growing awareness on the part of white journalists and newscasters of the revival of black nationalist ideas at this time.

Black power took a very specific form in the revival of the demand for a black territorial enclave within the United States. While Elijah Muhammad had used the principle of territorial nationalism in deliberately vague terms, and Malcolm X had not gone beyond specifying "five or six" states, the Republic of New Africa (RNA) made the demand quite explicitly. Organized in Detroit at a Conference on Black Government in 1968, the RNA brought together supporters of the idea. Robert S. Browne, one of the participants in the conference, had advocated the idea in 1966 and 1967, asking for a "separate homeland" in the United States. The RNA asked for the states of Louisiana, Mississippi, Alabama, Georgia and South Carolina, and $400 billion in reparations.[7]

Independent black institutions

In the period 1966-70 a great number of local organizations with nationalist or separatist objectives were formed. Over two hundred such organizations were represented at the 1970 Congress of African Peoples (CAP) held in Atlanta. Included were local chapters of national organizations such as SNCC, CORE, RNA, and black student organizations, community action agencies, black labor units, black educational institutions and churches, and organizations devoted entirely to cultural activities. The 1970 conference represented a continuation of an effort which had been going on for several years to bring some order out of the confusion of the hundreds of new groups. Earlier Black Power conferences in 1966 in Washington, D.C., in 1967 in Newark, and in 1968 in Philadelphia had failed to produce any significant permanent group. The 1970 Congress, presided over by Imamu

Amiri Baraka (LeRoi Jones), produced a diffuse "documentary" volume which incorporated a number of resolutions and reports.[8]

The very diversity of the institutions and positions taken made it impossible to define with clarity the ideological position of the congress as a whole. Baraka's left-nationalist opponents characterized him as a cultural nationalist with ill-thought-out political mottoes such as "It's nation time" and with an egocentric approach. While the RNA presented its position to the congress, so did the Nation of Islam and other organizations with less specific political goals. The 1970 congress approved a resolution recognizing the RNA as an African nation in the Western Hemisphere. The major political thrust of the CAP was to form coalitions and to suggest political action which would assist particular black candidates in municipal elections. The congress also called for a Black National Liberation Front which would consolidate the CAP with the League of Revolutionary Workers, the Black Panther party, and the RNA. The absence of delegates representing the Panthers gave evidence of the difficulties facing such consolidation, which was not achieved.[9]

Among the speakers at the 1970 congress were a variety of civil rights advocates and black politicians whose use of black nationalist rhetoric and concern for liberation of black people was perhaps more significant than their differing ideological and political inclinations. Julian Bond, Richard Hatcher, and Kenneth Gibson, all politicians, had each won office with varying degrees of white support. Jesse Jackson, Whitney Young, and Ralph Abernathy represented three separate civil rights organizations. Despite the established record of each of these leaders in working within the social and political system of the United States, each adopted a degree of nationalist rhetoric in calling for pan-African solidarity and the acquisition and selective use of power. The ideas and orientation of nationalism were once again gaining "respectability" as they had in the earlier periods of leadership by Cuffe, Crummell, and Delany.

An organization represented at the CAP, the Opportunities Industrialization Center (OIC), headquartered in Philadelphia, and led by the Baptist Reverend Leon Sullivan, was a national organization of black-organized skills training centers funded privately by contributions. The OIC local chapters received federal grants from the Department of Labor and Office of Economic Opportunity and sought membership from both black and white employers. Sullivan's style, which is reminiscent of Booker Washington's, represents another form of revival of specific black nationalist ideas.

Religion

The Nation of Islam continued actively to recruit followers after Malcolm X's death, and expanded its economic activities to include the purchase of several large farms in the South. As always, the exact number of temples and the size of the following were not made public, but the Nation's vitality appeared quite recovered after the decline of initial suspicions that Malcolm's death had been ordered by Muhammad. While no leader of Malcolm's popularity emerged from the movement, the elaborate organizational structure and numerous temples continued to provide training and experience to potential nationalist leaders.

Among Christians, a notable development in Detroit was the activity of the Reverend Albert Cleague. He renamed his church the Shrine of the Black Madonna, reviving the idea of the African Orthodox church established by George McGuire in 1924. In 1969 Cleague published *The Black Messiah*, in which he presented historical and religious evidence of the African origins of Christianity.[10]

Among non-Christians, the Falashas, or Commandment Keepers, have continued to be active, and a small group of Chicago-based black Jews, the Al-Beta Israel Temple, emigrated to Liberia in 1967. Several went on to Israel in 1969. Since 1966 the Yoruba Temple in New York, led by Ofuntula Oseijaman Ad-funmi, has been based on a full return to African religion, clothing, and customs. While small, its style may represent the full flowering of the cultural aspects of black nationalism.

Summary

Black nationalism, like other nationalisms, is no clear-cut guide to present action; it represents rather a cluster of related ideas than an ideology. In the decade after the death of Malcolm X, no single figure of his stature or of Garvey's emerged to unite the diverse kinds of following into a single movement. Baraka has made such an effort, but despite some successes in getting different kinds of spokesmen and leaders who use nationalist rhetoric and nationalist ideas to speak from the same platform, it appeared unlikely that radicals led by men like Newton and Seale could find a comfortable alliance with conservatives led by a figure such as the Reverend Sullivan. However, the evolution of the Black Panther party into a more conventional political organization by 1973 and 1974 suggested that some organizational unity was in the realm of possibility.

Although problems of leadership, problems of economic ideology, and questions of policy prevented the unity of such diverse followings around the cluster of shared nationalist ideas, the very diversity of approaches has helped to keep the doctrine alive. Taken as a group, modern black nationalists in the United States, drawing on their rich tradition, continued to show activity and vitality on each characteristic element of the pattern of classic nationalism as described by Boyd Shafer. RNA and the Nation of Islam worked towards control of territory and the establishment of sovereign government. Black politicans frequently utilized the rhetoric of sovereign control and self-determination in their campaigns. Several independent black institutions and the Congress of African People under Baraka's leadership have stressed common culture, common institutions, and hostility to opponents. Groups as widely different as the conservative OIC, the Church of the Black Madonna, the black Jews, and the Black Panthers evoked common pride. The Nation of Islam especially called for loyalty and devotion. All the groups advocated the study of black history, either authentic or mythical, or both, in evoking pride.

While most spokesmen using black nationalist rhetoric made reference to specific historical figures, it was common to find such reference taking on a ritual quality, in which names were invoked, much in the fashion that a white American politician might invoke the names of Jefferson or Lincoln, or a Russian politician the names of Marx, Engels, or Lenin. Whether or not a particular modern figure is in reality influenced by a particular historical figure whom he names is always problematical. The unlikelihood of direct influence is especially great when a complex figure like DuBois is mentioned, and when the purported source of his ideas is his writing rather than direct contact. While DuBois may more or less legitimately be considered the father of pan-Africanism, his endorsement of civil rights and integration, his use of political and judicial tactics, his evolving separatist side, and his eventual Marxist commitment were also part of his position. Similarly, Delany, Blyden, Crummell, Booker Washington, and Garvey did not represent a single position, and the invocation of their names, while it may serve a reasonable symbolic function, has little intellectual content unless the variety of the positions each took is analyzed and understood. The academic development of black studies which came as a by-product of increased black self-awareness in the late 1960s will certainly expose a generation of potential leaders to the rich variety of ideas that form part of the black nationalist tradition. A flow of ideas across the Atlantic characterized the roots of Liberian nationalism and Liberia's influence upon American black nationalist thought in the mid-nineteenth century. A similar international cross-fertilization characterized the development of some of DuBois's, Washington's, and Garvey's principles, and has been under way once again in the recent decade. Contemporary sensitivity to African and socialist developments suggests that the American black nationalist tradition will continue to move in the direction of allying black liberation with the liberation of all oppressed peoples.

NOTES

Chapter 1

1. John H. Bracey, Jr., August Meier, and Elliot Rudwick, eds., *Black Nationalism in America* (Bobbs-Merrill, 1970), liv; Harold Cruse, *The Crisis of the Negro Intellectual* (Morrow, 1968), 6.
2. Boyd Shafer, *Nationalism; Myth or Reality* (Harcourt, Brace & World, 1955), 7–8.
3. Theodore Draper, *The Rediscovery of Black Nationalism* (Viking, 1970), 14–47, criticizes emigration as a "fantasy," yet even his conservative estimates of emigration attest its appeal.

Chapter 2

1. R. K. Kent, "Palmares: An African State in Brazil," *Journal of African History,* 6 (1965): 161–75.
2. Ibid.
3. C. L. R. James, *Black Jacobins* (Random House, 1963).
4. James T. Holly, *A Vindication of the Capacity of the Negro to Self-Government and Civilized Progress as Demonstrated by Historical Events of the Haytian Revolution, and the Subsequent Acts of That People since Their National Independence* (New Haven, 1857). Jefferson, Lincoln, and other deportationists considered Haiti suitable. Cf. Brainerd Dyer, "The Persistence of the Idea of Negro Colonization," *Pacific Historical Review,* 12 (March, 1943):53–65.
5. Herbert Aptheker, "Maroons within the Present Limits of the United States," *Journal of Negro History,* 24 (April, 1939): 168.
6. Marion D. de B. Kilson, "Towards Freedom: An Analysis of Slave Revolts in the United States," *Phylon,* 25 (2nd Quarter, 1964): 175–87.
7. Lydia Maria Child, *The Oasis* (Bacon, 1834).

8. Cited in Henry Noble Sherwood, "Early Negro Deportation Projects," *Mississippi Valley Historical Review,* 2 (March, 1916): 494–95.

9. Ibid., 497–506; Winthrop Jordan, *White over Black* (University of North Carolina, 1968), 546–54.

10. Jordan, 555–57.

11. Ibid., 549–50, 566.

12. Sherwood, 500–502.

13. Christopher Fyfe, *History of Sierra Leone* (Oxford, 1962), 13–19.

14. Sherwood, "Paul Cuffe and his Contribution to the American Colonization Society," *Proceedings of the Mississippi Valley Historical Association* (1912–13), 6: 382; Robin Winks, *The Blacks in Canada: A History* (Yale, 1971), 67–68, 71, 75.

15. Benjamin Quarles, *The Negro in the American Revolution* (University of North Carolina, 1961), 177–81; Winks, 72–73.

16. Hollis Lynch, "Pan-Negro Nationalism in the New World before 1862," *Boston University Papers on Africa,* 2 (1966): 153.

Chapter 3

1. Peter Williams, *Discourse on the Death of Paul Cuffe, delivered before the New York African Institution, October 21, 1817,* Paul Cuffe Manuscripts, New Bedford Public Library, New Bedford, Massachusetts. This MS collection hereafter cited as PCM. Biographical information, Henry Noble Sherwood, "Paul Cuffe," *Journal of Negro History,* 7 (April, 1923): 153–229.

2. Massachusetts Archives, vol. 186, 134–36. Cited in full in Herbert Aptheker, *A Documentary History of the Negro People in the United States* (Citadel, 1963), vol. 1, 14–16. Spelling, punctuation modernized.

3. *Records of the Court of General Sessions,* Taunton, Mass., cited in Sherwood, "Paul Cuffe," 163; William O'Brien, "Did the Jennison Case Outlaw Slavery in Massachusetts?" *William and Mary Quarterly,* 3rd ser. 17 (1960): 219–41.

4. Cuffe to Pemberton, Sept. 14, 1808, PCM.

5. *Seventh Report of the Director of the African Institution,* cited in Sherwood, "Paul Cuffe," 179.

6. Paul Cuffe, *A Brief Account of the Settlement and Present Situation of the Colony of Sierra Leone, in Africa,* 1812, PCM.

7. Politics of this kind entered into the early meetings of the Boston African Institution. Cf. Prince Saunders to Paul Cuffe, Aug. 13, 1812. PCM.

8. Paul Cuffe, "To The President, Senate, and House of Representatives of the United States of America," June, 1813, *Niles Weekly Register,* Jan. 22, 1814.

9. Sherwood, "Paul Cuffe and his Contribution to the American Colonization Society," *Proceedings of the Mississippi Valley Historical Association,* 1912–13, 370–402; *Western Courier* (Louisville, Kentucky), Oct. 26, 1815.

10. Paul Cuffe to Robert Finley, Jan. 8, 1817, PCM.

11. He had earlier supported the idea of two states, one in America and one in Africa; Cuffe to Samuel C. Aiken, Aug. 7, 1816, PCM.

12. Samuel J. Mills to Paul Cuffe, March 12, 1817, PCM. It is not known

with certainty whether Finley met with Forten before or after the mass meeting. Katz cogently argues it was before, in William Lloyd Garrison, *Thoughts on African Colonization*, ed. William L. Katz (Arno Press, 1969) iii–xvi.

13. James Forten to Paul Cuffe, Jan. 25, 1817, PCM.
14. Prince Saunders to Paul Cuffe, Aug. 3, 1812, PCM; Williams, *Discourse*. See below, ch. 6, for Saunders's later career.
15. There is disagreement among scholars as to whether to regard Cuffe as a nationalist. Edwin S. Redkey, *Black Exodus: Black Nationalist and Back-to-Africa Movements, 1890–1910* (Yale, 1969), 19: "Neither Cuffe nor the Colonization Society appears to have harbored black nationalist ideas." On the contrary, E. U. Essien-Udom, *Black Nationalism: A Search for an Identity in America* (Dell, 1962), 32: " 'Negro Nationalism' found expression during the nineteenth century in the Negro-sponsored emigration movement as well as in Negroes' response (though limited) to the emigration scheme of the American Colonization Society. . . . Negro emigration from the United States was first sponsored by Paul Cuffe. . . ." Hollis Lynch agrees in "Pan-Negro Nationalism in the New World before 1862," *Boston University Papers on Africa*, 2 (1966); and in *Edward Wilmot Blyden: Pan-Negro Patriot* (Oxford, 1967) he calls Cuffe, Daniel Coker, Lott Carey, and John Russwurm "pan-Negro Nationalists." Another view is found in John H. Bracey, Jr., August Meier, and Elliott Rudwick, *Black Nationalism in America* (Bobbs-Merrill, 1970), 38. They find Cuffe primarily interested in African redemption, not emigration; they find "glimmerings of nationalist sentiment" in some of Cuffe's associates.
16. Cuffe statements from Sherwood, "Paul Cuffe", 187, 191, 202, 204.
17. Paul Cuffe, "Letter to the Imposter," [sic] Jan. 13, 1817, PCM.

Chapter 4

1. Archibald Alexander, *Colonization on the Western Coast of Africa* (Martien, 1846; Greenwood, 1969), 15.
2. Ibid., 82.
3. Ibid., 87.
4. Winthrop Jordan, *White over Black* (University of North Carolina, 1968), 567.
5. James Forten to Paul Cuffe, Jan. 25, 1817, PCM.
6. Ibid.
7. William Lloyd Garrison, *Thoughts on African Colonization*, ed. William L. Katz (Arno Press, 1969), 63.
8. Gilbert Barnes, *The Antislavery Crusade* (Harcourt, Brace & World, 1933, 1964), 214n.; Nathaniel Paul to William Lloyd Garrison, April 10, 1833, cited in Herbert Aptheker, ed., *A Documentary History of the Negro People in the United States* (Citadel, 1963), vol. 1, 140; Garrison, vol. 2, 28, 30, 43, 44, 45, 63, 64, 65–67.
9. Aptheker, *Documentary History*, vol. 1, minutes third convention 146, fourth 155, fifth 159.
10. Garrison, vol. 2, 4.
11. Aptheker, *Documentary History*, vol. 1, minutes first convention, 116, 117–18.

12. Barnes, 214n.
13. Garrison, vol. 1, 11, 15, 21, 28-32, 37.
14. Alexander, 382-83.

Chapter 5

1. "Abstract of a Journal of the late Samuel J. Mills," in *Second Annual Report, American Colonization Society* (Greenwood, 1969), 19-67.
2. Governor E. H. Columbine to Sherbro Island Headman, Aug. 1810, in *Second Annual Report, ACS,* 11; Archibald Alexander, *Colonization on the Western Coast of Africa* (Martien, 1846; Greenwood, 1969), 102-4.
3. Alexander, 102-4.
4. *Second Annual Report, ACS,* 36-7, 53.
5. Mills to ACS Board, April 4, 1818, in *Second Annual Report*, ACS, 35.
6. *The Journal of Daniel Coker, A Descendant of Africa. . . in the ship Elizabeth on a voyage for Sherbro in Africa* (Baltimore, 1820), 15-16; Alexander, 126.
7. *Second Annual Report, ACS,* 39.
8. *Second Annual Report, ACS,* 54.
9. *Seventh Annual Report, ACS,* 66.
10. Richard Bardolph, *Negro Vanguard* (Vintage, 1961), 48; C. V. R. George, *Segregated Sabbaths* (Oxford, 1973), 112, 148.
11. *Fourth Annual Report, ACS,* 17-21; *Fifth Annual Report, ACS,* 9-10; *First Annual Report, ACS,* 21.
12. Alexander, 171.
13. Ibid., 174.
14. Ibid., 175, 177, 181.
15. Ibid., 189-96.
16. Bardolph, 40; Alexander, 371-72.
17. J. B. Taylor, "A Biography of Elder Lott Carey, Late Missionary to Africa" (Baltimore, 1837) cited in Alexander, 231-46. Carey's name was also spelled Lot Cary.
18. E. Ayres to ACS Board, Feb. 18, 1824, in *Seventh Annual Report, ACS,* 115.
19. Alexander, 246; P. J. Staudenraus, *The African Colonization Movement, 1816-1885* (Columbia University, 1961), 90-92; C. H. Huberich, *Political and Legislative History of Liberia* (Central, 1947), recognized the constitutional significance of this event and of developing sovereignty, but did not treat its ideological significance.
20. Alexander, 286-87.
21. Ibid., 288
22. Ibid., 257.
23. Alexander, 339, 338-44.
24. Ibid.
25. Bardolph, 66, 67, 76.
26. Alexander, 336.
27. Penelope Campbell, *Maryland in Africa: The Maryland State Colonization Society, 1831-1857* (University of Illinois, 1971), 132-36, 144-45.
28. Ibid., 147-49.

29. Ibid., 151–53, 159.
30. Ibid., 215, 227, 233, 235.
31. Alexander, 460–62, 468, 532, 597–98;. Charles Sydnor, *Slavery in Mississippi* (Appleton-Century, 1933), 203–38,
32. Hollis Lynch, *Edward Wilmot Blyden, Pan-Negro Patriot* (Oxford, 1967), 38.
33. Henry Wilson, *Origins of West African Nationalism* (St. Martins, 1969), 19–21, 50–51.

Chapter 6

1. William and Jane Pease, *Black Utopia: Negro Communal Experiments in America* (State Historical Society of Wisconsin, 1953), 23–26; *Journal of Negro History,* "Documents," 3 (April, 1918): 163.
2. Pease, 23–26; "Transplanting Free Negroes to Ohio from 1815–1858," *Journal of Negro History,* 1 (July, 1916): 302–18. Colonies were reported in these counties: Brown, Jefferson, Harrison, Lawrence, Mercer, and Hamilton.
3. Pease, 27–28.
4. Pease, 30–32. For a fuller treatment of the communitarian movement as a whole, see Arthur Bestor, *Backwoods Utopias: The Sectarian Origin and Owenite Phase of Communitarian Socialism in America, 1663-1829* (University of Pennsylvania, 1970).
5. Pease, 28–38.
6. Prince Saunders, *The Haytian Papers* (Rhistoric Editions, 1969; original, Britain, 1816, and Boston, 1818), preface n. p.
7. "Memoir presented to the American Convention for Promoting the Abolition of Slavery and Improving the Condition of the African Race," in Saunders, 12.
8. Earl L. Griggs and Clifford H. Prater, *Henry Christophe and Thomas Clarkson: A Correspondence* (Greenwood, 1952), 124–25.
9. Ibid., 125.
10. Ibid., 226; Staudenraus 82, 117–18.
11. Griggs and Prater, 248–49.
12. P. J. Staudenraus, *The African Colonization Movement, 1816-1885* (Columbia University, 1961), 83.
13. Rayford Logan, *The Diplomatic Relations of the United States with Haiti, 1776-1891* (University of North Carolina, 1941), 217.
14. Staudenraus, 85–86.
15. Ludwell Lee Montague, *Haiti and the United States* (University of North Carolina, 1941), 71.
16. Charles Mackenzie, *Notes on Haiti Made during a Residence in that Republic* (London, 1830), 90.
17. Archibald Alexander, *Colonization on the Western Coast of Africa* (Martien, 1846; Greenwood, 1969), 263.
18. *New York Times,* Oct. 3, 1971, sec. 14, 8.
19. Merton L. Dillon, *Benjamin Lundy and the Struggle for Negro Freedom* (University of Illinois, 1966), 87–92.
20. Dillon, 93; Dwight L. Dumond, *Antislavery: The Crusade for Freedom*

in America (University of Michigan, 1961), 166.
21. Dillon, 95, 100, 142–43.
22. Dillon, 185–216.
23. Martin R. Delany, *The Condition, Elevation, Emigration and Destiny of the Colored People of the United States* (1852), as reprinted in Howard Brotz, ed., *Negro Social and Political Thought, 1850–1920* (Basic Books, 1966), 85.
24. Pease, 49.
25. Ibid., 46–62.
26. Pease, 65, 71; Robin Winks, ed., *An Autobiography of the Reverend Josiah Henson* (Addison-Wesley, 1969), 96–100.
27. Pease, 81.
28. Ibid., 113.
29. Ibid., 115, 117, 119; Henry Bibb, *Narrative of the Life and Adventures of Henry Bibb* (New York, 1849); Dumond, 335–42.
30. Fred Landon, "Negro Colonization Schemes in Upper Canada before 1860," *Transactions of the Royal Society*, 3rd. ser. 23 (1929): 73–80.

Chapter 7

1. Victor Ullman, *Martin R. Delany: The Beginnings of Black Nationalism* (Beacon, 1971), 153–54.
2. Howard H. Bell, "National Negro Conventions of the Middle 1840s: Moral Suasion vs Political Action," *Journal of Negro History*, 42 (Oct., 1957): 257–58.
3. Charles Sydnor, *Slavery in Mississippi* (Appleton-Century, 1933), 215–16.
4. Howard H. Bell, "The Negro Emigration Movement, 1849–1854, a Phase of Negro Nationalism," *Phylon*, 20 (2nd quarter, 1959): 132. Cf. Bell, introduction to *Search for a Place: Black Separatism and Africa* (University of Michigan, 1969), 4.
5. *Fifty-second Annual Report, ACS*, 53.
6. Fred Landon, "The Negro Migration to Canada after the Passing of the Fugitive Slave Act," *Journal of Negro History*, 5 (1920):22; for full discussion of population estimates, see Robin Winks, *The Blacks in Canada: A History* (Yale, 1971), 484–96.
7. Bell, "National Negro Conventions," 247, 250.
8. August Meier, "The Emergence of Negro Nationalism (A Study in Ideologies)," *Midwest Journal*, 6 (summer, 1952): 96–98; Meier analyzed these works: Easton, *A Treatise on the Intellectual Character and Civil and Political Condition of the Colored People of the United States* (1837), Pennington, *Text Book of the Origin and History of the Colored People* (1841), Lewis, *Light and Truth; Collected from the Bible and Ancient and Modern History, Containing the Universal History of the Colored and Indian Race* (1844).
9. Henry Highland Garnet, "An Address to the Slaves of the United States," in Herbert Aptheker, *A Documentary History of the Negro People in the United States* (Citadel, 1963), 231.

10. Hollis R. Lynch, *Edward Wilmot Blyden: Pan-Negro Patriot* (Oxford, 1967), 12.
11. Bell, "Negro Emigration Movement," 133; Bell, "National Negro Conventions," 250.
12. Garnet to Frederick Douglass, Jan. 21, 1848, cited in Benjamin Quarles, *Black Abolitionists* (Oxford, 1969), 217.
13. S. Wesley Jones to William McClain, June 12, 1848, *ACS Papers*, Library of Congress.
14. Garnet, *The Past and Present Condition and the Destiny of the Colored Race: A Discourse Delivered at the 50th Anniversary of the Female Benevolent Society of Troy, New York*, Feb. 14, 1848, 12.
15. Garnet to Douglass, in *North Star*, March 2, 1849; Ullman, 213.
16. Aptheker, *Documentary History*, "State Convention of the Colored Citizens of Ohio, Convened at Columbus, Jan. 10–13, 1849," vol. 1, 278; Bell, "Negro Emigration Movement," 138.
17. Aptheker, *Documentary History*, "A Douglass-Garnet Debate," vol. 1, 288–90.
18. Bell, "Negro Emigration Movement," 135, 136–37.
19. S. Wesley Jones to William McClain, Dec. 29, 1851, *ACS Papers*.
20. Carter G. Woodson, *The Mind of the Negro as Reflected in Letters Written during the Crisis, 1800–1860* (Russell and Russell, 1926, 1969), 141.
21. Bell, "Negro Emigration Movement," 139; Ullman, 135–36.
22. Landon, 24–25; Bell, "Negro Emigration Movement," 138.
23. Bell, "Negro Emigration Movement," 137.
24. Delany, as cited in Howard Brotz, ed., *Negro Social and Political Thought, 1850–1920* (Basic Books, 1966), 38.
25. Ibid., 47, 55, 60–64, 77, 80, 82, 85, 97.
26. James G. Birney, *Examination of the Decision of the Supreme Court of the United States, in the Case of Strader, Gorman, and Armstrong, vs Christopher Graham, Delivered at its December Term, 1850; Concluding with an Address to the Free Colored People, Advising them to Remove to Liberia* (Cincinnati, 1852), 45–46.
27. Bell, "Negro Emigration Movement," 139.
28. *Proceedings of the Colored National Convention, Held in Rochester, July 6, 7, 8, 1853*.
29. *Frederick Douglass's Paper*, Oct. 6, 1853, and following issues; Ullman, 153–55.
30. Aptheker, *Documentary History*, "A Negro Emigration Convention," 368.
31. Martin R. Delany, "Political Destiny of the Colored Race of the American Continent," appendix 3, *Report of the Select Committee on Emancipation and Colonization* (Washington, 1862), 37–50; Ullman, 155–57.
32. Delany, *Official Report of the Niger Exploration Expedition* (New York, 1861), 8–10; or cf. Bell, ed., *Search for a Place*, 33, 36.
33. John Cromwell, "Early Negro Convention Movement," *American Negro Academy Occasional Papers*, no. 9 (1904): 20; this source cites a private letter from Holly to Cromwell, but there is no other evidence to indicate that "commissions" were issued at the first convention.
34. James T. Holly, *A Vindication of the Capacity of the Negro Race for Self-Government and Civilized Progress as Demonstrated by Historical*

Events of the Haytian Revolution, and the Subsequent Acts of That People since Their National Independence: (New Haven, 1857), 5, 45–46.

35. Edward W. Blyden, *Voice from Bleeding Africa* (Monrovia, 1856).

36. Quarles, *Black Abolitionists*, 238–39; Ullman, 197.

37. *Weekly Anglo-African*, Sept. 3, 1859.; Ullman, 218, 220, 252.

38. *Weekly Anglo-African*, July 23, 1859, Ullman, 252–55.

39. Robert Campbell, *A Pilgrimage to My Motherland*, in Bell, ed. *Search for a Place*, 181, 201, 244.

40. Bell, ed., *Search for a Place*, 49, 51, 52, 61.

41. Ibid., 78, 248–49; Earl Phillips, "The Egba at Abeokuta: Acculturation and Political Change, 1830–1870," *Journal of African History*, 10 (1969): 117–31.

42. Lynch, *Blyden*, 163.

43. Bell, ed., *Search for a Place*, 121.

44. James Redpath, *A Guide to Haiti* (Boston, 1861), 9.

45. Ibid., 97.

46. Ibid., 175.

47. Ibid., 94–96.

48. Bell, "Negro Nationalism: A Factor in Emigration Projects, 1858–1861," *Journal of Negro History*, 48 (January, 1962): 43.

Chapter 8

1. C. H. Huberich, *Political and Legislative History of Liberia* (Central, 1947) is most complete on this period; a summary can be found in Hollis R. Lynch, *Edward Wilmot Blyden: Pan-Negro Patriot* (Oxford, 1967).

2. Lynch, *Blyden*, 3–6.

3. Ibid.

4. Blyden, "Liberia As She Is," in Henry Wilson, ed., *Origins of West African Nationalism* (St. Martins, 1969), 79.

5. Lynch, *Blyden*, 29–30. Blyden adopted a similar critical tone in his Liberian orations as well. See Wilson, ed., 23.

6. Blyden, "Africa and the Africans," in Christopher Fyfe, ed., *Christianity, Islam and the Negro Race* (orig. 1887; Edinburgh, 1967), 276.

7. Blyden, "Mohammedanism and the Negro Race," in Fyfe, ed., 1–24.

8. Lynch, *Blyden*, 31n.

9. See below, ch. 11.

10. "Calendar of the life of Alexander Crummell," Schomberg Collection, New York.

11. Alexander Crummell, *The Future of Africa* (Scribner, 1862; Greenwood, 1969), 130.

12. Ibid., 153.

13. Ibid., 100.

14. Ibid., 147, 217, 278.

15. Blyden, "Our Origin, Dangers and Duties," in Wilson, ed., 94.

16. Crummell, "Our National Mistakes and the Remedy for Them," in Wilson, ed., 108, 110, 113.

17. Crummell, "The Social Principal among a People" in *The Greatness of Christ and other Sermons* (Whittaker, 1882), 294ff.
18. W. E. B. DuBois, *The Souls of Black Folk* (1903, 1953, 1961), 157–65.

Chapter 9

1. Paul Schieps, "Lincoln and the Chiriqui Colonization Project," *Journal of Negro History,* 37 (Oct., 1952): 418–53.
2. Robert Zoellner, "Negro Colonization: The Climate of Opinion Surrounding Lincoln, 1860–1865," *Mid-America,* 42 (July, 1960): 145–46.
3. Jacob E. Cooke, ed., *Frederick Bancroft—Historian, With an Introduction by Allan Nevins and Three Hitherto Unpublished Essays on the Colonization of American Negroes from 1801 to 1865* (University of Oklahoma, 1957), 228–47.
4. Zoellner, 149.
5. Ibid., 150.
6. Aptheker, *A Documentary History of the Negro People in the United States* (Citadel, 1963), "The Negro on Lincoln's Colonization Plans, 1862," vol. 1, 471–75.
7. Willie Lee Rose, *Rehearsal for Reconstruction: The Port Royal Experiment* (Bobbs-Merrill, 1964), 200, 222–29.
8. Ibid., 320–28.
9. Ibid., 407.
10. La Wanda Cox, "The Promise of Land for the Freedmen," *Mississippi Valley Historical Review,* 45 (Dec., 1958): 413–40.
11. Vernon Wharton, *The Negro in Mississippi, 1865–1890* (University of North Carolina, 1947), 38–43.
12. August Meier, "Booker T. Washington and the Town of Mound Bayou," *Phylon,* 15 (4th quarter, 1954): 396; Harold Rose, "The All-Negro Town: Its Evolution and Function," *Geographical Review,* 55 (July, 1965).

Chapter 10

1. Walter L. Fleming, " 'Pap' Singleton: The Moses of the Colored Exodus," *American Journal of Sociology,* 15 (July, 1909): 61; for social factors, see James B. Runnion, "The Negro Exodus," *Atlantic Monthly,* Aug., 1879, 222.
2. Fleming, 65.
3. Ibid., 70; Glen Schwendemann, "Wyandotte and the First 'Exodusters' of 1879," *Kansas Historical Quarterly,* 26 (autumn, 1960), 243–48.
4. Fleming, 72.
5. Ibid., 74.
6. Ibid., 76.
7. Ibid., 79–80.
8. Aptheker, *A Documentary History of the Negro People in the United States* (Citadel, 1963), "Proceedings of the Convention of Colored Men held in . . . Parsons, Kansas, April 27–28, 1882," vol. 2, 684–85.

9. Mozell C. Hill, "The All-Negro Communities of Oklahoma: The Natural History of a Social Movement," *Journal of Negro History*, 31 (July, 1946): 257.

10. Glen Schwendemann, "Nicodemus: Negro Haven on the Solomon," *Kansas Historical Quarterly*, 34 (spring, 1968): 21–22.

11. Ibid., 23.

12. Ibid., 25–27.

13. Ibid.

14. Dora A. Stewart, *Government and Development of Oklahoma Territory* (Harlow, 1933), 37–38.

15. Ibid., 41–43; Hill, 266.

16. Hill, 261, 267; Eighty-fifth Congress, *Biographical Directory of the American Congress, 1774–1961* (Government Printing Office, 1961), 1191.

17. Hill, 261–67; Jere W. Roberson, "Edward P. McCabe and the Langston Experiment," *Chronicles of Oklahoma*, 51 (fall, 1973): 346–51; note that McCabe's name is variously reported as Edwin and Edward.

18. Hill, 267.

19. Ibid., 264.

20. *Outlook*, Jan. 4, 1908.

21. William E. Bittle and Gilbert Geis, *The Longest Way Home: Chief Alfred Sam's Back-to-Africa Movement* (Wayne State University, 1964), 21.

22. Ibid., 29.

23. Ibid., 37–39.

24. Ibid.

Chapter 11

1. Alexander Crummell, *The Future of Africa* (Scribner, 1862), 242–43.

2. Edwin S. Redkey, *Black Exodus: Black Nationalist and Back-to-Africa Movements, 1890–1910* (Yale, 1969), 25–27; E. Franklin Frazier, *The Negro Church in America* (Schocken, 1964), 42.

3. George Brown Tindall, *South Carolina Negroes, 1877–1900* (University of South Carolina, 1952), 155–60.

4. Ibid., 160, quoting *African Repository*, July, 1878, 77–78.

5. Tindall, 165–67.

6. Redkey, 35, 39.

7. Ibid., 162–69.

8. S. J. S. Cookey, *Britain and the Congo Question, 1885–1914* (Humanities, 1968), 35–36; P. McStallworth, *The United States and the Congo Question, 1884–1914* (Ph. D. dissertation, Ohio State University, 1954), 196.

9. Redkey, 53–54; Tindall, 161–62; Lewis Pinckney Jones, *Stormy Petrel: N. G. Gonzales and His State* (University of South Carolina, 1973), 67–69.

10. Redkey, 47–72.

11. Emma Lou Thornbough, "The National Afro-American League, 1887–1908," *Journal of Southern History*, 27 (Nov., 1961): 494–512.

12. John Hope Franklin, *From Slavery to Freedom* (Knopf, 1974), 316; Redkey, 272–75.

13. Redkey, 102–12.
14. Ibid., 250.
15. Ibid., 173–75.
16. Mozell C. Hill, "The All-Negro Communities of Oklahoma: The Natural History of a Social Movement," *Journal of Negro History*, 31 (July, 1946): 262.
17. William E. Bittle and Gilbert Geis, *The Longest Way Home: Chief Alfred Sam's Back-to-Africa Movement* (Wayne State University, 1964), 70–73.
18. Ibid., 73, 75, 160, 173.
19. Ibid., 196, 197, 208.

Chapter 12

1. August Meier, "Toward a Reinterpretation of Booker T. Washington," *Journal of Southern History*, 23 (May, 1957): 220–27.
2. August Meier, "Booker Washington and the Town of Mound Bayou," *Phylon*, 15 (4th quarter, 1954), 396; Harold Cruse, *The Crisis of the Negro Intellectual* (Morrow, 1968), 19–20.
3. John H. Bracey, Jr., August Meier, and Elliott Rudwick, eds., *Black Nationalism in America* (Bobbs-Merrill, 1970), 235; Harold Cruse, 21, 175–76.
4. George Shepperson, "Notes on Negro American Influences on the Emergence of African Nationalism," *Journal of African History*, 1 (1960); K. King, "Africa and the Southern States of the U.S.A.: Notes on J. H. Oldham and American Negro Education for Africans," *Journal of African History*, 10 (1969): 659.
5. Theodore Vincent, *Black Power and the Garvey Movement* (Ramparts, 1972), 54–55.
6. W. E. B. DuBois, *The Souls of Black Folk* (1903, 1953, 1961), 157–65; "The Talented Tenth," in Booker T. Washington and others, *The Negro Problem: A Series of Articles by Representative Negroes of To-day*. (James Pott & Company, 1903) 35–75.
7. Elliott Rudwick, "The Niagara Movement," *Journal of Negro History*, 42 (July, 1957): 177–200.
8. W. E. B. DuBois, *The Autobiography of W. E. B. DuBois* (International, 1968), 289; Elliott Rudwick, *W. E. B. DuBois: Propagandist of the Negro Protest* (Atheneum, 1969), 19.
9. DuBois, *Autobiography*, 162; Heinrich von Treitschke, "Races, Tribes, and Nations," as cited in Eugene C. Black, ed., *Posture of Europe, 1815–1940* (Dorsey, 1964), 240; DuBois, "The Conservation of Races," *American Negro Academy Occasional Papers*, no. 2, 1897.
10. Clarence G. Contee, "The Emergence of DuBois as an African Nationalist," *Journal of Negro History*, 54 (Jan., 1969): 48–63.
11. DuBois, *Autobiography*, 291–92.
12. Ibid., 293–99.
13. Shepperson, 309–10; cf. George Shepperson and Thomas Price, *Independent African: John Chilembwe and the Origins, Setting and Significance of the Nyasaland Native Rising of 1915* (Edinburgh, 1958).

14. DuBois, *Autobiography,* 330.

Chapter 13

1. Edmund D. Cronon, *Black Moses: The Story of Marcus Garvey and the Universal Negro Improvement Association* (University of Wisconsin, 1968), 3-21.
2. Theodore Vincent, *Black Power and the Garvey Movement* (Ramparts, 1972), 97; Amy Jacques Garvey, ed., *Philosophy and Opinions of Marcus Garvey* (1923; Arno, 1968), vol. 1, 9.
3. Cronon, 16-19; Vincent, 98-99.
4. Robert C. Weaver, *The Negro Ghetto* (Russell and Russell, 1967), 14-32; Garvey, vol. 1, 60, 84-87.
5. Cronon, 145.
6. Ibid., 178-80; Byron Rushing, "A Note on the Origin of the African Orthodox Church," *Journal of Negro History,* 57 (Jan., 1972): 37-39.
7. Garvey, vol. 1, 36. On Thorne: Robert Weisbord, "J. Albert Thorne: Back-to-Africanist," *Negro History Bulletin* (March, 1969): 14-16.
8. Cronon, 99-101.
9. Vincent, 101.
10. Cronon, 73-102.
11. M. B. Akpan, "Liberia and the UNIA: The Background to the Abortion of Garvey's Scheme for African Colonization," *Journal of African History,* 14 (1973): 105-27.
12. Vincent, 221; Shepperson, "Notes on Negro American Influences on the Emergence of African Nationalism" *Journal of African History,* 1 (1960): 299-300.
13. Vincent, 221-27.
14. Cronon, 154.
15. Among observers who have attributed the following of later organizations to appeals among Garveyites are: Vincent, in *Black Power;* Cruse, in *The Crisis of the Negro Intellectual* (Morrow, 1968); Roi Ottley, *New World A-Coming* (1943; Arno, 1968); E. U. Essien-Udom, *Black Nationalism: A Search for an Identity in America* (Dell, 1962).
16. Cronon, 212-19.
17. Ibid., 198, 199.

Chapter 14

1. E. Franklin Frazier, *The Negro Church in America* (Schocken, 1964), 20-28.
2. Roi Ottley, *New World A-Coming* (1943; Arno, 1968), 86-87.
3. Arthur Huff Fauset, *Black Gods of the Metropolis: Negro Religious Cults in the Urban North* (University of Pennsylvania, 1944, 1971), 31-40; Joseph R. Washington, Jr., *Black Sects and Cults* (Doubleday, 1972), 132-33.
4. Howard M. Brotz, *The Black Jews of Harlem* (Schocken, 1970), 15-40; Ottley, 137-50.

5. Arna Bontemps and Jack Conroy, *Anyplace But Here* (Hill and Wang, 1966), 205–8; Fauset, 41–51.
6. Sara Harris, *Father Divine* (1953; Macmillan, 1971), 1–19.
7. Ibid., 31–43.
8. Ottley, 83–99.
9. Fauset, 52–67.
10. Harris, 205–7.
11. Ottley, 116–19, 54–55; Harris, 49.
12. Ottley, 108–9; Bontemps and Conroy, 204; E. U. Essien-Udom, *Black Nationalism: A Search for Identity in America* (Dell, 1962), 58.

Chapter 15

1. Bontemps and Conroy, *Anyplace But Here* (Hill and Wang, 1966), 216; E. U. Essien-Udom, *Black Nationalism: A Search for Identity in America* (Dell, 1962), 48; Brotz, *The Black Jews of Harlem* (Schocken, 1970), 12.
2. Bontemps and Conroy, 223; Essien-Udom, 87; C. Eric Lincoln, *The Black Muslims in America* (Beacon, 1961), 33.
3. Lincoln, 15–16.
4. Essien-Udom, 83; Bontemps and Conroy, 225.
5. Lincoln, 211–12; Louis Lomax, *When the Word Is Given* (World, 1963), 63–66.
6. Lincoln, 212–18.
7. Essien-Udom, 185; Lincoln, 20, 93.
8. Essien-Udom, 347.
9. Ibid., 336, 338.
10. John Henrick Clarke, ed., *Malcolm X: The Man and His Times* (Collier, 1969), presents a useful collection of observations on Malcolm.
11. Charles E. Wilson, "Leadership: Triumph in Leadership Tragedy," in Clarke, ed., 27, 31.
12. Benjamin Goodman, ed., *The End of White World Supremacy: Four Speeches by Malcolm X* (Merlin, 1971), "God's Judgment of White America," 121–48.

Chapter 16

1. Cruse, *The Crisis of the Negro Intellectual* (Morrow, 1968), 351–99; John Bracey, "Black Nationalism since Garvey," in Nathan Huggins, Martin Kilson, and Daniel Fox, eds., *Key Issues in the Afro-American Experience*, 270.
2. Cruse, 361, 382, 387.
3. Max Stanford, "Towards A Revolutionary Action Movement Manifesto," *Correspondence*, March, 1964, 3, 5.
4. "What We Want—What we Believe," *Black Panther*, March 16, 1968 (cf. other issues).
5. Eldridge Cleaver, *Post-Prison Writings* (Random House, 1969); Frantz Fanon, *The Wretched of the Earth* (Grove, 1966).
6. James Boggs, *Racism and the Class Struggle: Further Pages from a*

Black Worker's Notebook (Monthly Review Press, 1970), 172.

7. Stokely Carmichael and Charles V. Hamilton, *Black Power: The Politics of Liberation in America* (Vintage, 1967); Bracey, 276.

8. Imamu Amiri Baraka (LeRoi Jones), ed., *African Congress: A Documentary of the First Modern Pan-African Congress* (Morrow, 1972), vii.

9. Ibid., x, 167–73.

10. Albert B. Cleague, *The Black Messiah* (Sheed and Ward, 1968).

SELECTED BIBLIOGRAPHY

The citations in the notes will direct the reader to specific sources. This commentary on a selected list of works may prove useful to the reader who wishes to pursue the subject in more depth.

Antebellum Nationalism and Liberia

The only sound sources on Paul Cuffe are several articles by Henry Noble Sherwood: "Paul Cuffe," *Journal of Negro History*, 7 (April, 1923), 153–229; "Paul Cuffe and his Contribution to the American Colonization Society," *Proceedings of the Mississippi Valley Historical Association*, 1912-1913, 370-402; "Early Negro Deportation Projects," *Mississippi Valley Historical Review* (March, 1916), 501. Sherwood does not treat Cuffe as a pioneer in black nationalism, but as example of an achiever in the context of American society. However, Sherwood's documentation is excellent.

Liberia has been thoroughly covered in the large study by C. H. Huberich, *The Political and Legislative History of Liberia* (Central, 1947). Huberich examined the question of the development of Liberian sovereignty from the point of view of international law, not of ideology. The story of the ACS is covered in P. J. Staudenraus, *The African Colonization Movement, 1816-1865* (Columbia University Press, 1961).

Until recently there was very little material available on Martin Delany, but Victor Ulman's *Martin R. Delany: The Beginnings of Black Nationalism* (Beacon, 1971) now fills the gap very well. However, the work suffers an absolute lack of citation to sources, although it is clearly the product of careful research into primary materials.

Blyden and Liberia are covered brilliantly in Hollis Lynch, *Edward Wilmo*

Blyden, Pan-Negro Patriot, 1832-1912 (Oxford, 1967), which served as the basis for the treatment of Blyden here. Unfortunately there is nothing of corresponding quality on Alexander Crummell, J. T. Holly, or Henry Highland Garnet as of this date.

From the Civil War to Marcus Garvey

Willie Lee Rose's *Rehearsal for Reconstruction: The Port Royal Experiment* is detailed and very well done. Henry McNeal Turner and the back-to-Africa and black-owned shipping ideas are explored in Edwin S. Redkey, *Black Exodus: Black Nationalist and Back to Africa Movements, 1890-1910* (Yale, 1969). This work is excellent and thought-provoking, for it shows both the mass interest and the leaders' interest in nationalist ideas in the period. Chief Sam is treated with sensitivity in William E. Bittle and Gilbert Geis, *The Longest Way Home: Chief Alfred Sam's Back-to-Africa Movement* (Wayne State University, 1964). Marcus Garvey is presented well, but with a touch of condescension in Edmund D. Cronon, *Black Moses: The Story of Marcus Garvey and the Universal Negro Improvement Association* (University of Wisconsin, 1968). Theodore Vincent, *Black Power and the Garvey Movement* (Ramparts, 1972) takes a muckraker tone and counters several of Cronon's interpretations. DuBois has been covered in two studies: Francis Broderick, *W. E. B. DuBois, Negro Leader in a Time of Crisis* (Stanford, 1959), and Elliott Rudwick, *W. E. B. DuBois: Propagandist of the Negro Protest* (Atheneum, 1969), both of which see the nationalist ideas of DuBois as a minor theme in his thinking. The recent opening of the DuBois papers should produce a whole new body of scholarship in the next few years on this complex figure.

Since Garvey

On the sects and cults, the literature is diverse and uneven. Three good studies are Sara Harris, *Father Divine* (Macmillan, 1971), Arna Bontemps and Jack Conroy, *Anyplace But Here* (Hill and Wang, 1966). On the Muslims and Malcolm X, the best work is still C. Eric Lincoln's *The Black Muslims in America* (Beacon, 1961) which should be supplemented with Alex Haley and Malcolm X, *The Autobiography of Malcolm X* (Grove, 1965).

General Works on Black Nationalism

There are several anthologies or readers. Howard Brotz, ed., *Negro Social and Political Thought, 1850-1920; Representative Texts* (Basic Books, 1966) contains some excellent selections from Crummell and Delany, among others.

SELECTED BIBLIOGRAPHY

Henry S. Wilson, ed., *Origins of West African Nationalism* (St. Martins, 1969), includes some writings by Blyden and other Liberian materials. John H. Bracey, Jr., August Meier and Elliott Rudwick, eds., *Black Nationalism in America* (Bobbs Merrill, 1970) is a fine collection of quite short pieces and selections.

Little in the way of synthesis of this material has been published. Harold Cruse has raised the issue as to whether the writing of black history has tended to diminish the significance of the nationalist and separatist side of black politics in *The Crisis of the Negro Intellectual* (Morrow, 1968). Theodore Draper, *The Rediscovery of Black Nationalism* (Viking, 1970), is an angry polemic against the whole concept of political black nationalism, rather than a survey of the history of the subject, as the title might suggest.

INDEX

INDEX

Black Panthers, 154–155, 157, 158
Black Power, 156
Black Star Line, 126
Blaine, James G., 106
Blake (novel), 72, 73
Blyden, Edward Wilmot, 5, 65, 73–74, 77, 80, 115; ideas and influence of, 80–83, 85–86, 106–108
Boatswain, 35
Boggs, James, 155
Boley, 99–100, 110, 114
Bond, Julian, 157
Boston Guardian, 117
Boyer, Jean, 51–52, 53
Bracey, John, 114
Branagan, Thomas, 11
Briggs, Cyril, 126, 129
British-American Inst. (Ontario), 56–57
Brown, H. Rap, 156
Brown, John, 72
Brown v. Topeka School Board, 146
Brown, William Wells, 65
Browne, Robert S., 156
Bruce, Blanche K., 94
Bruce, James, 128
Buchanan, Thomas, 42, 43
Burgess, Ebenezer, 31–34
Butler, Matthew, 107

Caldwell, Elias, 24–25
Campbell, Robert, 73–74
Campelar (settlement), 32
Canada, 5, 13–14, 29, 55–58, 60–61, 65–66, 68–72, 94
Carey, Lott, 35–38, 43, 45
Carmichael, Stokely, 154, 155, 156
Casement, Roger, 106
Cherry, F. S., 133, 135
Chicago Defender, 123, 129
Chilembwe, John, 119
Chiriqui, 87–88
Christian Recorder, 104
Christophe, Henri, 50–51
Clarke, Edward Young, 125
Clarkson, John, 13
Clarkson, Thomas, 13, 18, 50, 51, 52
Clay, Henry, 20, 24
Cleague, Albert, 158
Cleaver, Eldridge, 154–155
Cleveland, Grover, 95
Clinton, Sir Henry, 32
Coker, Daniel, 20, 21, 33, 34, 45
Coles, Edward, 47
Commandment Keepers, 134
Communism. *See* Marxism
Communist Party (USA), 138

Congo Free State, 105
Congress of African People (1970), 152, 156–157
Congress of Racial Equality (CORE), 151, 153
Conventions: 1831–1836, 27, 56; 1854, 69–71; 1856, 72; 1858, 72
Coolidge, Calvin, 127
Cornish, Samuel, 40
Craft, Ellen, 65
Craft, William, 65
Crisis, 118–119, 120
Crowdy, William S., 133, 135
Crowther, Samuel, 74
Crummell, Alexander, 5, 65, 77, 82, 83; ideas and influence of, 83–86, 102–103, 105, 117
Cruse, Harold, 114, 129, 153
Cuffe, Paul, 16–23, 30–34, 50, 58
Cultural nationalism, 4, 69, 81–82, 85, 118, 120. *See also* Black Nationalism
Curityba, 110
Cyprus, 95

Davis Bend, 91. *See also* Mound Bayou
Davis, Samuel, 62
Dawes Act, 97, 100
Dawn (community), 56–57, 58
Dawud, Talid Ahmad, 145
Deacons for Defense, 153
Delany, Martin, 67–74, 81, 103–104, 111
Deportation, 10–12, 25–26, 29, 88–89
Devany, Francis, 39, 45
Dewey, Loring, 52, 58
Dey people, 35
Diab, Jamal, 145
Divine, Father (George Baker), 129, 136–137
Dodge Revolutionary Union Movement (DRUM), 155
Doolittle, James R., 88
Douglass, Frederick, 63, 64, 67, 69, 75, 94
Douglass, Henry Ford, 70
DuBois, W. E. B., 86, 112, 116–120, 125–126, 129, 159
Duse, Muhammad Ali, 122

Easton, Hosea, 27, 62
Economic nationalism, 22, 39, 69; at Mound Bayou, 91–92; Washington's, 114–115; Garvey's, 122, 125–126
Emigration, 4–5, 19–21; advocates of, as faction, 60–76; to Haiti, 21, 27, 29, 50–54; to Mexico, 27, 29, 54–55, 58, 68; to Africa, after Reconstruction,

178

INDEX

INDEX